Th[...] WILTS[...]
Village Book

MICHAEL MARSHMAN

with illustrations by Wende Maunder

COUNTRYSIDE BOOKS
NEWBURY, BERKSHIRE

First published 1987
New expanded edition 1999

COUNTRYSIDE BOOKS
3 Catherine Road
Newbury, Berkshire

ISBN 1 85306 583 8

Designed by Graham Whiteman

Front cover photo of Castle Combe and
back cover photo of Aldbourne
supplied by Roger Holman

Produced through MRM Associates Ltd., Reading
Typeset by Techniset Typesetters, Newton-le-Willows
Printed by J. W. Arrowsmith Ltd., Bristol

ACKNOWLEDGEMENTS

This book is for my wife Ruth, who helped me to sing again, and for our children Megan and James, who did their best to interrupt me but who visited many villages enthusiastically, especially if there was the prospect of lunch in a public house, whose interior I needed to research.

My grateful thanks to Suzanne and Nicholas Battle of Countryside Books for asking me to write a new edition of this book and for the opportunity to expand it. I am also most grateful to the countless number of Wiltshire men and women who have provided me with information over the years. Much I have forgotten but some has remained and appears in this book.

Foreword

Among the 400 villages and hamlets of Wiltshire you are unlikely to find two that are alike. Our villages have not received the same treatment as most of our towns where, in the commercial centres, you could be in Anytown, Southern England, and the only distinction in the new housing estates is that provided by the builder rather than the locality. A few of our smaller towns, such as Bradford on Avon and Malmesbury retain their identity but it is in the villages that we can most easily find expressions of local individuality, be they architectural, horticultural or human.

The village has been the pattern of English life for around 3,000 years, for it was not until the 19th century that the balance of where people lived tipped in favour of the town and city. The settlements in the villages can be traced back over a thousand years for nearly all are recorded in the Domesday Book and many are recorded in Saxon land charters. Some have been in continuous occupation since Roman times, the Iron Age or even earlier; as a site which provided the necessities of water, shelter, fuel and good land was unlikely to be abandoned other than in the event of some natural or man-made catastrophe.

In this book you will find out a little about the history, people and buildings of each village, a view of the present day village and, here and there, my personal opinions on a settlement. In selecting villages to include I have tried to find representatives of all types, historical, topographical and economic. I apologise if the village where you live, or your favourite village, is not included but there are more than enough for two books of this size. Indeed, when we have been visiting villages my wife has exclaimed in amazement that I am not including the attractive village through which we are passing on our way to one which is to be in this book. My answer then, as now, was that some very pretty settlements have been left out in favour of ones which may not satisfy the aesthetic senses so well but which have an interesting history, a noteworthy industry or a pleasing local personality.

Our villages naturally show the variation of the underlying geology and because of this the older houses blend well with their local landscape. The county basically consists of the chalk plain and downs in the south and east with clay vales and low lands in the west and north but, around the edges, are lands seemingly borrowed from other counties. In the north-west are parts of the Cotswolds stretching as far south as Westwood while the south-west, the former butter country, has many similarities with neighbouring Dorset. The greatest surprise of all is in the south-eastern corner where there is a small part of the New Forest.

From these various landscapes the villages have grown naturally and although brick became common in the county from the early 18th century it made little impact on the stone villages but, instead, added a pleasing warmth to settlements on the clay and chalk. It is only in recent decades that mass produced bricks and reconstituted stone have found their way into the countryside.

For two centuries the countryside suffered a slow decline with an irreversible movement to towns and cities thus reducing rural businesses, shops and services. Recently this has changed a little as more and more people realise the advantages of living among green fields instead of suburban gardens. Sadly this migration back has meant that the children of many villagers cannot afford to live in their community after they leave home. The conflict between locals and newcomers is normally muted however and, it must be said, it is often the newcomers who take a very active part in local affairs, fighting to save the village school, maintaining rights of way and standing for the parish council. Newcomers and villagers need one another for the former bring new blood and ideas while the latter maintain the long thread of history of the community, its oral traditions and customs and its link with the land and the ever shrinking farming community.

It is man's use of the land which has shaped our landscape and its villages and changes here are going to cause changes in the community and in its appearance. Farmers are having to diversify; trout, milking ewes, angora goats, deer, forestry, farm parks, holiday villages and golf courses are some areas being explored locally. These activities are likely to provide more rural employment than do the large farms with their fields geared to machine rather than man. There are also an increasing number of small industries appearing as advances in electronic communication mean that it is no longer necessary for businesses to be in urban areas and people involved in most types of creative work can conduct much of their business by email. I experienced a little of this technology myself for although I physically visited each village and did most research using printed or archival sources, I also gathered some facts from local web pages using the Internet.

From a lifetime's reading I am very conscious of the people who have sung the praises of my native county, some who were born within its boundaries while others came from afar and appreciated its beauties. It is largely the work of writers and artists which shapes public perception of a district or a community. Few can think of the Lakes without at least one line of Wordsworth coming to mind or have a mental picture that is not coloured by childhood memories of Arthur Ransome or adult readings of Melvin Bragg's novels. Dorset will forever be associated with the prose of Thomas Hardy as are the Potteries with Arnold Bennett and Nottingham with D.H. Lawrence.

So it is with Wiltshire although our writers may not be so well known nationally and no great novelist has used Wiltshire as his setting. Chronologically our first writer is William of Malmesbury. A monk who preferred the post of librarian to that of abbot and who disregarded his Somerset origins to align himself with his adopted county so that history has given him the designation, 'of Malmesbury'. More than a mere chronicler of events, he deserves the description of historian and is still a well regarded and well used source.

'The father of Wiltshire history' is the appellation of John Aubrey. Born in 1626 at Easton Piercy in the parish of Kington St Michael he was a gentleman who, from his earliest years, exhibited a keen interest in antiquities, folklore and natural history. None of his writings was published in his lifetime and one of his two manuscript volumes of Wiltshire collections has been lost, but in bringing Avebury to the notice of the Court and scientific establishment he performed a notable service. Posthumous publication has shown what a good topographer he was and his writings, although scanty, are one of our chief sources for the 17th century. Unfortunately he was unlucky in both love and litigation and much of his later life was spent away from his county of birth.

Our next writer was also born in Kington St Michael, but not until 1771, and he was to edit Aubrey's *Natural History of Wiltshire* for publication. John Britton was the son of a prosperous villager although the family later fell on hard times which necessitated John's apprenticeship to a London wine merchant, in which situation he managed to read widely and become known to literary and artistic people. He became a topographical and architectural writer and with E.W. Brayley published a series, *The Beauties of England and Wales*. His *Beauties of Wiltshire* was followed by a volume on Salisbury Cathedral while in his *Autobiography* he gives a lively picture of Wiltshire village life in the late 18th century.

Sir Richard Colt Hoare was a wealthy member of the banking family and inherited Stourhead. Between 1810 and 1821 he wrote and published *The Ancient History of Wiltshire* and began work, with various collaborators and employees on *The History of Modern Wiltshire*. The six volumes of this work cover the southern half of the county and are somewhat variable in content but they do represent the only published attempt at a county history until we reach the second half of the 20th century with the excellent, and ongoing, *Victoria History of Wiltshire*. The best volume of *Modern Wiltshire* is Robert Benson and Henry Hatcher's *Salisbury*, which stands head and shoulders above the other somewhat pedestrian accounts. A final historian was Yorkshire-born Canon Jackson who moved to Leigh Delamare in 1845, having developed a great interest in the Hungerford family and their estates. Besides his personal publications he edited, and greatly extended, Aubrey's *Wiltshire Collections*.

We now turn from historians to writers on the topography and life of the county. Richard Jefferies, farmer's son, naturalist, journalist, country writer and mystic, has left us with superb pictures of life in north-east Wiltshire in the late 19th century. Born at Coate, he captured his own childhood in *Bevis* and that of the farmers and their labourers in *Hodge and his Masters*, but it is in his natural history writings that he shows his greatest powers of observation and descriptive writing. He inspired many other writers and has an honoured place in the county's biography.

Alfred Williams of South Marston came from a different background and worked long hours at the forge for the Great Western Railway in Swindon, thus gaining the nickname of the Hammerman Poet. Largely self educated, he studied many Eastern languages and translated works from those languages. His poetry was well received but our greatest debt to him is for collecting folk songs. Wiltshire seems to have been largely ignored by folk song collectors and without the transcriptions of songs and their variations that Williams made we would be poverty stricken indeed. Unfortunately that was often the state of Williams and his wife; there was never much money and his work and scholarship went largely unrewarded. He has left us riches in the legacy of his writings which, in books such as *Villages of the White Horse*, provide us with superb descriptions of the life, customs and work of local communities.

Another writer, whose tragedy was to be poor, was not born a Wiltshireman, nor did he ever live in the county for any length of time. Yet I feel that Edward Thomas had a great affection for Wiltshire, as evidenced in many of his writings. He had relatives in Swindon and often stayed with 'Dad' Uzzel in Hodson where he and Helen enjoyed a pre-marriage honeymoon, excellently portrayed by her in *As It Was, World Without End*. In his own writings it is perhaps *In Pursuit of Spring* which gives his best picture of the county. After his gradual discovery that he was really a poet the small collection of verses that he was given time to write include some beautiful work with Wiltshire settings. For although Wiltshire gave him many happy days with birds, animals and flowers, provided excellent walking on its downs and was the venue for cricket matches, it was the setting for much grimmer times. He had volunteered to serve in the First World War, although at his age and with his family commitments he had no need; perhaps his personal daemon of black despair and melancholy was responsible. Be that as it may, it was in Trowbridge Barracks that he became a Second Lieutenant in the Royal Artillery, around Codford that he received his final training before embarkation and at Hatch Farm, Tisbury, where he saw his infant daughter Myfanwy for the last time while she was staying with Ivy, Arthur Ransome's first wife. His death in the artillery barrage which preceded the Battle of Arras deprived us of any more sensitive poetry and prose.

Thomas was born in London but W.H. Hudson came from much further away, born within ten miles of Buenos Aires. Although he did not come to England until he was an adult he was, perhaps, more English than the English, with a far greater knowledge of their history and countryside. His great Wiltshire book is *A Shepherd's Life* which tells the story of James Lawes and his father in the fictional village of Winterbourne Bishop, really Martin and now in Hampshire. There is also much powerful writing on other parts of Wiltshire, in particular the Wylye Valley, and Hudson, who had the happy knack of being accepted by all country people, travelled extensively in the county.

So far our writers have been male but we now have three good women writers. *Salisbury Plain* is a beautiful and evocative portrait by Ella Noyes with illustrations by her artist sister. Both now lie in Sutton Veny churchyard within sight of the western slopes of that chalk massif. Ida Gandy was one of a large family, at the vicarage in Bishops Cannings, with a most interesting father and an artistic and unconventional mother. This upbringing is splendidly captured in *A Wiltshire Childhood* and other books set in the county. Late in life she returned to the county, living in Aldbourne and writing her last book on that village.

Edith Olivier was also a daughter of the rectory, in her case Wilton, and her father was a canon of Salisbury Cathedral. Apart from being a novelist in her own right she entertained a formidable literary circle, often much younger than herself, in the 1930s and 1940s at the Daye House and was justifiably proud in being the first woman mayor of the ancient borough of Wilton. Her writings on Wiltshire have been influential and her *Wiltshire*, although published in 1951, is still well used while her autobiographical *Without Knowing Mr Walkley* gives some excellent portrayals of local people and events.

It was Edith Olivier who persuaded A.G. Street to write and publish his first book, *Farmer's Glory*. This splendid book came out when farming was in a very depressed state and it, with its successors, raised in the townsman's consciousness the importance to him of the countryside. A.G. was a man of great integrity and an amazing amount of energy pursuing full time careers in farming, writing and broadcasting. He wrote many novels with country settings as well as factual books on farming. His daughter, Pamela, has also become a well known novelist, but not before providing us with her own book on the county, *A Portrait of Wiltshire*.

It was A.G. who first promoted Wiltshire and the countryside on the radio and he was soon followed by dear Ralph Whitlock. Ralph was also a farmer, from a family of farmers at Pitton, who became a writer on the countryside, farming, natural history and folklore. With Ralph, however, writing became a full time occupation and he had more than a hundred books published as well as thousands of newspaper and magazine articles. His *Folklore of Wiltshire* is a standard work on that subject while *Wiltshire* presents a good picture of the county.

I realise that I have written about three writers whom I knew and that brings me to four who are currently writing in the county and singing its praises. Ken Rogers is exceedingly well known in Wiltshire, being the retired County Archivist and the expert on the local woollen industry. His *Warp and Weft* and *Wiltshire and Somerset Woollen Mills* are required reading on this subject. A less well known but very influential writer on Wiltshire's history is Douglas Crowley, the Editor of the *Victoria County History of Wiltshire* whose volumes provide the authoritative study of any parish they have covered. Of our present generation the writer who has brought Wiltshire and its history to most people's attentions is John Chandler. With a large number of books to his credit he has done a great deal to make people interested in both their community and their county and has also been instrumental in promoting the county outside its boundaries. Finally Ken Watts, an Edward Thomas enthusiast who came to writing after his early retirement. So far he has produced two excellent books, on the northern and southern halves of the county, which appeal greatly to walkers.

These writers, and a few others, have been responsible for the picture of

Wiltshire that many people hold alongside their own experiences of the county. Certainly more and more people are living here and from being a little known county Wiltshire and its towns and some villages are now in the public consciousness.

Michael Marshman

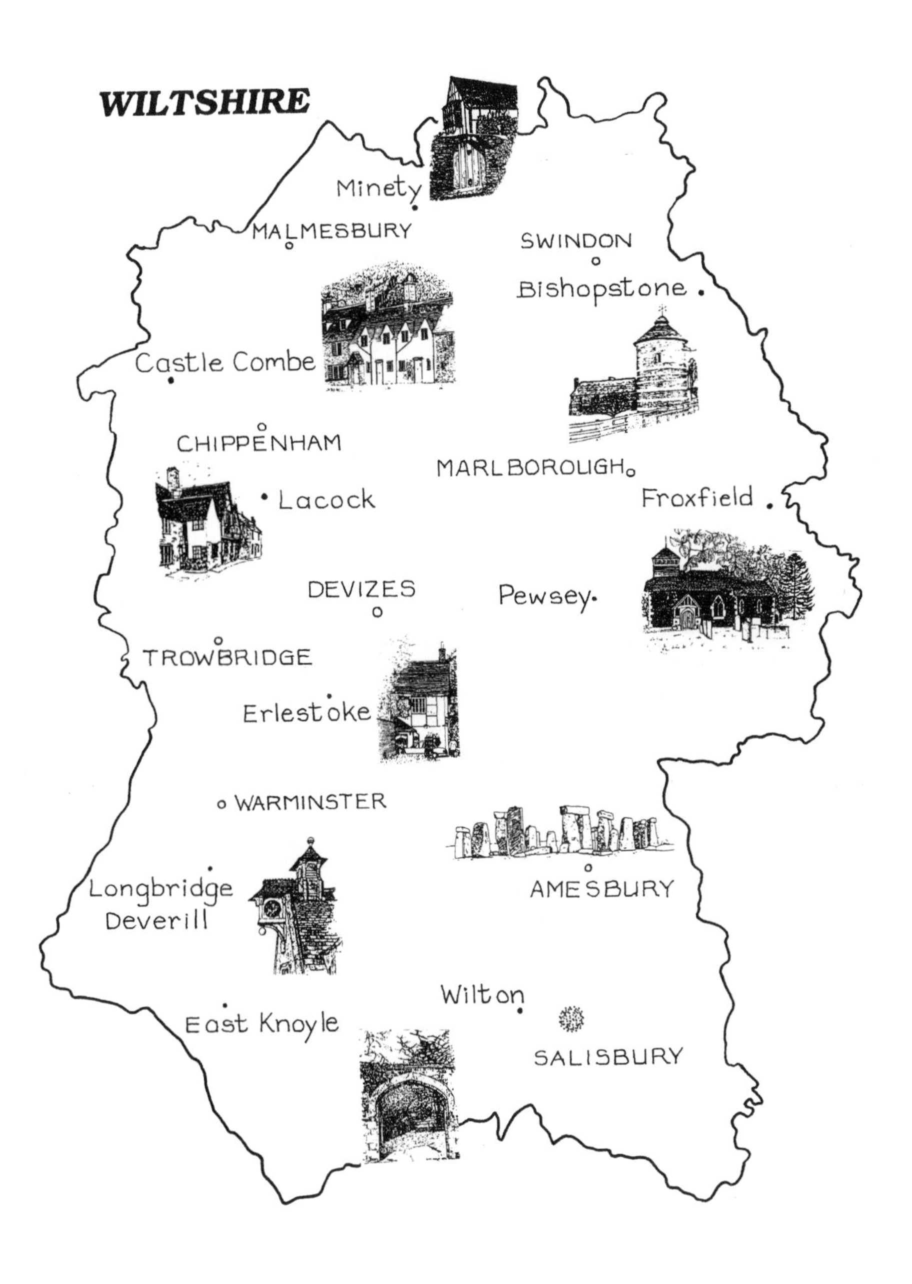
WILTSHIRE
Minety
MALMESBURY
SWINDON
Bishopstone
Castle Combe
CHIPPENHAM
MARLBOROUGH
Lacock
Froxfield
DEVIZES
Pewsey
TROWBRIDGE
Erlestoke
WARMINSTER
Longbridge
Deverill
AMESBURY
Wilton
East Knoyle
SALISBURY

ALDBOURNE

Aldbourne has a long and mostly prosperous history. It lies at the junction of five dry valleys where a tributary stream of the River Kennet rises to flow down a sixth valley. It is now a large village with much modern development and, to some extent, serves as a dormitory for Swindon.

In Wiltshire terms Aldbourne is an upland village and the way to approach it is through sheep pastures and wheatfields from Ogbourne, Ramsbury or Wanborough. Around Aldbourne is much evidence for early settlement including a Neolithic village at Upper Upham to the west and Romano-British field systems. Set high on the Downs, Upper Upham remained a small village but it shrank over the centuries until at the beginning of the 19th century only Upper Upham House, a farm and a cottage were left. The 20th century has seen new farm buildings and cottages added. Just to the south is the site of the deserted village of Snap; in the 14th century said to be one of the poorest settlements in the whole county. At the census in 1851 its population was 41 but soon after 1900 lack of work and lack of roads had caused it to become deserted.

In the middle of the village is a good square village green. The Green is probably the medieval market place and was certainly so used in the late 18th century. The Market Cross, restored after the fire of 1760, has stood on The Green since at least the early 19th century but there is some doubt as to its site before 1760.

To the south of The Green is the centre of the modern village, The Square. This is of an irregular shape and, again, most buildings date from the late 18th and early 19th centuries. Here is the village pond, certainly in existence by the 18th century and probably much earlier; in recent years it has been given a concrete bottom. Although many houses are recent, that is to say built in the last 200 years, they occupy known medieval house sites. This also applies to many of the surrounding farmhouses. For in medieval times this was a wealthy parish and was especially populous in the 17th century.

The great enemy of all early towns and villages was fire and doubtless Aldbourne suffered many that have gone unrecorded. That of 1760 destroyed 72 houses and caused the discontinuation of the medieval market. Ten years later in 1770 a total of 80 houses and 20 barns were consumed by fire, a very serious event as the community must have only just been recovering from the previous disaster. On both occasions there was much rebuilding and the fact that much of this was in brick and stone is indicated by the fire of 1817 only destroying 15 cottages, three barns and two malthouses. Many of the timber-framed, and tinder dry, houses had already been lost in the 18th century.

Needless to say there are still some early survivors, especially on the edges of the old village. The central part of Court House (to the north of the church) is of the late 16th century with stone mullions set in thick walls while inside, the ceiling beams are set in heavily moulded cases. Of the public houses, The Crown was first mentioned in 1735 but The Blue Boar not until 1822. There is, however, a tradition that the latter provided accommodation for the 15th century masons who built the Perpendicular church tower.

The industry for which Aldbourne is best known is bell founding and many Wiltshire parish churches can boast an Aldbourne bell. It is known that William and Robert Cor were operating a foundry in the grounds of Court House in 1694, which had successive owners until it became bankrupt in 1762. In 1760 Robert Wells, who was related to the Cors by marriage, opened a new foundry at Bell Court in the south-west corner of The Green. He made both church and small bells and between 1781 and 1825 his sons, Robert and James, made 200 church bells. The factory closed in 1825 when James was declared bankrupt.

In the 1790s the cottage industry of straw plaiting had been introduced by the Society for the Betterment of the Poor. This produced a material known locally as tucsin which was supplied to milliners. The industry flourished until the 1880s but had ceased by the beginning of the 20th century. A chair factory, in South Street, opened in 1887 and employed 40 people using ash, beech and birch from local woods. At the time of the First World War 100 chairs a week were being produced, but the factory closed during the hard times of 1927. Much more recently an egg packing factory provided much local employment, but has now moved to Lambourn to be closer to a junction of the M4.

For time out of mind villagers have been known as Aldbourne Dabchicks. The story goes that long ago a strange bird was found on the pond and nobody could identify it. Eventually the oldest inhabitant, a whiskered ancient, was brought out from his cottage in a wheelbarrow and after due deliberation, announced it to be a dabchick, a rare visitor to the downs. From that time the name has stuck and has been used jeeringly by the neighbouring villagers of Ramsbury, whose greatest insult was to tie a dead dabchick, obtained from the River Kennet, to the Aldbourne carrier's cart.

There is no feuding to match that of adjacent villages and the traditional

Aldbourne Feast normally ended in a running fight through the parishes with the Ramsbury villagers. This feast took place on or near the feast day of St Mary Magdalene, to whom it is believed the church was originally dedicated prior to the 15th century.

ALDERBURY

Settlement in the parish began in two separate areas which, in the 20th century, have joined together with ribbon development along the busy A36 Salisbury to Southampton road. At Alderbury itself is a delightful village on a tree-clad hillside overlooking the River Avon and its extensive water courses and water meadows. That it is a place of hills as well as trees can be seen from the names, School Hill and Tunnel Hill, as well as the evidence of your tiring limbs as you climb past the church to the main road. A seemingly later settlement is a farming one around The Three Crowns, at Whaddon on even higher ground. The Common is still marked on the map, reminding us of John Aubrey's remark, in the 16th century, 'They have tryed for coale at Alderbury Common'. In the 20th century there has been much development from the inter-war years onwards, including a large council estate, infill and more new estates.

To the north of the village, at Ivychurch Farmhouse, are the remains of the Augustinian Priory of St Mary. Founded in the 12th century by Henry II, it was here that Thomas Becket stayed during his quarrel with that king while the latter was at Clarendon Palace a quarrel that led to the murder of Thomas in Canterbury Cathedral. What remains today is the west front of the monks' church, incorporated into the walls of a 19th century garden, some Norman capitals in the west wall of the farmhouse, smaller fragments of panels and figures elsewhere in the house and more Norman capitals and piers in the garden.

There was probably quite a large Saxon church here as Alderbury was a royal manor and the head manor of a Hundred while the church was a mother church with dependent chapels. The later church, demolished in the 1850s, was a plain rough cast building with a wooden turret and a nave that was possibly early medieval. For much of its history, from 1110, it was under the jurisdiction of the Treasurer of Salisbury Cathedral rather than the Bishop. It was leased to others, 'Impropriate Rectors', for the benefit of the tithes and these rectors would have lived in, or let, the Parsonage or Rectory

House. They would also have appointed a vicar to carry out the necessary ecclesiastical work; one who held the office from 1663 to 1672 carried the splendid name of Onesepherous Bernard.

The present church was consecrated on 24th June 1858 and is in flint with freestone dressings. The dedication, to St Mary, maintains the name of the Norman priory. The spire is visible above the trees as you twist around the roads to find it and, when you do, you find the church set above the road with a small loop off the road in which carriages could stand whilst their passengers alighted for Sunday service. It is a mossy churchyard with many stone crosses while before the porch is an old and ruinous and much propped yew tree planted when the old church was young or, maybe, even when the Saxon one stood.

The Parsonage House was said to be old in the 16th century but the building standing in 1765 was probably built around 1600. It is to the south of the church, now named Court House, a most pleasant building of red brick and old tiles with a timber-framed wing to the rear. The windows must take a long time to clean as, on the ground floor, there are 42 panes to each window, with 36 on the first floor. A little further south, end on to the road is a nice red brick complex with some flint and hanging tiles. To the south-west is Alderbury House, a late 18th century ashlar-faced building, with a good red brick lodge on the road near the church.

At the top of School Hill are two timber-framed black and white thatched cottages and then we are on the main road. St Marie's Grange was built for himself by the architect Augustus Pugin after his marriage in 1835. He was only 23 and created a romantic dream come true, an ideal for Maria of the moated grange. In an extreme case of medievalism he even included a garderobe or privy, in the turret off his bedroom. He left the house in 1837 and it was altered and enlarged in 1841 in a style very similar to his original. On the first floor is some original Pugin glass while on the second is some early 16th century glass taken from Ivychurch.

On The Green is a fountain and water trough of 1902 commemorating the Coronation of Edward VII and indicating an appreciation of Lord Radnor, of Longford Castle, for providing a water supply. The Green Dragon was immortalised as The Blue Dragon by Charles Dickens in *Martin Chuzzlewit.* Unlike many of Dickens's inns, the name is obviously fictitious as I don't think there ever has been a Blue Dragon, even one whose sign had been faded to grey by the wind, rain and sun. Certainly in this part of the world the sign was green as the green dragon was part of the coat of arms of the Earls of Pembroke at

Wilton House.

The parish was well known for the manufacture of tiles and bricks from a band of clay also used at Downton and Redlynch. Records show that tiles were being produced in the 14th century while a brick kiln is shown in Clarendon Park on the 1773 map of Andrews and Dury. Whaddon Brickworks was founded in 1904 and in the 1920s Messers Hare and Tanner had two kilns which they fired about 15 times a year. Brick-making was carried out in the warmer weather and longer hours of daylight, normally between March and October.

ALL CANNINGS

The parishes of All Cannings and Bishop's Cannings lie side by side but their villages are three miles apart and there is no direct modern road between them. Both village churches can be seen from some distance and the tower of All Cannings shows well above the cornfields and houses.

The earliest settlement is Rybury Camp on the downs, two miles north-west of the present village. It is a Neolithic causewayed camp overlaid by an Iron Age hill fort. At the foot of the downs is another Iron Age site, All Cannings Cross, by the road from Allington to Stanton St Bernard. Excavated between 1911 and 1922 it was found to have 75 storage and rubbish pits, much pottery and many small artefacts now in the collections of Devizes Museum. The site is marked by Cannings Cross Farm whose outbuildings, in 1998, were being converted into housing.

Most of the village is set on what is now a quiet loop off the Patney road. It is an attractive place to live and this is borne out by the new houses built on the southern fringe of the village and the smaller development to the north. There is no old manor house but a later century compensated for this with The Grange, an attractive large house with pleasant walled gardens. Although not immediately obvious, it is built of Victorian concrete and, dating from the latter part of the 19th century, perhaps shows that this is better quality than that made in the 20th century.

There are many timber-framed cottages and farms of the 17th century, still mostly thatched. Some of these cottages, Rest Harrow, Rose Cottage and Sunnyside Cottage, are built end-on to the road as is the attractive Yew Tree Cottage, to the rear of which is the footpath leading to The Moor and the canal. Also from the 17th century is the large thatched Burden's Cottage and, what I feel is the most attractive of the timber-framed farmhouses, Rustic Farm.

The large church of All Saints shows some late Norman features but is basically of the 14th century with a 15th century tower and transepts. The latter makes the small-windowed chancel quite dark, while the nave is light. There are memorials to the Ernle family. That to Mrs Elizabeth Ernle, wife of the rector, who died in 1729 at the age of 39, states:

> 'She was a person that was endued with all the
> accomplishments both in Body and mind as render'd
> her an ornament to her Sex.'

and further,

> '. . . . . whose death looked upon as a public loss.'

Evidently a lady who had made a great impression locally. An earlier memorial to William Ernle, who died in 1581, has all the 'N' letters back to front on the main tablet but correct on the curved gable.

North-west of the church is the impressive old rectory which is dated 1642 and has additions from 1800 onwards. The church itself is at the southern end of a village which has grown northwards away from it. Next to the church is the pleasing village school where generations learned their letters and tables. With painted rough cast walls and slated roof, its stone tripartite window overlooks a good-sized triangular green where those same generations have played. In 1999 a new school was opened nearby. Today there are swings, a slide and wooden adventure play equipment which was grant aided by the Foundation for Sports and the Arts. From the green is a good view of the staircase turret of the church tower; a turret whose rectangular top houses the church clock. Back in the village street we are reminded of old trades. The Old Malt House is next to The Old Bakery, which still has its shop windows. Still thriving is the post office and grocer while on the other side of the road the village hall proudly bears Best Kept Village plaques for 1985,1988 and 1993.

ALTON BARNES & ALTON PRIORS

Seen from Walkers Hill, the twin villages of Alton Barnes and Alton Priors appear as one entity. To be honest they are scarcely big enough to make one village, let alone two, so we will consider them together. Saxon settlers were probably attracted to the site by the abundance of springs, the word 'Alton'

being derived from Anglo-Saxon and meaning farm by the springs. The good land around must have found favour in the eyes of these farmers. The random nature of the housing pattern may reflect the need to build on slightly higher and drier sites than the marshy ground that formed much of the village some centuries ago.

As recently as 1829 Augustus Hare, who had just been appointed rector of Alton Barnes, said in a letter that his first errand to Devizes was to beg a shoemaker to come and measure himself and his wife for waterproof shoes. In other letters he also comments on the quantity of ground water in the village. A fascinating village feature is the stone paths that cross open land between the churches and the scattered array of houses. It seems likely that these were first put down to protect walkers from the mud and water.

On the downs overlooking the villages are three notable features. The more recent is the Alton Barnes White Horse. Cut in 1812, it is a copy of that at Cherhill. It measures 166 feet high by 160 feet long and until recently the scouring of the horse was performed by local villagers. In 1987 the outline of the horse had become indistinct and the exposed chalk badly discoloured. Many tons of extra chalk were required but it would have been a massive undertaking to transport this up the hillside from the nearest road. Fortunately the Army came to the rescue and the chalk rubble was slung below helicopters and flown to the site.

The present horse is somewhat different in appearance from the original which was commissioned by Robert Pile of Manor Farm. A journeyman painter John Thorne, commonly known as Jack the Painter, agreed to execute the design to a depth of twelve inches and fill it with chalk rubble. After producing some drawings and getting John Harvey of Stanton St Bernard to do the labouring, Jack disappeared with the £20 fee that had been foolishly paid in advance; he was later hanged and Robert Pile finished the horse himself.

From the east, Walkers Hill, with Adam's Grave on top, has always reminded me of a female breast. Closer inspection shows the fancifully named Adam's Grave to be a chambered long barrow with deep side ditches. An earlier, and pre-Christian name was Woden's barrow, mentioned as 'Wodnes bearge' in a Saxon land charter of AD 825. The barrow was excavated in the 19th century when skeletons and leaf-shaped arrow heads were found. The third feature lies to the east of the Lockeridge Road and is the Neolithic causewayed camp of Knap Hill. It has been dated to around 2,760 BC and is certainly a superb defensive site.

There is pleasant walking around both hills and in spring and summer a fine array of wild flowers to be seen. Butterflies, including the Chalkland Blues, are a common sight. To the north, the linear feature of Wansdyke provides excellent walking and, again, there is much to interest the natural historian.

Although in the parish of Woodborough, the settlement at Honey Street has for a long time been associated with Alton Barnes. The wharf on the Kennet and Avon Canal was begun in 1811 and visually was one of the best complexes of canal architecture. Some of the buildings have now gone but there was a brick warehouse, weatherboard buildings (one with a clock turret and clock dated 1854) and a distinctive chimney, well known as a local landmark. There is a large canalside pub, naturally called The Barge, which is now approached through the sawmills which occupy the site today. The wharf acted as a local distribution centre for coal and building materials and there was some passenger traffic to Devizes. It is likely that local produce was also carried to Devizes Market. In 1862 the death knell of this traffic was sounded when the Berks and Hants Extension Railway opened their line to Devizes.

While the canal trade lasted, Honey Street was a proper canal community, looking to the waterway rather than to other local communities.

ALVEDISTON

Set at the upper end of the quiet Ebble Valley the attractive small and scattered village of Alvediston enjoys a tranquil existence. It was in such quiet valleys as this that the old Celtic families and names lingered long after conquest by Saxons and Normans. Such a family were the Gawens of the fine medieval Norrington Manor House. John Aubrey says that the family resided here for '450 and odd years' down to the year 1658 and mentions that the house was built in the time of Richard II. He also suggests that the name might be descended from the knight of the Round Table, Gawain.

The manor house that the Gawens built, possibly upon an older foundation, was at Norrington. Completed some time after 1377 it still stands; parts of it being the original building and the rest mainly 17th century. Whether Gawen really was Gawain cannot of course be known, but the name certainly is of great antiquity. Geoffrey Ashe believes that Gawain is more likely to have been a real person than many of the knights. He appears in a 13th century French romance, is one of the knights in Geoffrey of Monmouth's *The History of the Kings of Britain* (1135-1140) and most reliably, in 1125, William of Malmesbury mentions the finding of his tomb in Pembrokeshire during the time of William the Conqueror. If Gawain did exist it would be nice to feel that his descendants later settled on a peaceful Wiltshire manor.

In the church of St Mary another speculation leads one to suggest that the tomb of a knight of the late 14th century is possibly that of John Gawen. After 1658 the Wyndhams took possession of the manor and are represented by several monuments and memorials dating from 1688. The church itself is mostly of the 1866 rebuilding by T.H. Wyatt and the earliest remaining architectural features are 17th century.

The newer Manor House is not far from the church and, most unusually in stone country, is built of brick. It is 18th century and of two storeys with a fine shell hood over the doorway and is surrounded by pleasantly curving garden walls. It was the last home of the Prime Minister (1955–57), Sir Anthony Eden, whose tomb can be found in the churchyard.

The village name is unusual and there is great uncertainty as to its meaning. The usual suggestion is Aelfgeat's farm but some earlier forms of the name do not seem to agree with this. Within the parish the name of Trow Down has also caused some confusion. In the 10th century the name was 'Trogan' referring to the great hollow below the down and later forms are corruptions of this.

ASHTON KEYNES

Once Ashton Keynes, close to the county border with Gloucestershire, was set among lush water meadows on the banks of the infant River Thames. Large herds of dairy cattle grazed and fritillaries and many other wild flowers grew in abundance. Today the village is precariously perched on the edges of lakes which have engulfed thousands of acres of pastureland. For under those Thames-side meadows were the gravel beds that modern man has extracted. To me there seems to be a double sin here, for to build his despoiling motorways man has extracted gravel from and, in many eyes, ruined another part of the country. Some benefit will accrue from the leisure facilities of the Cotswold Water Park and the lakes will provide a home for waterfowl but to me, who loved the green meadows, this is now an alien and a blasted landscape.

The Thames is still just discernible, flowing between these lakes, and it provides one of the best features of the village, running past the front gardens of many houses whose residents can only reach the road by means of attractive bridges. This is in the High Road, and begins with Ashton House in the east where the river broadens and flocks of brown ducks are to be found. There is a mixture of old and new houses, perhaps the best of the old is what are now known as Nos 8, 9 and 10 The Grove, an early farmhouse with outbuildings.

In the beautiful Church Walk the Thames is quite a wide stream and it provides a most pleasing setting to Brook House, Ashton Mill and other fine houses with the smaller dwellings along Church Lane. At the confluence of the Thames with a smaller brook, at the end of Church Walk, is a pool, bounded by pretty two-arch bridges. Here I once saw trout up to 14 inches long. The fish in the brook, which also flows between houses and the road, are smaller but to compensate there is a sizeable flock of resident ducks.

The manor of Ashton Keynes was given by King Alfred to his daughter Aelfgifu, the Abbess of Shaftesbury. Later, to the east of the present church, a religious community grew up on the site of the present farmhouse. Church Farm is still encompassed by a moat from this early settlement while the church itself is surrounded by a bank and ditch from the same period. In the churchyard is one of the four ancient stone crosses for which the village is renowned. During the Civil War the tops of all four were smashed but the one in the churchyard was restored and dedicated as a war memorial in 1917, the year before the war actually ended. To approach the church from Church Walk you take a long path lined with chestnut trees which provide village children with a splendid crop of conkers each October.

The other crosses are at the end of Church Walk, to the south of The White Hart and by the former smith's shop. Today there is only one shop in this large village although the Beaconsfield Stores and butcher provide a wide variety of goods and the post office is in a private house next door. The street pattern is interesting and there is a Fore Street and a Back Street which seem to indicate early urban development which never fulfilled its potential.

There are two memories I shall especially retain. One is an amusing one of cats sitting on the bank of the Thames in Church Walk watching the small trout with longing in their eyes. The other is a poignant one. In the church porch there hung in the late 1980s a six inches to the mile parish map of 1924 marked with all the names of the now ravaged fields. It is no longer there but I hope that it has been kept safe.

ATWORTH

When approached from Bath and Box the village is seen with the distant heights of Salisbury Plain, with a wide cloudscape above, as a backcloth. On reaching the clock tower you arrive at a dividing line between two distinct parts of the village. Turn right along the minor road to Bradford on Avon and you will find yourself in the quiet original village centre; keep straight on along the main road to Melksham and you will pass the later ribbon development and meet far more traffic.

The clock tower itself is dated 1897 and was 'erected in commemoration of the longest reign in history' on the occasion of Queen Victoria's Diamond Jubilee. The following century used this prominent landmark as a war memorial. In the First World War 21 men of the parish were killed in action while a further 117 served their country and returned. The village was more fortunate in the next war as only one man was killed out of the 63 men and six women who donned uniform while the six who are listed from Chalfield all survived. Next to the tower is a former turnpike cottage en-isled by two branches of the road from Bradford and the main Bath road.

Settlement here was early. A Roman villa was found near the village school in the 1930s and the children helped to excavate it. In an area where wheat farming and dairying has always been important the discovery of corn ovens was especially significant. Later development, from the late 11th century, was linked with that of Bradford on Avon in whose Greater Parish Atworth was situated, thus being part of the vast estates of the Abbess of Shaftesbury for several centuries. By the time of Domesday there were two manors; Atworth Magna, the present village, and Atworth Parva now called Cottles from the Norman family of Cotel who held the manor. This once great family slowly fell and John Aubrey recorded that by the 1660s there were only poor people with the name Cotele left in the county.

Cottles House stands on a monastic site and the priest's house still exists. One former owner, Lady Constance who also owned Chalfield Manor, married four times. A contemporary account says she 'lived a naughtie life', some of it with her cousin Bishop Wyville and she seems to have been an unscrupulous woman with very loose morals. In the 20th century, the house was empty from 1935 and began to deteriorate and voices advocated demolition but, on the outbreak of war in 1939, the buildings were occupied by Stonar School which evacuated from Sandwich in Kent and has remained in Atworth to this day.

The parish lies on a thin layer of cornbrash overlaying Oxford clay and many wells have been dug down to the water-retentive clay. In the 1970s there were still 76 old wells and six public water pumps which were used during the drought of 1976 to supply water to many gardens. There have always been good supplies of building stone for local houses and the last quarry in the parish only closed around 1964.

The old area lies around the church of St Michael and All Angels and there was a Saxon chapel on this site in 1001. It was completely rebuilt in 1451 and the embattled saddle-back tower dates from this time although its oldest bell was cast in 1350 and claims to be the oldest in the county. In 1831 it was stated that the church had been unsafe and in a dilapidated condition for several years and was no longer large enough to hold the congregation. All but the tower was demolished and this still shows evidence of an infilled arch where the early nave roof joined the east wall. The new church, which was opened on 17th January 1832, is in the Early Gothic Revival style and is by H. E. Goodridge of Bath. The path leading to the doorway is irregularly flanked by 30 yews while inside is a stone pulpit, a gift from Melksham when their parish church was rebuilt in 1845, and pews of 1881 made by Mr F. Titt, the village carpenter.

The church now lies at the edge of the village and on two sides there are fields and a farm. Some landscape evidence remains to suggest that the church may have been surrounded by houses at an earlier time. From the church, Church Street leads to the Bradford Road. First, on the right, a two-storey house with gabled dormer windows in the roof, a porch with a steeply pitched roof and a date stone bearing the date 1676. Next, a nice row of stone cottages, some with mullions, one with a shell hood over the doorway and one with an inset stone dated 1716. An attractive approach to the church and on the corner of Bradford Road is The Forresters, joined to the row by a seemingly older tall house.

Along Bradford Road one passes the County Primary School, with the date 1828 on its small foremost building, and what seems to be the former schoolmaster's house attached. On the other side of the road is The Old Forge, the home of the late Professor Dowdeswell who inaugurated, and for many years was Chairman of, the Atworth History Society. This building which originally housed The Three Horseshoes and later The Hare and Hounds dates from 1650. Farther along is Poplar Farmhouse, very fine early 18th century with a good barn to the rear with nest boxes for pigeons on the end wall. There were twelve tall poplar trees to the front of the house but on a recent visit I could only count eleven.

The rest of the road contains early and more modern houses with some former workshops and small barns and then we reach the clock tower and Atworth Independent Church, built as the Congregational chapel in 1790 to 1792. It is a plain stone rectangular building with part of its graveyard on the other side of the footpath by the tower.

And so past the internationally known Botanic Nursery, which specialises in lime tolerant plants, onto the main road. There are several farms and former farmhouses along here and opposite the nursery there is still a platform from which milk churns were once collected. It is interesting to walk along this road mentally blotting out anything built after 1850. One is left with scattered farmhouses, barns, outbuildings and cottages built at different distances from, and at different angles to, the road. The 1773 map of Andrews and Dury shows some older buildings that have gone and a broad trackway leading south to Atworth Common. Near the common is a plaque, behind No 50 Bath Road, indicating the site of the village pound where straying animals were placed.

The White Hart Inn is a nice 18th century house of three widely spaced bays under a stone tiled mansard roof. In season there is a fine display of busy lizzies on every possible ledge and hanging from all suitable places. At the entrance to the car park the village post office is now sited in the old coach house. There is much modern infill and changes of use. Prospect Farmhouse has become Snapdragon's Nursery for young children while new houses, Prospect Fields, have been built in its grounds. The old Dowty factory site is now covered with houses while some older houses are now antiques shops and a hair salon. At the end of the village a minor road turns off at Purlpit, once an isolated settlement, towards Whitley.

AVEBURY

Many places have what could be called 'atmosphere'; the place in Wiltshire which most affects me is Avebury. One day, in spring or autumn, get up early and stand within the circle while most people are still abed. If you are fortunate, the sun will not yet have cleared the mist and the stones will loom up from the swirling white clouds like half-forgotten heroes out of ancient legend. You will be on a quiet island, an Avalon, where time seems to run at a slower speed and you will experience a sense of oneness with the past and with the people who raised the massive earthworks and the stones millennia ago.

For anyone encountering the site for the first time, the effect is tremendous. We are in an ancient landscape; man has occupied and shaped this countryside for over 5,000 years. Avebury itself is immense. The better known and celebrated Stonehenge is but a toy in comparison. The bank and ditch enclose an area of 28 acres; originally the bank rose 55 feet from the bottom of the ditch, the height of a five or six-storey building. The stone circle contains nearly 100 undressed sarsen stones and there are the remains of two further stone circles inside this. John Aubrey, who was responsible for bringing Avebury to the nation's notice, likened it to a cathedral while Stonehenge was a parish church.

The known prehistory begins at Windmill Hill, about a mile to the north-west of the circle, in early Neolithic times. Later in c3,250 BC this settlement was superseded by a causewayed camp. The use was seasonal when, in the autumn, herds of animals, mainly cattle with some sheep, goats and pigs, were assembled from a fairly wide area for slaughter. With little winter feed

Avebury

available, only a small number could be kept alive through the cold months. This site gives its name to the earliest known Neolithic culture in Britain. In the Neolithic and Bronze Ages the great henge monument, that we know as Avebury, was raised. Why it was built we can only speculate but, as with an ancient cathedral, it came into being because those involved believed in a purpose which had called upon them to create something that was possibly beyond the imagination of most of them.

The village did not spread into the Circle until the early 18th century, having grown up around the church and the two manor houses of Avebury and Avebury Trusloe. From 1930 houses within the Circle were demolished as they fell empty and housing growth was encouraged at Avebury Trusloe. In 1960 the policy became one of gradual clearance; most of the houses removed were those of the 19th century. In 1976 it was recommended that the remaining buildings should be allowed to stand. This seems to be right as the village was a development of the landscape and somehow harmonises with, rather than detracts from the prehistoric site. Many of the cottages have pieces of sarsen stone in their walls which helps this harmony.

In 1938 Alexander Keiller, who had bought and excavated Avebury, converted the coach house and stables of Avebury Manor into a museum. This passed to the National Trust and was named the Alexander Keiller Museum in 1966 when Mrs Gabrielle Keiller presented the contents to the nation. It contains nearly all the items that have been found in excavations locally, although not all are on display at any time. After an exhaustive tour of the museum, the henge and the stones you will be in need of refreshment which is well provided at Stones vegetarian restaurant in the Great Barn complex.

If you are in Avebury on a crowded summer's day and you feel a need for solitude, take the track that leads east-north-east from the double bend by the Red Lion. This takes you across the Ridgeway to Fifield Down and the little-known Valley of the Stones. Here the grey wethers, or sarsen stones, lie scattered just as they were deposited.

BIDDESTONE

If you were asked to imagine a perfect English village, you would probably picture a village green with large and small houses jumbled around it, maybe a duck pond, an old church, a centuries old manor house in mellow stone, and most probably a couple of pubs in which local games and meetings still took place. Such a village is Biddestone. It is my perfect Wiltshire village; a quiet honest village that is beautiful in its own right.

We'll start in the centre on the green. A road, fortunately not a busy one, runs through the middle of the large green. The pond is populated by a mixture of wild mallard and farmyard ducks. Not long ago they were breeding so well that homes for the surplus ducks had to be found on other village ponds. On the roads into the village there are now signs depicting the outline of three ducks and the legend, 'Slow Ducks Crossing'. They think highly of their ducks in Biddestone. Behind the pond is the handsome Pool Farmhouse in the local grey stone with two storeys and a three-storey gable. There is an interesting early circular window, while in the corner of the garden is a fine gazebo.

All around the green are fine houses and cottages in grey stone, none of them more recent than the early 1700s. Most of the roofs are of stone tiles but there is a thatched cottage on the edge of the pond. Short rows of stone cottages lead off at right-angles from the main frontages while, on the northern side of the green, there is Willow House, a fine early Georgian home with later wings at the rear. On, or near, the green are two pubs, The White Horse and The Biddestone Arms. The White Horse must be around 300 years old and is the base for many local sporting activities while also offering a varied menu for the traveller. The Biddestone Arms is a conglomerate building from different periods, while in the front windows is Edwardian etched glass with 'Smoke Room' on one and 'Bar' on the other. Here the visitor can also find food as well as liquid refreshment.

Biddestone once had two churches and two parishes. The church of St Peter was destroyed in 1840 (it was behind the manor house) and its bell turret erected in the grounds of Castle Combe Manor House. The church of St Nicholas is of Saxon foundation, although it is now basically a Norman church with early Norman work in the south doorway, the chancel arch and the font. The sanctuary is of the 19th century and unfortunately the east window does not relate to any other features. Most other windows are small and the light from the west window is obscured by a gallery so that it is easy to imagine yourself taken back several centuries in this intimate darkling atmosphere. There are pine box pews which, with the gallery, were made around 1712. Over the Norman doorway there is a carved tympanum and cross.

The gallery has an interesting history connected with the neighbouring village of Slaughterford. Their church had been badly wrecked by Cromwell's troops and remained ruined for 200 years. The faithful of Slaughterford came to worship at Biddestone but, like most villages sharing a common boundary, they did not get on together so the folk of Biddestone built them the gallery, with an outside staircase, so that they would not need to mix with their neighbours. The staircase is gone but the gallery remains to this day.

In 1998 Biddestone lost its school and the children now travel to a newly built one in Yatton Keynell. A reunion of former pupils was held after the end of term and many memories were exchanged. Among these were that children had to walk in along muddy lanes from Slaughterford and West Yatton and had to write out lines or miss their games if they had muddy shoes or boots. In 1956 maypole dancing was revived with all the children processing to the village green, while in 1959 the children, with the rest of the village, cleared out the pond and created the attractive feature we see today.

BISHOP'S CANNINGS

At 8,871 acres, Bishop's Cannings is the second largest parish in Wiltshire. Its most outstanding feature is the large and noble church of St Mary the Virgin, 122 feet long with a spire 135 feet high which stands proud above the surrounding cornfields and sheep pastures. There is also an infant spire atop the tower, allowing access from the stairs. This has provided the foundation for a story told against the village, in that seeing that one spire was taller than the other, they mucked the ground around the small spire to make it grow. But this is a story I have heard about other villages in other counties. Constructed of ashlar and slate, the church is originally 12th century but much altered in the 15th century. It was restored in 1883-84 at a cost of £3,600. The chancel is very long, being only four feet shorter than the nave which is very light and airy.

One of the most unusual features is a piece of furniture made like a single box pew for which there are many theories, such as a monastic carrel or a penitential seat. Inside and painted on a panel, in such a position as to be on the left of anyone seated at a small desk, is a 'hand of meditation'. Painted on five fingers and a scroll are brief admonitory sentences in Latin, such as: 'Thy end is bitter', 'Thy life is short' and 'Thou hast offended God'. The origin and purpose of this are much disputed and dates range from the 15th to 17th centuries.

The Wiltshire writer, Ida Gandy, was brought up in the village, being one of the vicar's daughters. Her book *A Wiltshire Childhood* published in 1929 gives a fascinating picture of country life at the end of the 19th century.

There are many humorous tales told about and against men from Bishop's Cannings. The classic one is, of course, that of the Wiltshire Moonrakers. A group of Excisemen came upon two villagers pulling a hay rake through the local pond. On being asked what they were about, they replied that they were raking for 'thic thur girt cheese', pointing to the reflection of the moon in the water. The Excisemen went on their way, doubtless laughing at the stupidity of the rustics. 'Girt vules' we would have said but, of course, the last laugh was with the simple countrymen, for the Bishop's Cannings men were smugglers and had tipped their cartload of brandy casks into the pond on the approach of the Excisemen. It was the unexpected return of these gentlemen which had surprised the retrieval of the contraband. Wiltshire people have always been proud to be called 'Moonrakers' knowing that 'we baint as simple as we seem'. Indeed it was the cloak of apparent simple-mindedness that saved many a Wiltshireman from transportation when confronted by a learned judge.

Some other local stories involve the supernatural. In Pig Lane there are no black dogs, headless horsemen or phantom coaches, but an enormous phantom sow which has been seen crossing the lane.

Tan Hill, at 980 feet one of the highest in Wiltshire, is in the parish. In 1499 the right of holding a fair here had been granted and fairs were held until the Second World War. It occurred on St Anne's Day on 26th July, according to the old calendar and, besides being a horse and sheep fair, there was horse racing and many amusements. Early on a summer morning came farmers, shepherds, drovers, dealers and gypsies. By 6 am the hill was covered with sheep, horses and people and the fair was in full swing. A great amount of business and pleasure was packed into a few hours for by three o'clock in the afternoon the fair was over. Tan Hill was once more its deserted self by nightfall and could slumber through the seasons for another year.

BISHOPSTONE (NORTH WILTSHIRE)

Just inside the county border and astride the Icknield Way is the charming thatched village of Bishopstone. It has a delightful setting around a small valley that leads down from Charlbury Hill and the Ridgeway. The stream has been dammed to make a mill pond and the main road crosses the top of this dam with a steep drop on the far side. The old three-storey mill is an impressive building in the village.

To the left of the mill a lane leads to the church passing, on the right, Court House which has a date stone inscribed: 'Daniel New TC: WP 1781' in its rendered rubble walls. The church of St Mary on the western side of the stream now seems a little isolated from the rest of the village. It is mainly Perpendicular with one window in the Decorated style while the north porch entrance is c1200. On the north wall of the chancel is a splendid Norman doorway with fine dogtooth carvings. It probably came from an earlier church on the site as did the plain Norman font.

The earlier houses are somewhat difficult to date externally as most of them are rendered. One of the few not rendered is Littlecot which is of whitish stone, possibly from Okus quarries, and has various additions which make up a charming homogenous house. Two other houses nearby exhibit their white stone, with later brickwork, as do other cottages near the mill pond.

This white stone has been copied in a fairly hideous recent small development where the blocks appear to be only one step up from breeze blocks. I can see no sympathy whatsoever between these houses and the rest of the village. One local pub is unusually called The True Heart, its sign showing Cupid shooting an arrow into a large heart, and it appears to be very late 18th or early 19th century. Next door is a most pleasant old farmhouse called Sarsens with fine thatched and rendered ranges. The adjacent Primitive Methodist chapel of 1886 provides a striking contrast in red brick with stone dressings.

Bishopstone is well provided with trees which greatly enhance the houses and show what has been lost in those villages which once had a high proportion of elms. A good spirit was shown in the local community effort which provided funds for the village hall.

BISHOPSTONE (SOUTH WILTSHIRE)

Bishopstone is set in the Ebble Valley on a strip of alluvium and river gravel enclosed to the north and south by chalk downs which are themselves overlaid in places with clay and flint. As befits a parish which originally contained six villages, this is a scattered settlement. With one exception the villages have grown together and Croucheston, The Pitts and Faulstone all seem to be part of Bishopstone. Netton lives on in the name of a street and Netton Farmhouse, a building of three bays of stone and flint chequerwork, which is dated 1637. The far-flung settlement to the west is Throope with a manor house, farm and cottages and, most surprisingly, the parish church of St John the Baptist.

The church is of rubble and ashlar construction and was rebuilt in the mid-14th century. The two-storey porch was added in the 15th century and the tower originally possessed a wooden spire. There is some evidence of an earlier 12th century church inside, where there is a Norman arch and window in the tower crossing. The church is large and in the Decorated style throughout and there is much here of interest. The north transept is still known as the Farmer's Aisle as this was where all the tithe paying farmers sat. In a recess in the north wall is a tomb decorated with carved crosses and a shield believed to be that of the founder of the church. In the west wall is the carved figure of a man depicted from the waist up which is believed to be 17th century but from the costume appears earlier. The chancel has fine stone vaulting and still has, by the altar, three seats for the priest, deacon and sub-deacon. Outside on the south wall of the south transept is an unusual covered

and arcaded tomb while in the churchyard is a most curious small circular tomb that is reminiscent of a giant chimney pot rising out of the grass.

The old rectory, now Bishopstone House, was built around 1815 and is a substantial building reflecting the time when clergymen had large families and entertained a considerable number of visitors. In 1843 a school had been built at The Pitts, containing carved medieval fragments in its gable. This was closed in 1977 when only 20 children were attending.

Naturally the chief occupation has been agriculture, although in the late 17th century John Aubrey mentions that on Flamston Down there was a quarry producing a spar from which glass was made. From the 1890s watercress was grown at Netton Marsh using pure spring water that gushed from artesian wells at a constant 51 degrees F. Watercress is still grown in these extensive beds, alongside the stream that runs past The Three Horseshoes, while the surrounding meadows and downs are used for sheep and cattle pasture and corn growing.

The River Ebble supported at least two mills until recent times. Croucheston Mill, which produced animal foodstuffs, closed down in the

1990s and, in 1998, was empty although water still rushed through the sluice gate outside while rooks cawed from nearby trees as they had through centuries of milling. Lower Mill is now a private house but had possessed 19th century machinery which, powered by the waterwheel, ground corn until the Second World War. The attached Mill House is 18th century or earlier. Finally a word about the village name. It indicates that the manor belonged to the local bishop, in this case the Bishop of Winchester, and here contained his demesne farmstead. It may have been this episcopal influence that has ensured the survival of this name for the modern village, while those of the other villages have been reduced to streets or local area names.

Box

Box is probably best known for its stone and its railway tunnel. According to legend, in the early 8th century St Aldhelm threw down his glove and said that if men dug where it fell they would find treasure. Stone may not have been the treasure that his followers had in mind but it has certainly provided employment and money for the village since that time. The Saxon church of St Lawrence at Bradford on Avon is built of this stone and the original foundation there was by St Aldhelm. The building of the Kennet and Avon Canal ensured that by 1810 Box stone could be easily transported to London while, in 1836, the building of Box Tunnel uncovered immense deposits of good stone between Box and Corsham. By 1900 there were nearly 700 men employed in the stone industry.

Box Tunnel was constructed by Brunel using 1,200 men and over 1,000 horses, a number increased during the final few months to 4,000 men. Over 100 men were killed and many more had been seriously injured when the two teams working from either end broke through the remaining rock to make a perfect join. The total length is 3,212 yards and the tunnel was officially opened in June 1841. The entrance is ornate and in the classical style. Devotees of Brunel gather at this entrance each year before dawn on 8th April to see the sun rising through the far end of the straight tunnel. Many people believe that Brunel chose a more difficult route just to ensure that this happened on his birthday.

The church of St Thomas of Canterbury is mainly 14th century, having replaced an earlier structure of 1200. In the churchyard is a good collection of table tombs and the triangular gravestone called the Pinnacle Stone. Local legend says that under it is buried a man whose hatred of his wife was mutual and she always maintained that when he died she would dance for joy on his grave. This unusual gravestone was his way of denying her this final triumph.

There are many good houses in Box and naturally they are built of stone. Springfield House, now warden-supervised flats, was originally The Old School of the late 17th century, while The Chequers is also of the 17th century. The lounge bar of this attractive pub was a butcher's shop until 1959 and some of the interior stonework is still blackened from the smoking of hams. If you visit in winter, telephone first as there are limited opening times.

In the 1980s only one stoneyard remained in the village, that of Carpenter and Sheppard Ltd. Once there were six, now there are none. On Box Hill to the north-east are the cottages of the miners who were working here until 1968; they are remembered in the name of the pub, The Quarryman's Arms. Inside are examples of the tools, mainly picks and saws, which were used to extract the stone. Now Box has other industries, including a computer firm and a successful business manufacturing golf balls and tennis balls in a candle factory that once provided the means of illumination in the underground quarries.

Box is now the home of Swindon-born David Hempleman-Adams, the mountaineer and explorer. He is the first man to climb the highest mountain in each continent and reach both the geographic and magnetic North and South Poles. He has many more expeditions planned but in between them lives here with his wife and daughter. A former famous resident was the Rev W. Awdry who at one time lived within sight of the entrance to Box Tunnel and remembered engines and other features which he used in his Thomas the Tank Engine books.

BRATTON

The best known feature of Bratton parish is its white horse, perversely known as the Westbury White Horse. True, it is facing Westbury and railway passengers would associate it with that town, for Bratton has no station, but it belongs to the village all the same. The present horse was cut in 1778 by a steward of Lord Abingdon who was surveying his master's estates in the area. He is believed to have obliterated a horse which could have dated to King Alfred's victory over the Danes in AD 878. The horse was further repaired and partly re-cut in 1853, while in the 20th century kerbstones and concrete ensured the permanency of the figure. On the brow of the hill is the Iron Age hill fort of Bratton Castle, 25 acres in extent with massive defensive banks and ditches. It was assaulted and taken in 1985 when part of the 'Peace Convoy' encamped here after being denied access to Stonehenge.

The arrival of this convoy created one of the biggest local disturbances of modern times. Villagers and shopkeepers felt themselves to be living under a state of siege. Visitors were deterred from coming to the White Horse and the Iron Age hill fort as the whole area became unsightly and odiferous. There were more police, DHSS officials and social service workers around the village than Bratton had previously believed existed. After the convoy moved on, a huge rubbish problem was left and many locals felt that it would be many years before the area was once again useable. Two years later the ordinary visitors returned and are themselves causing great damage by driving cars and motorcycles over the hillfort ramparts.

In 1986 a different problem occurred when the threat of a similar invasion caused the blockading of roads leading to the Plain. With the 'Peace Convoy' and with the War Department just over the horizon, Bratton has not enjoyed a peaceful time recently.

The village is mostly perched on a bed of Upper Greensand between the clay vale to the north and the chalk scarp of the Plain to the south. The church is perched highest of all, well above the modern village. Once it was in the hamlet of Stoke while only the area around Lower Road and Court House was called Bratton, and the part to the east at Stradbrook was known as Milburne. The medieval houses of Stoke are long gone and the church of St James stands high and lonely at the top of more than 100 steps. Being far above the village traffic, this mainly Perpendicular church is in a very lonely and peaceful place.

Much of the recent history of Bratton is that of two families: the Reeves and the Whitakers. The Reeves family owned the Bratton Iron Works which made agricultural machinery, while the Whitakers were clothiers and yeoman farmers. Their story is told in a most readable book by Dr Marjorie Reeves, *Sheep Bell and Ploughshare*. The families accumulated great stores of household items, toys and printed ephemera spanning some two centuries. This has been kindly given to Trowbridge Museum where parts of the collection are normally to be seen.

Most of the older houses are good, although there is space to mention only a few. Winters is most attractive, being of red and blue bricks with stone mullions and quoins. In its gabled end are two oval windows, possibly of the late 17th century. The lower is glazed in an ornate stone setting, while the higher one is smaller and simpler. Then the Georgian Yew Trees, where the Whitakers ran a small dissenting academy in the 18th century, and Pear Tree Cottage, of brick with stone mullions and quoins and with a fine stone doorway and studded door.

The beautiful brick and stone Baptist church owes much to the efforts of 18th century Whitakers. It was built in 1734 amidst the orchards which were such a feature of the village at that time. Enlarged in 1786, schoolrooms were added in 1818 and a vestry in 1856. There is a wealth of interesting historical material on Bratton and much of it has been researched by the village's own historian, Mrs Jean Morrison. The village also now has its own local history society publishing a journal. A well known feature of the village is its inn, The Duke, in whose garden a pair of whalebones has been recently re-erected after being missing for many years. It is of brick and rendering and stands opposite the Jubilee Hall of 1887.

BREMHILL

The situation of Bremhill is exceedingly pleasant. Grouped around a minor road, with little through-traffic, it sits on the eastern upper slopes of its hill looking across lush pastureland. Below the north-western side of the hill is the tiny settlement of Bremhill Wick, once much larger but now consisting of only a few scattered cottages and farms and a small modern development. The countryside about is traversed by footpaths and roads whose narrowness keeps them quiet and makes the village a peaceful place.

The Rev William Bowles, poet and eccentric, has left his mark on the church and vicarage. He was rector from 1803 to 1844 and made many Gothic additions to the vicarage, now Bremhill Court, and filled its gardens with grottoes and hermitages, a trait of the 18th century which had by then gone out of fashion. There was a considerable literary circle centred upon Bowood House and William Bowles was the literary guide and friend of the 3rd Marquess of Lansdowne, responsible for introducing many writers to the house. Much of Bowles's own poetry has been derided and unfortunately he was unable to resist any opportunity for breaking into verse on tombstone, wellhead, sundial or monument. Naturally much of this is poor, as witnessed by his inscription on the Maud Heath Monument (1838):

> Those who dost pause on this aerial height
> Where MAUD HEATH'S pathway winds in shade or light,
> Christian Wayfarer in a world of strife
> Be STILL and ponder on the path of life.

However, it was Bowles's published sonnets that influenced a whole school of poetry. Coleridge and Lamb were first attracted to poetry through them when aged about 17 at Christ's Hospital and later both Southey and Wordsworth thought highly of them.

There are pieces of verse by Bowles in many places locally. On the outer north wall of the church is a carved stone memorial to 'a poor old soldier', Benjamin Tremblin, who died in 1822 at the age of 92 and whose verse commemorates the notable actions and commanders he had witnessed. One habit of Bowles was his love of giving away copies of his works suitably inscribed. One day he gave a Bible to the wife of Thomas Moore; the Moores were living at Sloperton Cottage in Bromham and were part of the Bowood Circle. On opening up her Bible, Mrs Moore found it inscribed: 'With the Author's compliments'!

The road from Wick Hill passed through Bremhill Wick, East Tytherington and Langley Burrell to Chippenham. At Kellaways Bridge there is a stone pillar inscribed:

> 'To the memory of the worthy MAUD HEATH, of Langley Burrell widow, who in the year of grace, 1474, for the good of Travellers did in Charity bestow in Land and haufes about Eight pounds a year forever to be laid out on the Highway and Causey leading from Wick Hill to Chippenham Clift. This Pillar was fet up by the Feoffees, 1698. Injure me not.'

The most amazing feature is that after more than 500 years here, the Causeway survives.

Maud Heath is described as a 'market woman' although obviously one with substantial resources as she was able to provide this charity for her fellow market travellers and peddlers. At this time many low-lying areas could be impassable during the winter and there were many benefactions set up to improve the roads but very, very few have survived. On Wick Hill the Marquess of Lansdowne and William Bowles set up a monument to Maud Heath depicting her as a seated rustic figure on the top. She is looking towards Kellaways but as two trees have been allowed to grow up in front of the monument, she might soon find her view somewhat restricted.

It is pleasant to find a farmyard in the midst of the village, and one which is still heavily involved in farming. Unfortunately the well stocked stores and post office which I noted in 1988 now seems to have closed.

About two miles south-west of Bremhill was Stanley Abbey, a Cistercian nunnery founded in 1154. The mill here was the earliest known fulling mill in Wiltshire in 1189 and there was still a fulling mill working here in 1727. Between Bremhill and Stanley, Hazeland Mill is still preserved in working order by its owners. It is a three-storey stone building, the earliest part dating from the early 18th century with an addition of c1800. The narrow, and interesting, road crosses a narrow bridge afront the mill and makes a 90 degree turn alongside leat, pond and sluice gates.

BRIXTON DEVERILL

Brixton Deverill has very nice thatched stone cottages and a Manor Farmhouse. The church of St Michael dates back to the 13th century and tradition has it that it was at an earlier church on this site that King Alfred took communion the day before the Battle of Edington in the year AD 878. Fastened to the north wall of the church are some very attractive carved panels which formed part of the pulpit presented to Monkton Deverill church by Lord Charles Thynne in 1880. As that church is now redundant the panels, which are believed to be of Belgian origin and depict scenes from the story of Adam and Eve in the Book of Genesis, have been moved here. The canopied Norman font is also a recent presentation, having come from the church of St Giles in the deserted village of Imber in 1951 when it was finally decreed that Imber should remain a military firing area.

Over the hill to the south is Pertwood Down, with very fine Celtic field systems and lynchetts. The land has been left in trust by Jack Houghton-Brown so that it will never be ploughed and this example of prehistoric farming will be preserved. A relative of Jack Houghton-Brown is David Stratton, whose demonstration farm in the parish shows different ways of farming on the chalklands.

Here the Wylye river is a little wider than in the upstream Deverills and tends to spread itself over some low lying areas, particularly near the road bridge. Along the road Dredge's Farmhouse reminds us of this well known Wiltshire and Somerset border name and of a time, not many years ago, when around half the Frome cricket team were named Dredge. The Old Rectory is of stone with a slate roof while next door, the one-storey building end on to the road sports an old yellow Automobile Association sign. This states that Kingston Deverill and Longbridge Deverill are both one and a half miles away, London is 99½ miles and motorists are reminded 'Safety First'.

BROADCHALKE

In Broadchalke one is very close to that great Wiltshireman, John Aubrey. Until forced to sell because of his father's debts and various financial losses, Aubrey had a dearly loved small farm here. He was also churchwarden, helping to restore the then ruinous church and, having a musical ear, wrote of the bells: 'One of the tuneablest rings in Wiltshire, which hangs advantageously; the river running near the churchyard which meliorates the sound.' It is indeed a watery place with many springs and small watercourses besides the River Ebble, of which Aubrey wrote: 'There are not better trouts (two feet long) in the kingdom of England than here.' He goes on to say that he introduced crayfish into the river but they did not survive; maybe fortunately as one of their favourite foods is trout spawn.

To read Aubrey is to learn much about the past of Wiltshire. Having lived through the Civil War and the Restoration, he knew the countryside both before and after that disruptive period. With the return of Charles II he spent much of his life in London so it was mainly of pre-Civil War Wiltshire that he wrote. Besides being a great writer of prose and an archaeologist, he is an important social and economic historian. Commenting that his farm at Broadchalke had been reduced in value by £60 a year he is able to ascribe it to the failing price of wool brought about by the decline of trade with Turkey and the fondness of women for silken clothes rather than woollen.

One of the best ways to approach Broadchalke is over the watershed between the rivers Nadder and Ebble on the road from Fovant through Fifield Bavant. The dramatic valley setting is strongly emphasised and with the settlements being well hidden within folds of the hills, it gives an older more desolate impression than is really the case. Today settlement at Broadchalke is scattered on either side of the river. The 20th century has seen watercress beds made in the valley bottom and much new housing outside the historic village centre.

Most of the older houses are on the southern side with the church of All Saints prominent. It was basically built at two periods: late 13th century and from c1360-70, and is a truly massive seeming structure. West of the church is the attractive Kings Old Rectory of stone with brick chimney and Elizabethan mullioned windows. The archway here is believed to be pre-Reformation. Nearby is the early 18th century brick Reddish Manor, once the home of Cecil Beaton, while about a mile further west by the river is Garston House of the 16th and 17th centuries with some walls three feet in thickness.

There are several cob walls around, some of them still thatched, and many pleasant gardens. One modern house, on the eastern side of the village, has used both cob walls and hurdles as fencing to enclose its boundaries. Although not far from Salisbury the village maintains a garage and a shop incorporating family butcher, post office and stores and offering a wide range of services. By the river is the new Broadchalke Surgery while on the other side of the road The Queen's Head has both a non-smoking restaurant and a Village Bar. A recent addition has been a plank bench and bar outside, near the door; this takes us back a few centuries to a time when the men of the village would stand outside the alehouse or sit on the ale bench to drink. Education for children of primary school age is provided in the flint and brick built village school.

To the south-west, and high on the downs, is the village of Bowerchalke. An artificially widened stream flows on the south-east side of the road between the two villages and this was once full of watercress beds. To the south is Marleycombe Hill with its defensive earthworks, field systems and, to the south-west, a settlement site that pre-dates the present village. There are several attractive houses in Bowerchalke; the church of The Holy Trinity is largely Perpendicular although the dedication is from 1297.

One present day resident is Inka Steven who began life in a Russian labour camp and survived to become a singer and actress. She is now a painter and sculptor and raises a great deal of money for multiple sclerosis charities. She has the disease herself but each year stages an event, Inka's Extravaganza, in the village. In 1998 there were top chefs and many celebrities attending and the event raised £40,000.

BROAD TOWN

On a sunny autumn day turn west from the Devizes to Swindon road, through Broad Hinton canopied with leaves turning to browns and yellows, and fall over a steep hillside into Broad Town. I say fall but the road was built before the internal combustion engine was invented and so zig zags down a scarp slope at a gradient suitable for horses. The land drops nearly 100 metres and spread out below is the linear settlement of Broad Town and the beginning of the flat countryside of north-west Wiltshire that once produced so much cheese.

To the north-east of the hillside you have just descended is the Broad Town white horse, which is best viewed from the road on either side of the church although the horse faces the town of Wootton Bassett some three miles distant. There is some dispute as to the origin of this horse. It is believed to have been cut in 1864 by William Simmonds of Littleton Farm on his own land. Speaking in later life he said that he had intended to gradually enlarge it, a process which, if he had carried it out, would have produced a very distorted horse. However, in 1919 there was a claim from a curator of the Imperial War Museum that in 1863, when he was a schoolboy in Wootton Bassett, he and a friend had scoured it. An elderly relative had told him that it had then been in existence for some 50 years.

Clearly there is no way of reconciling these accounts and one is left with the question, did William Simmonds re-cut an old horse in 1864 and, with the passage of time, believe that he had created it? The horse is 78 feet long and 57 feet high and is far more natural in its proportions than most of its kind. In 1991, after a village appraisal, the Broad Town White Horse Restoration Society was formed. At this time the horse had become somewhat overgrown and the Society carried out a restoration and now perform an annual cleaning.

The village name means 'great farmstead' and was used in contrast to Littletown, whose remaining buildings lie below the white horse. The ecclesiastical parish was only created in 1846 out of parts of Broad Hinton and Clyffe Pypard and it did not become a civil parish until 1884. Thus Christ Church with its little bellcote was built in 1846. It is isolated from the main part of the village and is well shaded by yew trees at the front. It is more open at the back where it adjoins fields but it is easy to drive past without realising it is there. The early domestic dwellings are scattered and are mainly thatched, or were formerly thatched. One of the earliest buildings is a one and a half storey timber-framed house with old thatch which has been covered with wire to stop the depredations of nesting birds. There are other timber-framed cottages in Chapel Lane and on the main road, including the L-shaped Laurel Cottage which has pheasants astride its well executed thatched ridge.

Farms are in and around the village and there has been a fair amount of modern infill. It is interesting to note that footpaths lead up the drives and through the gardens of several of these new houses, surely indicating the open and scattered nature of the original settlement. Opposite Chapel Lane is one of the early farmhouses which seems to have been originally thatched. The tiled roof has curves, especially around a first floor window, that were never meant for a tiled or slated roof. It is a sure indication that these curves were once covered by thatch which moulds itself easily to rounded forms. The house is Broad Town Farmhouse and a remarkable family once lived here.

Geoffrey Grigson was the seventh son of a Cornish vicar who worked in Fleet Street as a journalist and, later, in broadcasting. He lived in a cottage in the village at first, in the 1930s and in 1939 his first volume of poetry was published. He was to become a respected poet, critic, anthologist, travel writer and a writer on natural history and the countryside. He is one of the writers I wish I had met, but now, alas, it is too late. His output was prodigious and varied and included, *The Englishman's Flora*, *The Faber Book of Nonsense Verse*, *The Oxford Book of Satirical Verse*, *The Shell Country Alphabet* and several collections of his own verse. In 1957 he wrote *The Wiltshire Book*, a history and guide to the county with good monochrome photographs. In it he lamented the fact that the Kennet and Avon Canal was likely to be abandoned but I am sure that he enjoyed being proved wrong in later years.

To many people Jane Grigson is better known than her husband. She restored pride to English food and cooking and was one of the leading cookery writers of her generation. Her books are well loved and well used in kitchens throughout the land and most are still available in paperback. Her untimely death in 1990 robbed us of the books which she would have written for her own pleasure but she and Geoffrey have left us another influential cookery writer and broadcaster in their daughter Sophie.

BROMHAM

The village of Bromham lies in a triangle, formed by the junction of the A3102, Melksham to Calne road, and the A342, Devizes to Chippenham road. There are four hamlets within the parish: Westbrook, Hawk Street, St Edith's Marsh and Nether Street - the latter to the east of the Devizes Road. The main settlement is clustered around the church, while houses and farms line most of the roads.

The appearance is such that one feels that a handful of dwellings was broadcast by an inexpert sower over a wide area and where each one landed it was allowed to take root and grow. The simile is apt, as from the 17th century market gardening has been the chief occupation. This came about with the dramatic decline of handloom weaving in the depression of the 17th century. A once prosperous industry was decimated and it was said that in 1622, 44 looms were lying idle and there were 800 unemployed in the parish.

The parish was fortunate in having a light friable soil and for 300 years produce has been supplied to neighbouring towns. Under the Small Holdings Act, Wiltshire County Council acquired land in the parish and by 1940 had created 77 holdings. These typically supported the owner, his wife, two married sons and a labourer. The main livestock was pigs and poultry, the dung from these bringing increased fertility to the market gardens.

By 1986 there were just two full-time farms left: Horse Lane and Low Hawk Street, and one part-time. All the rest had been amalgamated and merged.

Market gardening has meant that many of the present population are employed within the parish; a rare event in a Wiltshire village. The industry is still very labour-intensive with many crops raised, planted, hoed and harvested by hand. There are also associated small industries, such as the manufacture of garden sheds, while a fairly recent development has been the establishment of workshops for furniture designer and maker, Mark Wilkinson, who is based at Overton House with workshops in the High Street.

The church of St Nicholas lies in the centre of the village on the site of a Norman church. The most memorable feature of the church is the Tocates and Beauchamp Chapel, later known as the Baynton Chapel. It is a fine example of mid-15th century elaborate and richly decorated Gothic with original painted ceiling and oak screens, while some pieces of late 15th century glass remain.

In the north-east corner of the churchyard is a timber lock-up. An unusual sight in Wiltshire, where all other remaining lock-ups are built of stone, and a reminder of a time when the wrongdoers of Bromham were incarcerated here before being taken off for trial and a possible sojourn in Fisherton or Devizes gaol.

Also in the churchyard is a Celtic cross, marking the grave of the poet Thomas Moore (1779-1852). Moore spent the later years of his life at Sloperton Cottage in the hamlet of Westbrook. Another well-known resident is commemorated at Battle House, to the north of the church. At this appropriately named residence, from 1820 to 1831, lived Sir William Napier, the historian of the Peninsular Wars.

During the 18th century visitors and entertainers from outside the village cannot have arrived in any great number. We can therefore picture the excitement in 1735 when it was announced that a steeple flyer, Thomas Kidman, would visit the village and fly down from the church steeple. Doubtless crowds gathered early, many walking in from some miles away, and the favoured few were accommodated at first floor windows in the surrounding houses, and maybe in a small covered stand erected for the better-off. Peddlers and sellers of foods and drinks would have a most successful day and many a labourer was tempted to spend money he could ill afford on a fairing for his wife or sweetheart. Children were everywhere, but especially perched on top of the tombstones to see over the heads of their elders. A taut rope was stretched from the top of the steeple to the ground. 'Could a man really fly down that rope and live?' was the question on all lips and wagers on the success and survival of the steeple flyer were made.

The hour arrived and the flyer was tied to a board, through which the rope passed by means of a groove, and despatched head first upon his terrifying descent. He had calculated well in the strength of his rope and the speed he was likely to attain but had, unfortunately, left the state of the steeple out of his considerations. Halfway down, the steeple gave way! The flier was thrown off course, but fortunately his fall was broken by a churchyard tree and he escaped serious injury. The event, and narrow escape from death of its chief participant, provided conversation for many a long month and those who had bet on its failure went away happy, although those who had bet on the demise of the flier may have cast disappointed glances at the life-saving tree.

In the Civil War, Bromham had been visited by the outside world in a less pleasant fashion. Between 1643 and 1645 there were many battles and skirmishes in or near the parish. One of the chief Wiltshire Parliamentarians was Edward Baynton who lived in the ancient family mansion, built during the reign of Henry VIII. It was said that stone from Devizes Castle was used in its building and that it was as big as the Palace of Whitehall while the ironwork alone had cost £5,000. Henry VIII had been entertained there and James I had visited it on three occasions. The head of the Baynton family at the time of the Civil War was apparently a very quarrelsome character who spent nearly as much time arguing with his fellow Parliamentarians, particularly Sir Edward Hungerford, as he did fighting Royalists. He was regarded with suspicion by many, some harbouring thoughts that he might be a traitor. If he was, he received little thanks from the Royalists, who burned his magnificent mansion in 1645.

BROUGHTON GIFFORD

I always think of Broughton Gifford as the village around the common, although in truth most of the houses now lie on the road to Holt between the common and the church. Neither Broughton Common nor Norrington Common to the north-east were ever enclosed. Broughton Common was formerly known as Broughton Marsh and there was still a pond on it well into the 20th century. Today it is drained and in the winter is the pitch for the village football team.

The settlement around the common has led to a northwards drift of habitation from the original site around the church. The church of St Mary the Virgin dates from the 13th century and is Early English in style. Until recently hollow ways and house platforms of the early village could be seen in the field on the other side of the road from the church.

Naturally the Baptist chapel of 1806 is near the common where it keeps company with some very fine houses. At the junction of Mill Lane is The Manor House, dated 1622. It is a beautiful stone house with gables and stone mullioned windows and is shaped as an 'L'. Hollybrook House is late 18th century with broad mullioned windows and lower one-bay wings. On the south side of the common is Broughton House dating from the late 16th century. To the north is Gifford Hall, a fine L-shaped building of c1700 on the site of a 16th century building.

In the 16th and 17th centuries this was the home of numerous clothiers and weavers. Handloom weavers were still in existence in 1860 but by that time there was very little work for them and they were in a depressed state, both mentally and economically. Encroachment on the waste had led to the erection of many small cottages and hovels around The Common, few of them with any sanitary provision. This caused many outbreaks of disease. The scarlet fever epidemic of 1851, the year of the Great Exhibition, led to 17 deaths.

During the 17th century Broughton Gifford had been a relatively important place and was well known locally for its geese. No rogue had tried 'to steal the common from these geese' and in fact until quite recently local people were known as 'Broughton Ganders'. There is a story from long ago that a Broughton man once called in the blacksmith to shoe his geese so that they would not go lame whilst walking to market! The story apparently indicates local stupidity but I am sure the meaning behind it reflects the economic importance of the geese and the desire to keep them healthy and well-fed on their journey to a goose fair.

BURBAGE

The passing motorist must think Burbage a very long village and he might be forgiven for wondering if he has actually driven into an adjacent community without realising it. Indeed, at over a mile long, it must be one of the longest villages in the county, being made up of four settlements which for many centuries were separate entities. The 20th century changed that and there has been much building in recent decades which has amalgamated most of the old habitation sites. Although this development has brought some light industry most of the population of just over 1,400 find employment in Marlborough, Swindon or Hungerford.

The increase in the number of villagers has brought new shops, a hall and a club to the village while the local inns are also thriving. Burbage now has its bypass and this has considerably reduced the 1,000 heavy goods vehicles which used to pass through every day. As parts of the High Street have no pavements, a walk to the pub or shops was once a hazardous undertaking.

The Victorian church of All Saints was built in 1854 and is in local flint with a stone pattern. The tower and the west porch entrance come from a much earlier building and are probably 14th or 15th century. A notable feature in the parish is the canal wharf which has the last surviving wharf crane, once privately owned, on the Kennet and Avon canal. Lying to the west of the village, where the road from Marlborough climbs over the canal, both wharf and crane have undergone restoration in recent years. Nearby is the 1,512 foot long Bruce Tunnel through which there is no towpath. Horse-drawn barges were pulled through by their crew hauling on chains fixed to the tunnel walls.

The village is on the edge of present day Savernake Forest and close at hand are small forest settlements which retain great individuality. The small village of Durley is hidden in the woods and is still little known. There is also the large estate church of St Katherine, Savernake (1861) and a renowned cricket team which plays under the name of the forest.

The Forest itself was leased to the Forestry Commission for 999 years by the 6th Marquess of Ailesbury in 1939. He retained the title of Hereditary Warden of Savernake which had been held by his family since William the Conqueror appointed Richard Esturmy as the first Warden. The female line brought the Forest to the Seymour family in 1535. The two best known members were Jane, who followed Anne Boleyn as Henry VIII's Queen but was to die in 1537, twelve days after giving birth to the son that the King so desired, and Edward who was created Duke of Somerset and Protector of the Realm before his fall from grace. In 1676 Savernake again passed through the female line to the Bruce family who have retained it ever since.

BURTON

The small village of Burton is in Nettleton parish so perhaps I should really be writing about Nettleton. However, Nettleton church is at Burton, which is also my wife's maiden name, so I am going to write about that village. The name is one of the commonest place-names in England, meaning 'farm by the borough', and this one was so named by 1204. The settlement is in a slight valley formed by a feeder stream of the By Brook and there is a pleasant collection of houses around the three roads. On the main road is Burton Farm, whose geese will hiss at you as you walk past on the pavement. In the afternoon sun they come out and sit on the grass by the nearby telephone box and become much more sociable.

There are two pubs in the village. The Plume of Feathers is a free house dating back to the 16th century run, in 1998, by Nick Stripp and Wendy Harrison. Nick is an Australian who brings a touch of the Orient to Burton with delicious Thai cooking. More good food is on offer at The Old House at Home. While enjoying your food you can study a wide range of sporting and musical mementoes or, in good weather, sit outside in a terraced garden high above the road.

The church of St Mary has Norman work in the north arcade and a

Perpendicular tower in the Somerset style with decorative window work in the top stage similar in design to that found on the central tower of Wells Cathedral. This is only found in five churches in the county; West Kington, also in Nettleton parish, nearby Yatton Keynell, Devizes St James and Westwood, which gave its name to the style. A variety of periods are represented inside. There is a Norman circular font, a Perpendicular stone pulpit, a 17th century communion rail and Georgian box pews in the north aisle.

In the mid 17th century John Aubrey stated that in the churchyard there was an old epitaph 'not long since legible' inscribed,

> Here lies a traveller old Madam Bene
> Honest Charles Hales his wife I guess
> She was his dear one, we'll not belie her
> And so's mine too; would she lay down by her.

Make of this what you will but it was certainly the sort of epitaph which delighted Aubrey.

This is a long settled area and was important in the extensive Roman occupation of the Cotswolds. In the parish is the Shrine of Apollo which was excavated between 1956 and 1971. A small circular temple was built in the 1st century AD which by the 3rd century had been rebuilt in a much larger and grander octagonal form. The hostelry, which had existed from soon after AD 140 was replaced by a much larger building at some time after AD 250. Other associated buildings were a priest's house, a shop and domestic buildings.

It is likely that the shrine had a pre-Roman significance and that the Romans took over an existing Celtic holy place, as would happen later to their shrines when Christianity arrived. The principal deity was Apollo but there was also an association with Diana which indicates that this was probably a centre for healing. Other cults represented included Silvanus, Mercury and an unidentified one which could have been a local deity. The 3rd century rebuilding with a larger hostelry indicates that the shrine throve and it must have been well used by the owners of the large villas in present day Gloucestershire and Wiltshire who, while paying due homage to their household gods, felt that on special occasions an offering should be made to Apollo. The shop would have sold them images of the gods and, doubtless, other items of religious significance which they could have taken home with them.

CASTLE COMBE

What is there left to say about Castle Combe? There have probably been more visitors to it, more photographs taken of it and more words written about it than any other village in the country. Being voted the Prettiest Village in England in 1962 was perhaps the worst thing that ever happened to this beautiful and once peaceful village. I suspect that none of the villagers could foresee the far-reaching effects that this award would have on their lives. The announcement had been made in the Sunday papers and by lunchtime the narrow street was jammed solid by traffic generated by people wanting to see the unspoilt village.

Four years later, when the village had returned to a slightly quieter existence, it was chosen as the location for the production of *The Story of Doctor Doolittle* by 20th Century Fox. Parts of the village were rebuilt, the By Brook was made into a fishing harbour, complete with seven boats, plastic cobbles were laid over tarmac and Rex Harrison and Anthony Newley were there every day. This generated even more visitors and, since

that time, with an increasing amount of private transport, it has become difficult to enjoy a visit to Castle Combe in the spring, summer or autumn.

For many centuries the villagers were involved in the cloth industry, producing a red and white cloth known as 'Castlecombe' and using the water power of the By Brook to operate their fulling stocks and wash the wool. Weaving was carried out in the cottages and in the 16th century 50 new cottages for weavers, fullers and dyers were erected. By the end of the 17th century the waters of the By Brook began to decrease in volume and many weavers went elsewhere. By the beginning of the 19th century the woollen industry was concentrated in other larger towns and Castle Combe returned to an agricultural existence.

The castle, which gave the village its name, began life as a Roman fort and was used by the Saxons before becoming a Norman stone castle in 1135. By the mid-14th century the castle was ruined and being used as a stone quarry for building materials for village houses. Today all that remains are earthworks of a motte and four baileys with a little masonry.

Half a mile south-west of the castle is the present Manor House, dated 1664 but very much altered by the Victorians so that it appears a house of fantasy, quite out of keeping with the village. In 1947 the then Lord of the Manor put up the whole village for auction. The Manor House became a hotel and the cottages were sold in groups of two or three, or individually.

Within the grounds of the Manor House is a walled garden. Three years ago it was a two acre wilderness of weeds and brambles, now it is an organic farm run by S&J Organic Growers. Husband and wife team Steve Merritt and Juliet Fay cleared the site and using traditional methods such as crop rotation, dressings of manure and compost and growing clover leys, raise a large selection of vegetables. These are sold through a box scheme, at farm gate sales and at a monthly market in Bath. Also in the garden are two flocks of organically fed Warren hens and a herd of pigs; a range of smoked and cured hams, gammon and bacon and specialist sausages is sold

There are many architectural gems in the village, although most have now been over-restored and prettified. At the centre of the village stands the well known Market Cross, date of building unknown but in existence by 1590. The church of St Andrew is basically Perpendicular and in the tower is a rare faceless clock made by a local blacksmith in 1380. Many houses were rebuilt in the 15th century and these probably still exist under later facades. Of special note are the Dower House of 1700 and The White Hart, half-timbered under its facade and still on its original site. Despite much controversy the Castle

Combe Motor Racing Circuit is still in existence to the south-east of the village and provides local people with a rare opportunity to watch motor sport.

Castle Eaton

Castle Eaton is a quiet pleasant village set around a rectangle of streets with the newer buildings along the road that takes the through traffic away. The village is also bounded by a loop of the infant River Thames which, at this

point, is beginning to grow up. It is a gentle shallow meandering stream with trout sheltering under the streaming ribbons of waterweed. The surrounding countryside is very flat but not uninteresting with good pastures and trees.

The river flows around the church of St Mary, which is approached by a nice little winding path from The Street. At the entrance to the churchyard is the base and stump of the old cross, but what catches the eye is the Victorian bell turret and spire above the eastern end of the nave.

By the church is Manor Farm, where the church key can be obtained whilst admiring the good range of stone and brick barns. Leading from the farm entrance is Long Row, a short street which has a long row of eight stone cottages. Now roofed with asbestos tiles, their upper windows look very much like weaver's lights. Round the corner in The Street is Longcot, probably originally three cottages, with an old cast iron water pump on the pavement side of its garden wall. In the middle of the village is The Red Lion, one of the largest buildings. It is 18th century, of brick with a Cotswold stone tile roof, and its size probably indicates that The Street carried all the 18th century traffic. A most unusual feature is a Petanque Club which plays in a specially constructed area in the gardens.

Although petanque is a national pastime of France it has a long history this side of the Channel. It is likely that it was a form of this sport that Sir Francis Drake played on Plymouth Hoe before setting sail to meet the Spanish Armada. Certainly he played with round bow-cannon balls on gravel and bowls in its modern form did not exist until 1856. In modern times, petanque clubs have existed since 1966 and the British Petanque Association was founded in 1974. Most clubs are in the central and eastern parts of southern England and Castle Eaton certainly has the only one that I have seen in Wiltshire.

There are some new houses, which do not conflict with the appearance of the old village, and a new village noticeboard. The latter was erected in 1995 to mark the fiftieth anniversary of the Second World War and is sited before the small village hall.

THE CHALFIELDS

While the Chalfields are not exactly villages, they are so interesting and attractive that they deserve an entry to themselves. Great Chalfield can be approached by a road winding through pastures and cornfields from Holt or

Bradford Leigh to the south, but the best way to come to the Manor is through the lodge gates at Broughton Gifford, off the South Wraxall road. Then one travels down a broad tree-lined approach to the Manor gatehouse. The modern road takes a kink to the right but the footpath continues between its avenue of trees across a field. At the end, set in idyllic rural surroundings, is a moated Tudor manor house with a small church and other old, though slightly less ancient, buildings. The whole group gives a good picture of what much of Wiltshire looked like 200 years ago.

The manor house was rebuilt by Thomas Tropenell, a wool merchant, who acquired the property in 1437 but was not in secure possession of it until 1467. The original house, built by the Percy family, was by this time in a dilapidated condition so Tropenell created 'one of the most perfect examples of the late medieval English manor house, mellow in its buff stone and happily balanced in the composition of its facade without being pedantically symmetrical' (Pevsner). This was completed about 1480 and the remains of the earlier fortified house can still be seen in the curtain walls and tower bases that enclose the church.

In 1908 a fresco of the 15th century was discovered under the whitewash of the dining room. This depicted a bearded man and must surely be a contemporary portrait of Thomas Tropenell. The face is both astute and thoughtful, whilst appearing a little secretive, giving some substance to the opinion of one of his fellows that Thomas Tropenell was a 'perilous covetous man'. While this might have been true, he was a good businessman and also an artist. The evidence for this can still be seen in the manor house and church. To establish his title to his property he compiled the famous Tropenell Cartulary (published in two volumes in 1908) of leases, lawsuits and settlements relating to his estate. This collection is of great historical importance and tells us much about medieval life.

His house is full of fascinating details, amusing ornaments and gargoyles. There are a pair of wrestlers carved on the wall nearest the gate, while in the gallery are three stone masks with hollow eyes and mouths designed so that ladies could watch their husbands feasting in the great hall below without being seen themselves. One defensive measure was the low wicket gate at the front. On entering one was obliged to duck one's head and if your intentions were hostile it would be an easy matter for the door warden to get in a blow at your exposed neck.

For two years during the Civil War the manor house was garrisoned for the Parliamentary forces. From 1644 to 1646, 200 men and 100 horses from the

Malmesbury garrison were somehow accommodated. In 1645 the manor was unsuccessfully besieged by Royalists in April, while in July the Chalfield garrison surprised the Royalist garrison of Lacock while they were on a foraging party and defeated them. The Parliamentarians themselves conducted a food levy from the surrounding parishes and were supplied with bread, cheese, bacon and beer, with ducks coming from nearby Broughton Gifford. Long after the depredations of Parliament, the Manor is now looked after by the National Trust.

To the west lies Little Chalfield, approached by a narrow road that leads through ploughland to Little Chalfield Manor. A stone Georgian building of three bays with a slate roof and iron porch, this also has a most tranquil setting with only its farm, barns, two stone houses and two 20th century houses to keep it company. The approach road is lined by an avenue of trees, mainly chestnut and beech, while another avenue lines the grassy track of a former entrance.

CHARLTON (NEAR MALMESBURY)

That Charlton is on the edge of the Cotswolds is immediately apparent from the stone cottages roofed with Cotswold stone. There is a splendid looking village street, where the gaps have been filled with new houses constructed of Bradstone which does not look too out of character compared with the houses of two or three centuries earlier. On the road to Minety stands the lonely, but well frequented Horse and Groom. Of the late 17th century, it has three steep gables with small oval windows that are unusually set in a horizontal position. Set around are some barns well converted to domestic use, while nearby are some good modern houses in natural stone.

Off Park Street, to the west, is the church of St John the Baptist. At the end of Park Street, and providing its name, is Charlton Park, former seat of the Earls of Suffolk. The original house belonged to the Knyvetts (a good monument to Sir Henry Knyvett, died 1598, and family is in the church) and was brought to the lst Earl of Suffolk by his wife. There is some doubt as to the date of the present house with the earliest date given as 1607, although the building appears later. The interior is mainly Georgian, begun c1772, but some of it was not completed until the 20th century. The hall was started some time after 1783 but was left unfinished for many decades. This is a fine exuberant house which in 1939 passed from the ownership of the Suffolks and became a school. After 1950 it was empty for 25 years and, although a Grade I listed building, was in danger of being demolished. It was rescued by Christopher Buxton, of Period and Country Homes, who, in 1975, took on its renovation and conversion into 18 apartments at a total cost of £1.5 million.

At a much earlier period two well known people were associated with the house: John Dryden (1631-1700), the poet and playwright, married the elder daughter of the Earl of Berkshire, a family closely allied to the Suffolks, and he often came to Charlton for the fishing. His son, Charles, was born here in 1666 while a year later his *Annus Mirabilis* is dated as having been written at Charlton.

A less reputable connection was with an illegitimate daughter of Lord Berkshire, called Mary Davis, who Pepys says was born here. She became, between 1663 and 1668, a most popular actress and dancer on the London stage and certainly attracted the attention of Charles II. One contemporary commented that she had raised herself from the bed of the common ground into the royal bed, while Pepys laconically said of her father, 'he hath got her for the King'. Her reign as a favourite mistress was fairly brief as she fell foul of Nell Gwyn who did not take kindly to rivals. The story goes that Nell invited Mary to supper and laced her sweetmeats with jalap, a very potent purge. The effects of this not unnaturally upset the King, who dismissed her with a pension and a daughter that he had fathered.

CHARLTON (VALE OF PEWSEY)

Charlton is approached by a narrow road from the main Devizes to Amesbury road and is well protected from casual traffic by the road narrowing considerably between the church and the high wall of Charlton Farmhouse. As the road ends at the River Avon anyway, there is little traffic to disturb the peace of the village.

At the western end of the village an overgrown lane leads back to the main road and the village pub. To generations of Wiltshiremen, and many others who were stationed at Upavon during the war, this is The Charlton Cat. In 1986 it was sold and, with no local justification that I could see, was called The Sweeney. After a Vale of Pewsey campaign The Charlton Cat was reinstated as the pub name. Originally it was The Poore's Arms, from the name of the lords of the manor of neighbouring Rushall. Their coat of arms was supported by leopards and it is believed that a badly painted inn sign of these animals first caused the inn to be described as the Charlton Cat.

As The Charlton Cat it is famous for its association with the village's own poet, Stephen Duck. He was born in 1705 and received schooling until the age of 14, when he worked on the farm as a thresher, mower and reaper. By the time he was 20 he had a wife and child and also a burning desire to improve his mind. He worked overtime to get money to buy a book or two and worked harder than others in the fields to get half an hour of daylight off to read the *Spectator*. He was helped by a village friend, who had been in service in London, bringing home a score of books. With the aid of a dictionary he read the whole of *Paradise Lost*; many of us since that time have needed the services of a dictionary when we first tackled that epic.

He wrote much in heroic couplet and in 1730 his verses were brought to the attention of Queen Caroline, when he was described as 'lately a poor thresher in a Barn in the County of Wilts at the wages of four shillings and sixpence per week'. He received royal patronage and the Queen made him a Yeoman of the Guard, the Keeper of Duck Island (in St James's Park, London) and had him educated for the Church. All this was a pleasant change from the tremendously hard winter work of threshing grain with a flail in the barn. Of his good fortune Swift somewhat sarcastically wrote:

> 'The Thresher Duck could o'er the Queen prevail,
> The proverb says 'no fence against a flail',
> From threshing corn he turns to thresh his brains,
> For which her Majesty allows him gains;
> Tho' 'tis confessed that those who ever saw
> His poems think them all not worth a straw.
> Thrice happy Duck! employed in threshing stubble
> Thy toil is lessened, and thy profits double.'

It is true that his conventional verse became submerged under artificial subjects and he used too much classical imagery. His best work is his earliest and most especially *The Thresher's Labour*, whose subject was suggested by the Rector of Pewsey. One image that comes from his farm labouring days, rather than his classical reading, is of prattling women whose tongues moved faster than their rakes when haymaking! The Duck Feast in his honour started in 1734 when the then Lord Palmerston gave a small field, later called Duck's Acre, whose rent paid for a supper for twelve Charlton threshers every year at The Charlton Cat.

Stephen Duck's end is sad. In 1752 Queen Caroline gave him the rectory of Byfleet in Surrey but only four years later, on 21st March, he drowned himself in the Kennet at Reading in a fit of madness or melancholy. We can speculate as to whether he pushed himself too hard to rise from his labouring friends into the circles of Pope and Swift. It was fitting, as I'm sure he would see, to end his days in a river whose source is not many miles north of his birthplace.

CHERHILL

Cherhill is dominated by its white horse and its monument. The white horse was cut in 1780 by Dr Christopher Alsop, the guild steward of Calne. The proliferation of white horses in Wiltshire is usually ascribed to the influence of the Uffington white horse upon various landowners who owned a chalk hill on which such a figure would add grace to the neighbourhood.

Dr Alsop cut this horse in the following way. Firstly he placed a number of flags delineating the outline at ground level on the hillside. He then went about a mile away to the top of Labour-in-Vain Hill where he directed the repositioning of the flags so that the horse would appear lifelike from a distance. To effect his commands he made use of a speaking trumpet and, when he was satisfied with his design, the work of construction could begin. The turf was cut and removed and the space left filled with chalk from a quarry on the other side of the hill. A hollow ring of turf was left for the eye with the eyeball being made with broken glass bottles. The sun's reflection on these could be seen from a great distance.

The second man-made structure is the Lansdowne Obelisk. Erected in 1845 by the 3rd Marquess, he who built the Maud Heath Monument at Bremhill in 1838, it commemorates his ancestor, Sir William Petty, the 17th century economist. For many years it was in a sad state of repair but was restored in 1990. There was one other impressive feature here: the timber-framed Cherhill Barn, 110 feet long with side aisles. In the 1930s it was pictured as being on a stone base with weatherboard walls and huge stone slates on the roof. It was demolished in 1956. Its peculiarity was walls of upright oak studding.

The village lies to the north of the A4 road, formerly the turnpike, between Calne and Beckhampton. There are some interesting street names. Broth Lane is so called from a time in the 19th century when soup was provided at the vicarage during times of hardship. When the soup was ready a bell was rung and the needy came along the narrow lane leading to the vicarage from The Street. The road at the north-east, leading to the main road, was known as Rubble Lane in the 19th century from the practice of carting chalk rubble from Cherhill Down into the village.

At one time a row of elms used to line the main road near to the Old Bush Inn. It was sometimes customary for village men to hide in this tree and to fish for sides of bacon and sacks of corn or cheeses off the tops of the wagons. On one occasion a missing side of bacon was discovered hanging down the chimney of a thatched cottage. On another occasion two men, George and William, wanted a cheese and devised the following ploy. George entertained the wagoner in the inn while William moved the cheese to a previously arranged hiding place, before joining them. But after a while George went out to answer a call of nature and moved the cheese to another hiding place. On later going to divide the cheese, George contrived to appear as shocked at its disappearance as was William, who obviously believed that there was honour among thieves!

For time out of mind there was a Club Fete in Cherhill. The Black Horse was the headquarters of the Club, whose members made weekly contributions as an insurance against sickness and unemployment. Every year on Whit Wednesday the members, preceded by a band, marched around the village with the idea of attracting new recruits. This was thirsty work and necessitated a return to The Black Horse for refreshment. After a while the refreshment would take effect and the members would end the day dancing in the main road. At the end of the 19th century the Club Fete was such an important event that most villagers took it as a holiday. With the gradual improvement of the labourer's lot, the Club became less important and the Fete ended just before the outbreak of the First World War.

CHILMARK

Chilmark is best known for its stone. The quarries here provided the building material for both Salisbury and Chichester Cathedrals and Wilton House. The 13th and 14th centuries saw the greatest use of Chilmark stone but a millennium earlier the Romans had made use of the quarries. Stone continued to be extracted up to the 19th century but the building of the Kennet and Avon, and the Wiltshire and Berkshire canals in the north of the county, allowed quarries producing Bath stone access to a cheap form of transport. In 1839 an estimate for the cost of stone for the new Houses of Parliament put the cost of Chilmark stone at five shillings and threepence per cubic foot in London while Box stone was only one shilling and elevenpence. The quarries continued to be used until 1939 but in 1937 they were taken over by the Ministry of Defence for storage use by the RAF.

It is RAF Chilmark that dominated the parish, although fortunately not the village. Above ground there is little to see apart from boundary fences, railway lines and a few buildings. Most of what went on was hidden from public gaze in the maze of tunnels, galleries and the main vault covering 13 acres below ground. Although a feeling of disquiet may have been engendered in many local minds about possible activities at the site, it is at least an excellent place to see untroubled rabbits at play while sheep safely graze. Now that the base is largely empty, the recently opened Teffont Quarry is extracting excellent stone on part of the site.

The village itself is dominated by its church. Built of the local fine-grained sandy limestone, it has looked over its village for the last 600 years, although the first church on this site would have pre-dated the present one by many centuries. The present dedication is to St Margaret of Antioch, a memory brought back from a warmer land by local men who took part in one of the Crusades.

From the highpoint of the churchyard we can see that the houses are spread around the gentle slope below, a most attractive pattern of stone buildings. Just to the south of the church is Chilmark Manor, of the 17th century. Elsewhere in the village there are 17th century stone cottages with mullion windows, and a stream running between the road and many of the houses; a pleasing feature found in several Wiltshire villages.

On the B3089 road, just to the north of the village, is the ancient Black Dog Inn, dating from the 15th century with some interesting architecture and good food. In the field opposite this inn was held a great annual sheep fair on 20th July, St Margaret's Day. The fair is mentioned by John Aubrey in the 17th century and the field is still called Fairmead.

Within the parish, and near the borders of Fonthill Park, is the isolated and appropriately named settlement of Ridge. An upland settlement with only a few houses, it has survived, whereas most of these outlying hamlets disappeared some centuries ago. Although four roads still lead there, it is a lonely place and receives few visitors other than those concerned with work on the land.

CHILTON FOLIAT

A visit to Chilton Foliat sets me thinking about names. Originally it was probably Cilla's farm, receiving its surname from the Foliat family who owned the manor before 1300. In the chancel wall of the church there is a tomb with the effigy of a knight, cross legged and with his shield and sword. This is believed to be Sir Sampson Foliat but the name has endured here far better than the family that bore it. Then there are the house names. Many of these indicate the former use of the building, such as The Old School, The Old Forge with its lovely undulating tiled roof, Tanyard House and The Old Post Office. The comparatively recent Methodist church of 1932 did not survive too many decades before it also became a house of man and was renamed The Old Chapel. The forest has left its mark with Stag Hill, the late 18th or early 19th century Stag House and the more modern Stag Service Station.

But a sunny day with cotton wool clouds hanging motionless in a sky as blue as the Virgin's snood is no time to consider nomenclature. It is a time to lean upon the parapet of the bridge and watch broad Kennet flow below you. There are waterfowl here. Swans, ducks and coots provide entertainment for the idler and if you are lucky you will catch a glimpse of a large trout, facing upstream out of the main current, as he waits for the waters to bring down food. Downstream the river has been further widened into a small lake and as you gaze over this, with your knees on the sign informing the world that the bridge was widened in 1936, you become aware that your elbows are resting on much-carved stone. Here many a lad has whiled away the time awaiting his lover's tryst by carving their initials in the stone or, at other times, groups of youths left a permanent mark between throwing stones in the river and gawking at passers-by when there was little else to do.

By the bridge a leat takes some of the water under the late 18th century mill which is now all one with its 19th century Mill House. Also here is the mysterious Bridge House. Was it an inn? Was the part fronting the river, with its rain water heads dated 1766, built as an assembly room? Was it a house extended into a grander villa in the mid-18th century?

One Sunday morning in September I watched as villagers hurried along the road to Harvest Festival in the church of St Mary. They, most especially the children, carried produce of all kinds through the thatched lych gate, along the path between the twelve pollarded lime trees and through the church doorway. Much of the church, particularly the west tower, is of c1300 with additions and alterations in the 14th and 19th centuries. It is of flint with dressings of Bath stone and has a splendid semi-circular wagon roof of the early 17th century. Inside are many monuments to long gone Leybournes and Pophams of Littlecote and the latter family had their own pew adorned with their hatchments.

Much of the village is around the main street and the older houses are a mixture of flint and brick with roofs of old tiles or thatch. Even the bus shelter is thatched, as is the Village Store which offers part exchanges and house clearances. Next door is The Wheatsheaf, early 19th century with a straw pig upon its ridge and brick and flint walls below the thatch. The attractive village hall of 1895 has hanging tiles above lower courses of flint while a little farther on is The Square, seven good thatched cottages in an L-shape.

Apart from the church the earliest remaining building must be Chilton Cottage. Once three cottages and now a single house, it is from the early to mid-15th century and was restored between 1975 and 1977. Timber framed upon a flint sill and with brick and plaster infill, it was originally an open hall house. Its dates have been established by Carbon 14 dating corrected by dendrochronology, and some thatch has been dated by C 14 to between 1580 and 1670.

In the mid 1980s the village became famous through the BBC television series, *The Victorian Kitchen Garden.* Although Chilton House is in Berkshire much of its gardens are in Wiltshire and it was here that Head Gardener Harry Dodson and Peter Thoday, the expert from the University of Bath Horticultural Department, presided over a very popular series.

CHISLEDON

The parish of Chisledon is extensive and contains the communities of Badbury, Burderop, Coate, Draycot Foliat and Hodson as well as the fast growing village of Chisledon itself. The older part of the village lies in a sheltered hollow where there are cottages of chalk and sarsen stone typical of a settlement on the edge of the downs. The oldest building is the large church of the Holy Cross and its most ancient part is a small Anglo-Saxon window which has been set into a pier in the arcade. Externally the church is largely Perpendicular but inside are features that date from c1200.

In the churchyard are memorials to the Jefferies family; the best known member having been born at Coate Farmhouse in 1848. Richard Jefferies is perhaps Wiltshire's most famous country writer and spent his boyhood in the fields, on the downs and around Coate Reservoir. Much of this younger life is evocatively recaptured in *Bevis* which, along with earlier works, I find free of the slight artificiality of some of the later books which seem to present the country and its inhabitants in the way that the townsmen and the establishment wished to see them, rather than as they really were.

Occasionally Jefferies was not a very good writer, although he was an excellent journalist, but he was always extremely good at observing and recording the detailed life of the countryside. It was these written observations that delighted and inspired a greater writer and poet. Edward Thomas knew this area intimately, often spending holidays with his grandmother at Swindon and later introducing his future wife, Helen, to the Wiltshire countryside that he loved. Edward had become friends with an old Wiltshireman, David Uzzell, known in the local fashion as 'Dad' in respect to his grey hairs. They enjoyed many long walks and 'Dad' taught Edward the many names of birds, animals and flowers. It was probably the face of David Uzzell that was in his mind many years later when he began his poem *Lob* with the words,

'At hawthorne time in Wiltshire travelling
In search of something chance would never bring.
An old man's face, by life and weather cut
And coloured - rough, brown, sweet as any nut,
A land face, sea-blue-eyed — hung in my mind
When I had left him many a mile behind.'

In Edward Thomas's day Swindon was a good clean, hardworking railway town and he esteemed it above all others in England. He walked many a mile in what was then open country between Swindon and Wootton Bassett. One place he knew especially was Hodson with its delectable thatched cottages in a tiny valley that seems to belong to the world of faerie.

Times have changed. Urbanisation has approached nearly to the door of Coate Farmhouse, which itself has been most fortunately preserved as a museum to Richard Jefferies and the Swindon writer Alfred Williams. Coate Water is now a country park and even the brick tower of Chisledon windmill (c1820) has been removed to a business park at Windmill Hill in the West Swindon development. Hodson, however, is still secluded in its valley.

CHITTERNE

Approaching from Warminster you traverse a typical section of high Salisbury Plain country before rolling down a long spur into the valley of the Chitterne Brook. As you descend you look across to the modern Valley Farm before dropping down the last steep incline into the village. I feel that Chitterne is more akin to lost Imber than the other neighbouring villages of the Plain, Tilshead and Shrewton, for here too the valley sides rise steeply to the high plateau where the houses and gardens end.

In such an isolated community you would expect some good stories; I know of three, from different centuries, and they are all true. One evening early in June 1668 the diarist Samuel Pepys and his party set out from Salisbury to travel to Bath over the Plain. The route they were following passed to the east of Chitterne but as dusk fell their guide missed the track and they entered a 'town' as Pepys wrote, later referring to it as 'Chiltren'. Here they found an inn and beds which were 'good but lousy, which made us merry'. I had thought that 'merry' may have had a different meaning in the 17th century but the Complete Oxford English Dictionary disagrees so I can only assume that the amorous Pepys found other diversions for merriment during a sleepless night. They were well pleased with their mistake for, had they not found Chitterne they would have passed the night in their coach upon the open Plain.

The early 18th century parish registers provide the next story. An entry in the register for the church of All Saints reads, 'John Bridmore and Anne Selwood were married, the aforesaid Anne Selwood was married in her smock without any clothes or headgear on'. This is a very late survival of a custom whereby when a man married a widow he did not become responsible for the debts of her late husband. The idea was that she brought nothing with her from her former life but to preserve some decency she wore her smock. Smock weddings were once commonplace and there was a strong belief that if a man married a widow in any fashion other than this he took over the debts of the former husband.

On Chitterne Down is the Robber's Stone. This records the death of Benjamin Colclough who dropped down dead after being pursued across the Plain after robbing Farmer Dean at Imber on 21st October 1839. His companions, Thomas Saunders, George Waters and Richard Harris were all captured and sentenced to transportation for 15 years. A most unsuccessful attempt at highway robbery as all the malefactors were on foot which gave them little chance of escape if their plot went awry.

Chitterne once had two churches and these were situated in parts of the village which still wear separate identities today. The church of All Saints was sited in the part of the village around the minor road leading north from the Warminster to Shrewton road. In 1861 the old church was demolished and a new one erected on a site presented by Walter Long. The church is a substantial one in flint and stone in the Perpendicular and Decorated styles with an embattled west tower. Inside there are some good monuments including one to Matthew Mitchell who went to sea in 1718 at the age of eight and retired as a commodore in 1747; he lived at Chitterne Manor. The other church, dedicated to St Mary, lay in the eastern part of the village on the main road. After the building of the new church, which has a joint dedication, much of the church of St Mary was pulled down in the 1860s.

To find the remains you must take the track, to the east of The King's Arms, and pass through a kissing gate into a graveyard. Here, standing alone, is the chancel of the old church. Built c1450, it has been retained as a mortuary chapel and, as well as its original furnishings, contains some fragments of late medieval stained glass from the demolished church of All Saints. It is a tranquil setting with a farm and farmyard on two sides and with apple trees flanking the lane. The ecclesiastical parishes were joined in 1861 but it was not until 1st March 1907 that the civil parishes were amalgamated.

In 1998 a new village hall is being built, next to the present church, as a millennium project. In front of this is a small triangular village green and on the other side of the road is the large Parish Council Playing Field.

Nearly all housing is around the roads and the enclosed situation is apparent from the old farmyards in the village rather than post-Enclosure ones in the new fields. There are good buildings from four centuries, the earliest being The Gatehouse with parts from the 16th century and stables, with a loft over, from the same period. Both Chitterne Lodge and Chitterne House are in chequered flint and stone of the late 17th century and the latter has a datestone over the door inscribed, 'Health and Peace this House Increased 1635 G.D.'. White Hart House, a former inn which could well have been the one that accommodated Pepys, has a datestone of 1651, while The Manor is mid-17th and The Round House, on the main road, late 17th century.

The present public house is The King's Head, on the main road in the eastern part of the village and presenting some very attractive floral displays to the passing traffic. It is a mid-19th century building and appears in the directory for 1848. At this time, when the population was rising to 691 in 1851, there was also a beer retailer in the village. Population peaked in the census years of 1861 and 1871 when totals of 710 were recorded. Since then there has been a steady decline to the 289 recorded in 1991. The mid-19th century figures must represent the high point of chalkland farming since when agricultural depression and increasing mechanisation has reduced the numbers of men working on the land. It must have been a sober village as only one public house and one beerhouse were sufficient for 700 people.

CHOLDERTON

Although on the edge of Salisbury Plain, Cholderton has the feel of Hampshire within it and indeed the border is only a quarter of a mile away. It is a pleasant tiny village, a mixture of flint and brick, thatch and tile, mostly set along the Marlborough to Salisbury road. It is also set on either bank of a small stream but for most of the year this is hardly noticeable for it is a winterbourne and much of its bed becomes choked with vegetation in the summer. One local house name, Drybrook Lodge, expresses it nicely.

For me, the real treat in this village comes at the approach to the church. A narrow lane leads off from the main road and along the left hand side is a line of one-storey cob cottages, mostly thatched. A rare surprise and unusual, for although the far one now has an upper floor, it is the roof space that has been used and the roof itself has not been raised. The church of St Nicholas is then approached along a mossy path, shaded by four yews, to the only door set in the west wall.

The story of the church is most interesting. The old church was in a ruinous state by 1840 and needed rebuilding when the rector, the Rev Thomas Moyley (1836-1846), chanced upon the old oak roof of a church that had been destroyed in the 15th century. The fact that this find was on a quay at Ipswich did not deter the rector! He went to a great deal of trouble to bring it to Cholderton and build his new church under it. The total cost was £6,000, of which the Rev Moyley provided £5,000. So the mid-19th century church has a medieval ten-bay roof with hammerbeams.

North of the church is Cholderton House, while back in the village is the early 18th century Manor House. The latter has an extensive farmyard by the War Memorial with tiled cob walls and early stalls and outbuildings. A former farmyard at the southern end is that of the pleasant white-painted

Cholderton

Holly Tree Farm House, while the thatched Crown Inn has a thatched wellhead.

Recently an international equestrian star lived in Cholderton with his 13 horses and four staff. New Zealander Mark Todd, MBE, established his yard here after working in Chippenham, Malmesbury and Mere. The 1984 Olympic three-day event champion competed all over the world but found this quiet corner of Wiltshire ideal for training and bringing on his horses. Nowadays the Country Leisure Group, which make glass fibre mouldings, employs 24 people in the village.

CHRISTIAN MALFORD

One of the more unusual of Wiltshire's 'double-barrelled' village names has the meaning of 'a ford by a cross' and it is mentioned in land charters, often as Cristemalford or similar variants, from AD 717. There are the remains of a cross in the garden of the house named Croscote on The Green, but this is medieval and the early cross is likely to have been on, or near, the site of the present church which overlooks the River Avon.

The church is dedicated to All Saints and has 12th century origins although much of the existing work is of c1300 and the 15th century with an 18th century west tower. The clock in the tower was given by John Hiscocks in 1855 while the well kept gutters and downpipes are dated 1881. From a time before church clocks were common is the scratch dial which can be seen on the buttress at the south-east corner of the chancel. There is a very large churchyard, part of which is clear and this might account for the gravestones which have been used as paving through the lush grass and trees. Here there are good chest tombs including a handsome group from the 18th and 19th centuries, to the Hull family of Ridgeway Farm. A later monument, to members of this family, who died around the year 1900, has intricate carvings of a dove and passion fruit flowers entwined round a cross. The church register dates from 1653, because an earlier register was burned in 1693 when the house in which the curate was living was struck by lightning and set on fire.

The pattern of the village presents an interesting problem when conjecturing its original form. The present pattern is much the same as it was in 1773 when Andrews and Dury published the first accurate large scale map of the county. From the church, east-north-east, runs Church Road to The

Green and thence on to Thornyend. The Green heads north to the Main Road, along which are sited most of the larger houses and farmhouses, which in turn leads north-east to Friday Street and Upper Town. Both old and new houses are widely scattered and set within their own gardens. At the western end of Main Road, at the end of Avonweir Road was Christian Malford Mill. Near the church was the manor house, the seat of Henry Herbert in 1773, which is now demolished. Normally with this village pattern one would have expected the settlement to have been moved, or grown away, from the church but here, one feels, the present pattern is likely to be similar to the original. Development to the west would have been curtailed by the river, which is also the parish boundary.

Along Main Road are Beanhill Farmhouse of the late 17th and early 18th centuries, Great Ridgeway Farmhouse of c1700, The Mermaid Inn, formerly Mermaid Farmhouse of the early 18th century, and Swallett Farmhouse of the early 18th century. Around 1700 was an important time for farmhouse building and perhaps indicates the time when much of the land in the parish was enclosed. Also on this road are some late 17th century timber-framed buildings, including Malford House, and Swallett House of the early 18th century.

The Green was mentioned in 1327 when it was the home of Rosemond atte Grene, a reminder to us that this surname was given to people who lived on, or near, a green. Writing about the village John Aubrey says, 'Here is, in the green, a very faire Church-house, where at Midsummer is a famous Revell'. Aubrey was very keen on recording village revels which obviously held great attractions for him and which were an important feature of rural life, allowing licensed promiscuity and mayhem for a short period and thus acting as a safety valve for people's emotions. The fair church-house later became the village poor house and had gone by the mid-19th century.

Some houses on The Green were built in the 19th and early 20th centuries when the small amount of remaining unenclosed land was enclosed. From a much earlier time is The Old Malthouse, built in 1673 of stone rubble with a roof of good Bridgwater tiles, while No 70, with its triangular garden, could well have originated as a small cottage built on the waste. There is a nice brick house of the late 18th or early 19th century which has the nameboard from Dauntsey railway station in its garden, while Westfield House is a good example of a modern village house in a traditional style. The parish now has much modern housing, much of it infill but some on the sites of earlier dwellings.

The new houses must account for the two classrooms, toilets, a staffroom and an office which have been added to the 1856 National School in 1998 and 1999. The pleasant red brick school has preserved an old notice giving the names of a previous headteacher and caretaker and added large painted wooden figures of clothed bears, a badger and a squirrel to the walls. Near the church is both an old and a new rectory. The former was remodelled c1816 by John Provis and has a 17th century cottage to the rear. The plans for the remodelling are in the County Record Office and show that the work was not executed exactly as planned.

For amenities the village still has a post office and store while the parish council maintains a recreation ground. The village hall, built largely of tin and painted an eye catching lime green, provides a venue for many events and organisations. Apart from farming there is little employment although in the 19th century many people would have worked in a six-storey cloth mill which was built c1800 on the Avon and worked to c1850; it had been demolished by 1885.

CHUTE

In the east of the county is what remains of Chute Forest. The small settlements of Upper Chute, Lower Chute, and Chute Cadley were all originally established in forest clearings that had been hacked out by men with axes. This is still deserted country which receives few visitors, but it is becoming more heavily populated. The modern parish of Chute Forest contained no village until the 20th century, only Chute Lodge and various farmsteads.

The only church remaining in use is that of St Nicholas at Upper Chute. It was built by J. L. Pearson in 1869-72 and is in flint and brick. A relic of the previous church can be seen in the floor before the chancel, a grave slab of 1792 to a long-lived inhabitant, one William Meadows, who was as old as the century when he died. The empty and redundant church of St Mary (1875) stands at the end of a little lane in Chute Forest. In 1976 its six bells were transferred to St Nicholas.

Most of the settlements have their big houses around which the cottages cluster. Standen House is of the late 18th century; built in grey brick it has an impressive presence. Chute Lodge is a substantial brick house, c1760, with many fine features both inside and out. There are various alterations, made when the house was a Borstal and later a school, but the property was restored in the 1970s. Fronting its park is Conholt House, the only one without attendant smaller houses. As it stands it is an early 19th century building of grey brick, but this was only an extension to a late 17th century house which was demolished in the 1950s. One has the impression that it might be a little lonely living in Chute Forest but Lower Chute has its village hall and Upper Chute a surprisingly large pub, The Cross Keys, at the top of the village and doubtless there is more neighbourliness than in larger villages.

To the north of the village runs the impressive Chute Causeway. Originally the Roman road from Winchester to Mildenhall, it is now overlaid by the modern road but survives as a distinct causeway. From here there are superb views of the surrounding downland and forest but at times, so local legend has it, a ghost may also be seen. It is that of a rector of Chute who died of the plague in the time of Charles II. He apparently persuaded those of his parishioners who had the sickness to go and live in an isolated camp by the Causeway. He promised to bring them food and other supplies but then abandoned them once he had cleared them from the village. Those that survived the plague died of starvation. His ghost is seen constantly trudging up the hill on the journey he could not bring himself to make when he was mortal with all the fears and weaknesses of the flesh.

CLYFFE PYPARD

As its name suggests, the village is built into the hillside and the view down its village street towards the church is the stuff of picture postcards. The church of St Peter itself has a beautiful setting, being below a wooded part of the hill called Clyffe Hanging. Dating from the 15th century, the church was somewhat over-restored by William Butterfield in 1873-74, when he also rebuilt the chancel. These have been the lands of the Goddard family since 1530 and there are plenty of memorials to them. Two Tudor statues to members of the family are in the unusual medium of chalk while somewhat later the Rev F. Goddard made a very good job of carving the font in 1840. More recently the great architectural and art historian, Sir Nikolaus Pevsner, and his wife, were buried here.

Nearby is the brick Manor House of the Goddards, which was mostly rebuilt in 1880, while the old stone gabled rectory of 1839-40 now has the new brick rectory of 1980 as a companion. Further up the village street The

Goddard Arms bears further witness to the local family. A more recent member of the family was Canon E.H. Goddard who did much work for the Wiltshire Archaeological Society and compiled a bibliography for the county of printed material published up to 1928. An abridged version of this was published in 1929 and is still well used today.

A natural event that was long remembered occurred here in the 1850s. A whirlwind swept over the hill above the village and uprooted hundreds of trees close to the houses. It was a truly terrifying visitation with large tree trunks being tossed around like matchsticks and every cottage in danger of a tree falling onto the thatch.

Several small settlements are nearby, the largest being Bushton to the north-west. Manor Farmhouse, of brick with stone dressings, is dated 1747 but may be a little earlier. That this area was more heavily populated 600 years ago than it is today is evident from two deserted villages at Bupton and Woodhill.

CODFORD

The village of Codford has been formed by the union of the two parishes of Codford St Mary and Codford St Peter. This, which began as the growing together of two adjacent villages, was formalised when in 1928 the union of the benefice of the two Codfords was approved, while six years later the two civil parishes became one. Most refreshingly both churches are still in use.

The church of St Mary lies at the southern end of the village while at the northern end is the church of St Peter. Much of this is the 1864 rebuilding but the tower and south aisle are Perpendicular. The glory of this church is to be found in the north wall of the chancel. Standing only four feet high, it is a 9th century Saxon tapered shaft. The carving is very fine and this remarkably well preserved piece was probably part of a cross shaft although the depiction is less easy to understand. There is a man, holding a mallet, with his head thrown back looking at a stylised branch that he is holding aloft.

It was in this church that I was reminded of P. G. Wodehouse's story of the Great Sermon Handicap. In it a group of young men from a vicarage reading party made a book on the lengths of the sermons of the incumbents of surrounding parishes. This was in the days when the winner preached for 50 minutes and the occasion was irreverently brought to my mind when I saw a collection of picture books for the use of children during the service.

Like several Wiltshire villages, Codford was transformed during the First World War by the erection of enormous army camps around the parish. At first these were tented and as the winter of 1914-15 was exceptionally wet the conditions were chaotic. Many colonial troops died of meningitis and there was much flooding, with roads being barely passable. Hundreds of workmen were entrained from Salisbury to build 15 better camps and their horse teams and traction engines churned the already deep mud into quagmires. The village itself became full of temporary shops, cafes and barbers to cater for the troops while agriculture and normal village life became very limited and difficult.

As in other camps there was an influenza epidemic after Armistice Day and as a result there are 98 Anzac graves in the small war cemetery across the road from St Mary's church. The majority of victims were New Zealanders, who are buried in the west of the area, while the Australians are in the east. Nearby is the Anzac Hut which was once the home of the lst Codford Scouts, Cubs and Brownies but now appears to be disused. Other survivors are various huts and buildings to the north and east of Codford St Peter.

Codford has a long tradition of good social life and entertainment which is perhaps best seen in amateur drama and theatre. The Codford Amateurs reached the London final of a competition organised by a national newspaper after the Second World War and were eventually placed fourth. In 1948 the Woolstore Theatre Club was formed; in 1963 they purchased the old brick woolstore, thus making Codford the first village to own its own theatre, and the club still stages around four productions a year, including a pantomime, and they have built up a very large store of costumes.

Other aspects of village life are thriving. There is both a post office and shop and the Codford Stores and Off Licence, while there is also a garage selling motor caravans and an antiques shop. Since the village bypass has been built it is a pleasure to walk down the main street and pause by the old Warminster Roads turnpike milestone, 'Salisbury 14 Warminster 7', and watch the village football team playing on the recreation ground. Recent additions to business and social life are the Codford Business Centre, the village hall and the Sports and Social Club. A reminder of the past is on the house called The Old Bakery. It still has a sign, 'Wilts & Dorset Motor Service Ltd. Parcel Agent' in the splendid red which was the colour of their buses.

COLERNE

From the A4 road in Box take the little road to Ditteridge and Colerne, cross the By Brook and follow the twists and turns and the signposts to Colerne. If you like a steep descent take the short route across the Lid Brook, otherwise take the longer road that first swings east before heading north-west to the village. This is the way to approach Colerne for from these roads you see it in its glory as a hill top village. *The Village on the Hill* is the apt title of two volumes by the Colerne History Group and the village stands proud at about 540 feet above sea level overlooking a steep coombe.

The defensive nature and settlement potential of this site have long been recognised. Iron Age man built a promontory hillfort on Northwood Plain around 100 BC while a little later the Romans, or Romanised Britons, occupied several sites and built a villa. The Saxons settled here and by 1086 Colerne was a large manor. In 1447 Henry VI granted a market and a fair to the Warden and Scholars of New College, Oxford, who owned the manor from 1389 to 1877. The market was held every Friday and the fair on the eve, day and morrow of St John the Baptist, the patron saint of the church.

The church dates from the 1190s, the eastern end of the present nave, to 1280, chapel, north aisle and clerestory, to 1450 when the tower was built. This slender west tower is an enduring image as it stands against the sky when you approach from the south. The church was somewhat over restored in 1877 but surviving are vaulted sedilla niches, medieval tomb recesses and two fragments of a cross shaft. These are 9th century and very fine with a motif, as Pevsner says, of 'wildly intertwined dragons'.

If you are lucky you can park in the old Market Place before the church. There are good houses everywhere. Nos. 1 and 3 Market Place date from before 1600 while Daubenys is a medieval long house. The Manor House, to the north-east of the church, is dated 1689. The old Rectory looks fairly plain from the front but at the rear has splendid Venetian windows. In the middle of the Market Place is a small enclosed green with a monument, 'Erected by subscription to record the grateful appreciation of the benevolent acts of Richard Walmesly Esq. of Lucknam 1893'. Lucknam Park lies about a mile and a quarter from here and is part Georgian but largely heavily Victorian.

Leading off the main road is Tutton Hill with a nice row of cottages fronted by a raised pavement, or a sunken road. Parsonage Farm has a steep pitched roof while lower down, by Tutton Hill House, is a pump and a water trough for horses fed by a open stream. Other cottages are in short rows at right angles to the road and most have splendid views across the valley to the hills rising beyond Box.

This was a fairly isolated community to which modern services came late, but which isolation ensured a stable community with many long established village families, the core families of population studies. This was to change in the 1930s when plans for airfield expansion for the country began. In 1936 a three-man team arrived in the village to assess potential sites and found a suitable area of 800 acres. The first contractors arrived in June 1939 and the Camp's maintenance role began on 1st January 1940 with building work hardly started. The aircraft operated from grass strips before the runways were made and there were many ATA pilots, including Amy Johnson, ferrying aircraft.

Colerne became the RAF's first permanent jet fighter base in January 1945 with the 19 new Gloster Meteor IIIs of No 616 (South Yorkshire) Squadron. This was the only jet operational during the war. On the whole the village felt 'The Camp' was a good thing, with job opportunities, new and increased local services and possible marriage partners. One effect was quite dramatic. In 1931 the population had been 844, by 1951 it was 2,035 with a very large service settlement north of the airfield. RAF Colerne closed in 1976 and the Camp was handed over to the Army for use as a barracks. The population drop was substantial; from 3,142 in 1971 to 2,221 in 1981.

One result of the Camp seems to have been The Vineyard Restaurant, at the face of an old quarry. In October 1945 Iris Fuller received permission to open a catering establishment. On the first day a plywood sign announced, 'The Vineyard is Open for Teas and Suppers'. Six customers arrived from the Camp on the first afternoon and the venue was soon so popular that the bus company put on an extra bus on Sunday afternoons. In 1948 the 17th century cellar was restored as a restaurant while a good write up from Fanny Cradock in the 1950s ensured national renown with many American customers. In 1966 Iris Fuller sold the restaurant to Ben Warris, of the comic duo Jewel and Warris, and his wife.

COLLINGBOURNE DUCIS

It is hard to imagine that the two Collingbournes, Ducis and Kingston, were once medieval forest villages, when Chute Forest reached out towards ancient Savernake. One glimpse remains. If you approach from Tidworth and Ludgershall you will reach the brow of a hill and see Collingbourne Ducis embosked below you. The only part of the old village visible above the trees is the slender church tower, although the newer houses on the Salisbury road are outside the small wooded area. They are situated in the Bourne valley and, although the River Bourne rises at Burbage, to the north, it is a winterbourne for much of its length and summertime visitors to the Collingbournes will find only a dry bed where the waters of a small stream should sparkle. Both parishes included several small settlements; at Ducis there was Cadley and Sunton, with Brunton and Aughton at Kingston.

Collingbourne Ducis has some most interesting buildings and features. Mainly thatched with a mixture of timber framing and brick walls, one house has a thatched human figure on its roof instead of the more usual bird. Sunton Cottage is of brick and flint and has really deep overhanging thatch which at one point sweeps down nearly to ground level.

The Last Straw (formerly the Catherine Wheel) is a thatched free house with a restaurant and tea room, while opposite is one of the few remaining one-storey cottages I have seen in Wiltshire. It is of flint and cob, with a little timbering and is thatched with crowns atop the ridge giving the clue to its name, Crown Cottage. Linden Cottage is of flint and has a door stone inscribed 'RWE 1694'; there is a thatched well head in the garden. Appropriately Old Lime Farm is surrounded by lime trees while a little further south is the Blue Lion Inn, built of red and blue bricks with a slate roof. It looks Georgian in its symmetry and is attached to an earlier thatched brick house.

The Tidworth road continues to follow the winterbourne and has a nice old milestone inscribed 'To Marlborough X miles/To Andover X miles'.There are some interesting houses on the other side of the road from the stream bed and this road is a little less busy than the main one.

The road to Salisbury turns 90 degrees here shortly to leave Collingbourne Ducis. Here stands the church of St Andrew, 13th century but rebuilt and restored in 1876-77. Inside are memorials of the Seymour family, ancestors of those who later held great power in the land, while in the Perpendicular tower, near the bells, a medieval incumbent constructed nest boxes to save the expense of building a dovecote. Nearby is the school which now serves both Collingbournes. Its roof is strikingly different in this area as it is slate in alternating grey and purple bands.

Along the very busy Marlborough to Salisbury Road there are various industries. In the early 20th century Mr Hosier of nearby Wexcombe, had invented a mobile milking parlour and the business, and until recently Hosier Farming Systems, flourished only four miles from the home of its creator. Now there is the Country Centre, a large retail complex selling industrial workware, outdoor wear, animal feeds, calor gas and other necessities for rural life, and an engineering works, while at Cadley is the surprising sight of several desert and safari expedition vehicles owned by Exodus Expeditions who have their base here. The name of Hosier still flourishes with several farmers including Hosier Bros. at Waglands Farm in the parish.

COLLINGBOURNE KINGSTON

Collingbourne Kingston is very much smaller than Collingbourne Ducis and still has a large farm in the middle of the village. Manor Farm has a substantial yard with outbuildings and a good-sized thatched weatherboard barn and now offers farmhouse bed and breakfast. Parsonage Farm is a farmhouse with stone mullion windows. The church of St Mary is largely Perpendicular with remnants of the 13th and 14th centuries. Inside, blocking the south-east chancel window, is a large monument, a veritable pile of stone, an appropriate memorial to Thomas Pile (died 1500), and wife, and their son Sir Gilbert Pile (died 1626) and his wife.

Surprisingly in a small village there were two public houses until recently, the Cleaver Inn, a Wadworth's house of red and blue brick, and the slightly later Windmill Inn, a Whitbread house of red brick. The Windmill, like its London namesake, has now closed and is a private house. The village has long had a reputation for hospitality. In 1604 the rector and 18 parishioners petitioned for the granting of a licence to Robert Fay to keep a victualling house. The reason given was that many travellers became lost on the downs and sought shelter in the village.

Just beyond Manor Farm and set on a slight rise is the old school, redundant now that the village children have to travel to Ducis. Unlike most of its kind it has not been turned into a private house but is a licensed restaurant, The Old School House. Within the parish the settlement at Brunton appears to be larger than the main village. Here there is an attractive mix of houses of various periods which includes the fine, brick built Brunton House of c1700.

One man believed to have been a native of the Collingbournes was William Collingbourne. Living in the reign of the unpopular King Richard III, he wrote satirical rhymes concerning the King and his ministers. He pinned these rhymes upon church doors so that all the parish, or at least the few who could read, might appreciate them. It was Collingbourne who wrote the well known couplet,

> 'The Cat, the Rat and Lovel the Dogge,
> Rule all England under a Hogge.'

Sir William Catesby, Sir Richard Ratcliff and Lord Lovell were the chief ministers of Richard III, whose crest was a boar. The King was not amused and Collingbourne was indicted for sedition, found guilty and hanged.

CORSLEY

Corsley is really the parish without a proper village or centre. It has lots of hamlets and small settlements: Corsley Heath, Longhedge, Lane End, Lye's Green and the Whitbournes, besides Corsley itself in the north.

After the Reformation much of the parish was bought by the Thynnes of Longleat and, while rebuilding Longleat House, John Thynne built a manor house here in 1563, part of which is incorporated in the present Manor Farmhouse including the quadruple gabled stone front. The present parish church of St Margaret is of 1833 and replaced a medieval church which had become increasingly neglected.

Property at Corsley was at the centre of a dispute after the death of Sir John Thynne, the builder of Longleat, in 1580. To his wife Dorothy he had left one third of his plate and the contents of Longleat plus monies, cattle and 100 sheep from his Corsley estate. On 21st May Sir John died, some hours after he had learned that his demise had already been reported in London, leaving Longleat and its estates to his eldest son John. Dorothy was John's stepmother and she had little time for him. On his arrival at Longleat he was refused entry into her rooms.

Dorothy was convinced that the Corsley property was hers and she and her servants remained locked in part of Longleat for two days, bringing the running of the house to a standstill. After departing to Corsley she continued to make trouble for the new owner and his young wife until she eventually married Carew Raleigh, the brother of Sir Walter.

The stone-built Corsley House of 1814 was the home of Byam Davies, a retired barrister. In 1909 his daughter, Maud, published her *Life in an English Village*, an investigation of rural poverty inspired by Sydney and Beatrice Webb. The local indignation at the publication of 'confidential' village information persuaded Mr Davies to buy up all copies of the work and caused Maud's departure for London, where she took up social work. Tragically she died beneath a train there only three years later. Needless to say, this is now a very rare work but copies are available and it is well worth reading for its excellent portrayal of a Wiltshire village.

Both Whitbourne Springs and Longhedge have many rubble cottages of the 17th and 18th centuries, while Longhedge Farm now houses the Longhorn Western Riding Stables. At Temple Whitbourne is the church of St Mary, built in 1903 in the 'Arts and Crafts' style, and the earlier stone rubble and brick Baptist chapel of 1811.

Corsley Heath has probably the greatest concentration of population, is on the greensand and, like Longhedge and Lane End, was originally built on the common land. It is on the main road between Warminster and Frome and possesses a post office, stores, garage and The Royal Oak Inn, which is mainly 18th century, being extended in the 19th century. Another pub is at Lye's Green, the picturesque Cross Keys, while at Lane End, where John Wesley preached in 1772, there is a long association with Methodism and therefore probably temperance, although The White Hart has survived there and looks out across the county border into Somerset.

Farming has always been of prime importance, alternating between pasture and arable at differing periods. The most recent change was during the Second World War, from dairying to corn growing. There have been various small industries from the times of the 18th century enclosures and these included fulling, weaving and dyeing, a silk mill, maltings, a brickworks and the Corsley Wagon Works. More recently the southern part of the parish became Lord Bath's Safari Park.

In the east is Cley Hill with a smaller hill to its north-east. The barrows and univallate hill fort on the larger hill gave rise to the local verse:

'Big Cley Hill do wear a hat
Little Cley Hill do laugh at that.'

Today Cley Hill is best known for its association with unidentified flying objects, first reported in 1965 and written about by local journalist Arthur Shuttlewood in *The Warminster Mystery* and several other books. The area still attracts many UFO hunters, some of whom keep all night vigils.

DILTON

Dilton provides the supreme example of a village which has shrunk and almost vanished while its child of the common land has prospered and grown into a village of some 2,000 plus people. The original village, now known as Old Dilton, is in the narrow upper valley of the Biss Brook, south-west of Westbury. It is easy to see why settlement shifted away from here. There is little flat land and the village would have been hemmed in by its open fields making expansion impossible. The surrounding, higher, chalklands were suitable for the plough and within reach of the houses and farms. Today no-one passes through Old Dilton except by design. It is at the junction of three very small roads from Upton Scudamore, Hisomley and Chalford, but it is doubtful if the residents of those places would travel by that route. So the farm and the few houses and cottages that remain enjoy a fairly traffic-free existence.

There is one other building, in my view the best and most surprising. The church of St Mary escaped the hands of the Victorian renovators and has preserved its furnishings intact from the 18th century; there were some

St. Mary's
Old Dilton

advantages to being forgotten and neglected in the 19th century! Inside is a three-decker pulpit, high box pews with three medieval ones surviving, large square family pews and both a west and a north gallery. The church is unlocked during the daytime and an absence of recent stained glass means that it is very light inside. A visit will provide a very clear picture of the conditions of worship prior to 1800.

The increase in population had led to squatters' cottages on the common and marsh and by the 14th century this was the main concentration of population, although Old Dilton remained the more important for several more centuries. Gradually cottages and farmhouses there became derelict as people moved away from the old village, while in the late 18th century there was great expansion at Dilton Marsh. This was largely due to the local cloth industry which, at that time, involved weaving taking place on looms in the cottages, houses and attached workshops of the weavers. The trade was controlled by the clothiers, who provided the wool and finished and sold the cloth. Many of the houses on the edge of the common can still be recognised by their long front gardens between the houses and the road, indicating the land they were allowed to keep at the enclosure of the common. Some still have the single storey loom shops attached to the rear of the house. The weaving was killed off by the mechanisation of the processes and their concentration in factories in the local towns. Like many similar villages Dilton suffered great poverty through this industrial innovation.

Because of the origin of the settlement, many Dilton houses tend to be small and are of brick. However, Chalcot House, refronted in the late 17th century, is large and set in parkland.

Eighteenth century Dilton was associated with my own family name and in 1768, just outside the parish in Westbury Leigh, was born Joshua Marshman. His parents were both members of the Baptist church and although Joshua received only rudimentary education (his father was a weaver) he had a great thirst for knowledge and practised a pre-Victorian form of self help. At the age of 15 he was errand boy for a London bookseller, in which job he found some opportunities for reading. However, he was unhappy and returned to Wiltshire where he worked at the loom with his father but by the time he was 18 he had read 500 books, giving special attention to Greek grammar and divinity.

Aged 26 he was appointed master of a school at Broadmead, Bristol, where he joined the classes of the Baptist Academy studying the Classics, Hebrew and other Near Eastern languages. On his offering himself to the missionary service he was sent to the Serampore Mission Station in India with Mr Ward and Dr Carey. Here Joshua learned Bengali, Sanskrit and Chinese. The latter was learned from Chinese servants and from it he was able to make the first translation of the New Testament into Chinese. It was not particularly good but it was the very first attempt and not bad for the son of a Wiltshire weaver. With his colleagues he also printed and published the first eastern newspaper, *The Mirror of News*, whose first edition appeared on 31st May 1818.

In 1811 he had been made a Doctor of Divinity by an American university but Wiltshire did not see Dr Marshman until 1826 when he was again able to see the once familiar Westbury White Horse and talk to the friends of his youth.

DINTON

The story of Dinton is interwoven with the stories of some important families in the land. From 1547 to 1918 the manor was in the ownership of the Earls of Pembroke, to whom it had been granted by the Crown after the execution of the former owner, Sir Thomas Arundell. In 1609 Edward Hyde was born in the old Rectory (now Hyde's House, a National Trust property). He was to become the first Earl of Clarendon and Chancellor to Charles II. His daughter married the future James II and was the mother of both Queen Mary and Queen Anne. The Hydes had originally come from Cheshire and Edward's father, Henry, in 1597 married Mistress Marie Langford, the daughter of a Trowbridge clothier, whose family was one of the most important in the Wiltshire wool trade. Thus, from relatively lowly rural beginnings, a family became the greatest in the land within three generations.

Among other well-known families were the Lawes and Ludlows. Thomas Lawes was a vicar choral of Salisbury and the father of two well-known musicians of the day. They were both Masters of the King's Musick and Henry wrote the anthem for the coronation of Charles II and the music for Milton's *Masque of Comus* and *Zadok the Priest*. Henry was born in Dinton and buried in Westminster Abbey. The Ludlows were a large family, two of whom went to America in 1630. Robert Ludlow drafted the constitution of Connecticut and George Ludlow became a prominent member of the Council of Virginia and a tobacco planter with a 17,000 acre estate.

The final well-known family, the Wyndhams, arrived at the end of the 17th century and early in the 18th century were owners of 1,000 acres of the parish.

At the beginning of the 19th century they replaced the old manor house with the present Philipps House and at the same time a younger son, George Wyndham, emigrated to New South Wales. Naming his estate Dalwood, after Dalwood Farm in his native village, he received much livestock from his father, often accompanied by Dinton and Teffont families who settled in Australia.

Lying in the Nadder valley, Dinton is a fertile productive parish. The strip of greensand that runs through it is especially suited to market gardening and the area produced much fruit from a large number of orchards in the 18th and 19th centuries. The 17th and 18th centuries had also seen a considerable amount of money spent in making water meadows which, with their production of early spring grass and higher yields, had brought great prosperity to the farming community. Some of these meadows were still in use until 1962. It is interesting to note that in 1910 a successful tobacco crop had been grown in the parish and was most probably used by one of the Salisbury tobacco manufacturers; a reminder of George Ludlow who had left the village to become an important American tobacco planter.

There have always been important economic routes through the parish. The old Roman road from the Mendip lead mines to Old Sarum runs through Grovely Wood, where it can still be traced, while to the south of the wood runs the Ox Drove. This latter is an ancient green road by which cattle from a very large area were driven to markets at Wilton and Salisbury. The present main road through the village is a result of the turnpike acts and heavier and faster traffic. The original route from Salisbury to Hindon took the present minor road along the ridge to the north between Dinton Park and Marshwood. Doubtless the change caused a shift in settlement southwards onto lower ground adjacent to the new road.

It was not until 1958 that any house here was connected to a mains water supply, although in 1904 Lord Pembroke had constructed a reservoir and provided piped water to his tenants. Others used wells, pumps or ponds.

On the main road towards the eastern part of the village stands Little Clarendon, a very nice two-storey stone dwelling with a three-storied gable and a room above its porch. It is believed to be 15th or 16th century. In a building attached to the farmyard here is the present Catholic church. The pre-Reformation Catholic church still stands at the top of the village but is now of course Anglican. This church of St Mary the Virgin is a most dignified building which has stood spiritual guard over its village for 900 years. It is essentially 12th century, although the chancel was rebuilt in the mid-14th century and further repairs and additions made in the mid-15th century. In the second half of the 19th century the church was in a very poor condition and was extensively restored by William Butterfield.

All in all Dinton shows most of the good features of the classic English village. It has retained many of its early houses both large and small. Four properties: Dinton Park, Hyde's House, Little Clarendon and Lawe's Cottage are owned and conserved by the National Trust. Dinton Park contains Philipps House, owned by the National Trust. The village is thriving, with a well stocked shop, a primary school, a recreation ground, two pubs, a village hall and a vineyard; it is also now the home of the monthly glossy journal, *Wiltshire Life*, located at Jesses Farm.

DONHEAD ST ANDREW

Donhead, or Down Head, meaning the top of the downs. The name refers to both Donhead parishes rather than the villages; indeed, the church and early settlement of Donhead St Andrew is in a hollow and looks across the valley to Donhead Clift. It also looks up to the church of St Mary, a fact which gave the two settlements the early names of 'Nether' and 'Over' respectively. The two churches are quite close to one another, considering the parishes are fairly large, and in her study of the villages Diana Ladas suggests that this was for the convenience of Shaftesbury Abbey so that both would lie on the route from Shaftesbury to the nunnery's grange at Tisbury. For Donhead was part of an endowment of the abbey and was valuable and prosperous in Saxon times.

Prosperous enough for eight mills to be working at the time of the Domesday Book, the buildings of four of which still remain. Many families remained here for centuries and the Gould, Gold or Gole family were possibly here at the time of Edward the Confessor although there is no documentation for them before the 16th century. Other families have taken their names from within the parish; Brook Waters was the home of Walter atte Broch in 1225 and William atte Broke in 1338, while in 1225 Ferne House was the home of Philip de Ferne. Much later Ferne House was the home of several generations of the Grove family, who rose from country gentry to aristocratic grandees before losing their fortune in one generation. One member of the family, Harriet, was greatly in love with her cousin, the poet Percy Bysshe Shelley, who was a visitor to Ferne. Her diary and those of other members of the family have been transcribed, edited and annotated by Desmond Hawkins, a keen conservationist, a great man of literature and a lover of Cranbourne Chase, in *The Grove Diaries* (1995).

In the parish today there is a confusion of roads for the unwary stranger and after passing the church and continuing along St Bartholomew's Street, wondering why the street is so named when the church is dedicated to St Andrew, you suddenly find yourself in the hamlet of St Bartholomew's Hill, in the parish of Semley, enjoying splendid views over the Vale of Wardour. The hill, and the road to it, are named after a nearby Catholic chapel, for the Arundells of Wardour were a great Catholic family. As you look down on the wooded parish in which you could become lost, be grateful that the last wolves here were killed in the reign of King John, for which service the King, whilst staying at nearby Clarendon Palace, rewarded the hunter with 15 shillings.

Today the village is widely spread with ribbon development along most of the roads but, despite the scattered nature of the houses, most people walk to church along the narrow roads. There is much stone and thatch including The Forester, a free house whose name gives a clue to the earlier nature of this landscape. Next to the pub is, most appropriately, Brewer's Cottage while other cottages are to be found either end on to the road, such as Sparrow Cottage, or facing the road like Orchard Cottage. The settlement pattern seems to indicate house sites cut from the forest once the area around the church had been filled.

The church of St Andrew is of local green sandstone with its most interesting feature being a tall narrow Norman arch in the east end of the north wall of the nave. The low west tower was rebuilt in 1893 but other features date from Perpendicular to the 17th century, although much of the chancel was rebuilt in 1838.

Apart from the River Nadder which separates the twin parishes there are other streams and ponds. Some have been made into very attractive garden features while Mill Lane leads to the pleasant Kelloways Mill on the Nadder itself; from here you can take a waterside footpath leading back to the church.

DONHEAD ST MARY

This is also an aquatic place with a Watery Lane, Spring Cottage, a streamlet and pools by Shute House, a former mill pond in Charlton Lane and, of course, the Nadder. Here though the church stands high and proud above its village, in the churchyard you are at the same level as the thatched roofs of Berrywood Lane and can look out over them to attractive countryside and the scattered houses of St Andrew set amidst trees, fields and hills. In the churchyard itself there are pleasant trees, including a variegated holly and berry laden ordinary hollies. The stone of the church is much covered with lichen, a good indicator of the clean air here, and many of the older grave markers are moss covered and seem to be sinking into the lush verdant ground. It is not only flora to be found here for the church itself is one of several colonised by bats. Here a safe habitat is provided for Serotine, Brown Long-eared and Lesser Horseshoe bats.

Pevsner has found evidence that there was an aisleless Norman church here in the 12th century to which were added aisles in the latter part of that century. In the 13th century the nave was given a clerestory, a feature which is rare in Wiltshire. The Perpendicular period was responsible for the west tower and the chancel chapels, and so here we have the church of St Mary which has seemingly grown organically and not been greatly altered or rebuilt in any century. The font is Norman, the pulpit Jacobean and the painting of the Virgin and Child is Italian, the only foreign intrusion if one discounts the Norman replacement of the Saxon church.

Much of the attractive nucleated settlement is on higher ground around the church. To the north-west is the Old Rectory, parts of which date from the 16th century although the three-bay south front is from the early 18th century. A spring in the gardens here is believed to be a holy well. The former school is now the village hall but the boot scraper, set in the wall by the doorway, reminds us of the time when children traipsed along unmade roads and muddy lanes and cleaned their boots before entering to sit in wet clothes in the schoolroom. On the other side of the road is The Old Library with a small thatched building that was doubtless the village reading room. Opposite the church is another house betraying in its name its former occupation, The Old Stores, in red brick, attached to the stone Church Hill Farm, which now seems to be a farm in name only.

Further north, along the ridge of higher ground, is the massive and imposing Shute House with the thatched Shute Farm, enjoying views of its fields, across the road. Back in the centre is Pilgrim Cottage with stone mullions and a large garden near which a footpath leads through pleasing fields to St Andrew. There is an unusual old conservatory with blue and red coloured glass on the front of Church Hill House while below is a nice row of houses along a small private road. The part of the village below Church Hill is also pleasant and culminates in The Old Malthouse, a substantial stone building, and the stone built Methodist church within quacking distance of the ducks on the Nadder. To the east is Donhead Hall, an early Georgian house in ashlar which was once the home of the grandson of the artist Sir Godfrey Kneller, who had owned property in the neighbourhood. More recently, at Lower Coombe, Jill Pearce has set up Donhead Publishing whose specialist books are aimed at building conservators, preservation specialists, architects, surveyors, planners and academics.

This is a parish of deep sunk lanes with high banks and walls and one path has given its name to a hill which rises to 241 metres in the north of the parish. Tittle Path Hill is believed to have been originally Sticklepath, or steep path, which it certainly is as it climbs alongside Donhead Clift. The interestingly named Pigstrough Lane is believed to commemorate the place where the Abbess of Shaftesbury kept her pigs, although I feel that the name is probably a little more modern. But in this ancient landscape who can tell.

DOWNTON

Around 1205 Peter des Roches, Bishop of Winchester, created a new town to the west of the River Avon. It was a borough by right and is still called so. These 13th century boroughs were profitable concerns as the burgesses paid their rents in cash, instead of holding land against feudal labour and produce. Today The Borough has two long rows of houses set very far apart across the street and a broad strip of grass, a curiously impressive piece of medieval new town planning. The course of the road is interrupted by several small bridges crossing small streams of the Avon before the main river is reached.

One curious sight is to be seen on the northern side of The Borough, at the side of the house that until recently was The Three Horse Shoes. In a cottage garden a selection of murals and a very effective miniature village have been created, using only broken crockery and sea shells.

A strange historical fact concerns the political history of Downton. Like many small boroughs it had become a pocket borough by the end of the 18th century. In 1826 the poet Robert Southey was elected but declined the seat, the position being that William, Earl of Radnor (Liberal) offered the seats available on condition that those elected voted for the borough's disenfranchisement.

Downton must owe much of its present prosperity and town-like appearance to various industries that have flourished here. Lace was produced as a cottage industry and there has been a long history of flour milling and paper-making, particularly at two mills on the River Avon, the western one having been used for the latter manufacture from 1710. From 1885 Wiggins, Teape, Carter and Barlow produced handmade paper until the end of the Great War. The mill was then occupied by Mark Palmer & Son, the last of the Downton paper-makers. East Mill was used by the Jellyman family from 1830 to 1860 for the production of paste boards; later it became an electricity generating station.

In 1919 the Southern Tanning Company built an impressive four-storey building of 19 bays, at the rear of which was a waterwheel, ten feet in diameter, used to agitate the tan pits. Until recently the latter could be seen working, from the main road, the B3080. The tannery was taken over by the Downton Tanning Company in 1930 and a more recent factory wing has been added at the rear. Products have included sole leather from ox hide and leather for riding equipment and belts. The handsome main building is creeper clad and with the Tannery House opposite provides a fine industrial presence in the village. Unfortunately the economic conditions of the late 1990s seemingly proved too much for this business which closed in October 1998. However, the Hogsback Brewery is thriving and Downton has the only cider maker in Wiltshire.

Opposite the tannery buildings the present has dealt kindly with other former industrial buildings. By a sluice gate is Waterside Mill, offering bed and breakfast, and, on either side, two private houses, The Corn Mill and The Old Mill. Commerce thrives with a bank, many shops and several pubs while culturally the people are served by a library.

Much of Downton is a very watery place and you are never far from the river, a side stream or a mill leat. Apart from aiding the rise of industry, the abundance of water maintained considerable fisheries from the 13th century onwards. These produced coarse fish, trout and salmon and in 1782 it was said that five hundredweight of eels could be taken in a single night; these latter sold at 2d a pound, making a total of £4. 3s. 4d, a respectable amount of money for one night's work.

In the 1980s a new controversy came to Downton concerning the River Avon. It had been noticed for some years that the number and quality of fish, especially trout, had been declining; this in one of the better trout streams in the country. Several local people put the blame on the trout farms that proliferated in the vicinity of the village. Citing possible causes as chemicals, fish diseases and food additives being swept from the farms into the river, they went on the offensive. The owners of the farms, mainly large local landowners, denied this and said that the small quantities of fish were a result of overfishing. All in all a modern example of the old conflict between landowners and other interests.

DURRINGTON

Enclosed on three sides by a loop of the River Avon and sandwiched between the army camps of Larkhill and Bulford, is Durrington. The old village lies at the north around the church of All Saints. Rebuilt in 1851, many earlier features were used in the present church. From the Norman period a doorway and gable, from the 13th century a lancet window and from the 15th century a Perpendicular west window. The interior is much as it was before the rebuilding. The tower screen, benches and parts of the reader's desk are all Jacobean. Sometime near 20th August 1693 the church, or parts of it, were said to have blown down in stormy weather. Later, prior to the rebuilding of 1851, the *Wiltshire Archaeological Magazine* quoted a report saying that there was a defaced font of poor character, high pews with much good oak carving of the 16th century and a western gallery. During reconstruction a painting of St Christopher on the west wall was broken.

Near the church is the substantial base of the old village cross, now supporting a war memorial. This stone cross was once the scene of the villagers' May Day festivities. Durrington folk, being independent minded, kept up the tradition according to the old calendar and thus held their celebrations on 13th May. On May Day Eve the men would cut a may bush from the downs and take it to The Nag's Head where the maypole was stored for most of the year. After some ale to slake the thirst brought on by climbing up and down the hillside, they tied the bush to the top of the pole. A procession then carried the maypole to the remains of the ancient cross where it was chained to the stones. On the evening of May Day there was a feast and the men of the village danced around the pole to the sounds of pipes and squeeze boxes.

Apart from their keeping of the old date there seems to have been an even greater independence of spirit shown here. May Day was one of the great pagan festivals, yet here it is taking place at the cross which was planted to drive out the old religion. Maybe, as in many other places, Christianity coexisted with its native rival, taking over some of the events of the earth goddess. On the other hand, Stonehenge is not far away and perhaps the old religion remained strong and was able to continue before the very gates of the church.

In the main village street there are several early farmhouses and cottages of this once small village but most of the 4,000 population live on the housing estates to the south.

South of the village, and crossed by the main Marlborough to Salisbury Road, is the very large earthwork of Durrington Walls. It is a Neolithic henge monument built c2,500 BC and is related to its contemporaries in the Stonehenge sphere of influence. Just to the south is a smaller henge monument, 250 feet in diameter, called Woodhenge. The two settlements of 4,500 years ago were most probably the forerunners of the modern village; providing accommodation for those involved in Stonehenge as today the village does for those involved in the armed forces.

EAST KNOYLE

Until recently, when travelling south to Shaftesbury, East Knoyle was apparently a double bend, where one met lorries in the middle of the road, and then a long straight road flanked by ribbon development. Appearances are deceptive though, for the village is scattered throughout a large parish with several outlying settlements. The way to enjoy East Knoyle is on foot and this is now an extremely pleasant undertaking in all parts of the village since the new bypass has been opened.

The post office was once run by Mrs Stamp and called Wren's Shop, one of the many commemorations marking the fact that Sir Christopher Wren was born here. On the opposite side of the road is a pleasant small stone monument also recording this. Authorities differ as to the date of Wren's birth, putting it at either 1631 or 1632. It is the latter date that is entered in the parish register and as Sir Christopher's father was the vicar, we must suppose that he would know. Sir Christopher himself maintained a link with the parish until 1662 when he surrendered a small copyhold of inherited land.

Up the hill past the post office there is another reminder of the great architect. Wren Cottage is appropriately perched on the hillside but hovering

Wendé Maunder
East Knoyle

just above is Kestrel Cottage. At the top of the hill is an entrance to Clouds House. This was built for Percy Wyndham in 1881-86 for £80,000 but had to be rebuilt in 1889-91 for a further £35,000 after it was burned down in 1889. In 1938 the house was drastically reduced. It lost much of its steep roof, three dormers with gables, bay windows and large parts of the service wing. The story of the house and its family is told in an excellent book by Caroline Dakers. The house now accommodates a rehabilitation centre working with alcoholics and drug addicts; it is a large local employer with 59 staff.

Down in the village stands the church of St Mary the Virgin. Every century has made alterations and additions from the 11th century onwards. There is nothing out of the ordinary about this church until one looks into the chancel. Here is something unique in an English parish church: plaster decoration on all walls. Beyond the altar is Jacob's ladder with ascending and descending angels, on the west wall the remains of the Ascension of Christ, on the south the sacrifice of Isaac and on the north a man kneeling in prayer. There are also many inscriptions and verses. These were designed by Dr Wren, Sir Christopher's father.

Dr Wren, an ardent Royalist, lost his living during the Civil War and the facts about the plasterwork emerged at his trial in 1647. Prior to that he had designed a building in 1634 at a cost of £13,000 for Queen Henrietta, consort of Charles I, and he was also the architect of a new roof for East Knoyle church. The trial took place at Longford Castle in 1647 when Dr Wren was tried for 'heretical practices' before the Faulstone Committee, but doubtless his real crime was of being a Royalist. Evidence was given by Robert Brockway, a plasterer, of Frome St Quintin in Dorset.

From this it appears that in 1639 Dr Wren had provided Robert Brockway with all the designs required for producing the wall plasters. These included a depiction of the Trinity that has now gone. It is believed the ceiling was also used for this plasterwork and that may have been the setting for the missing design. Some of the Commonwealth thought highly of Dr Wren but, even so, he was fined £40 and his living sequestrated. It is interesting, however, that whereas so many church fittings that offended Puritan eyes were destroyed, the plasterwork remains. Another early item of note is a church chest, dated 1616, which had been purchased for ten shillings. It possessed five locks, each key being held by a different person. In 1982 the church received a gift of the carved centrepiece of the reredos that originally stood in Wren's church of All Hallows in Bread Street, London. It is displayed as a memorial given on the 350th anniversary of his birth.

EDINGTON

Edington holds an honourable place in the history of Wessex, for it was here, most people believe, that King Alfred defeated the Danes under Guthrum in AD 878. The battle of Ethandune was a turning point for Englishmen after the Danes had believed themselves conquerors of Wessex by the winter of AD 877. There is a strong possibility that a horse was carved in the chalk hillside to celebrate this victory; a horse of 'the cart breed' according to Sir Richard Colt Hoare and which has now been overlaid and destroyed by that cut in 1778 and known erroneously as the Westbury White Horse.

But it was the medieval period that gave Edington its greatest glory. In 1351 William of Edington, the then Bishop of Winchester, founded a priory which was converted into a religious house for the Bonshommes (an order of the Augustinian rule). Directed by the Bishop, the church of St Mary, St Katherine and All Saints was built and consecrated in 1361. It is a splendid church which takes some time to absorb. Suffice to say that besides the architectural joys are a wealth of good and interesting furnishings. Near the church is the house known as The Priory which could be either pre- or post-Reformation. Flanking the road is a massive stone wall, the boundary of the monastery, while inside is the large rectangular pond used to supply fish for the table.

There are two less noble events connected with the village. In 1314 William of Edington, the then vicar, had to promise 'to abstain from further connexion with Edith, Harlot and four other women'. We will be charitable and assume that he was providing similar help to that given by William Gladstone to fallen women in the 19th century. Less pleasantly, in 1449, during Jack Cade's rebellion, the Bishop of Salisbury, William Ayscough, was celebrating mass in the church when a mob broke in shouting, 'Death to the Bishop'. He was carried outside, dragged up the hill and stoned to death. Later a chapel and hermitage were built on this spot but now they are gone.

The village today has no obvious centre and is built around a small network of roads below the Westbury to Lavington road. A separate settlement to the east is Tinhead (originally Ten Hides) and here there is one superb building, Beckett's House, once the home of the textile historian and Wiltshire writer Kenneth Ponting.

The old turnpike road from Bath to Salisbury ran through Tinhead and the 18th century brick-built George was a coaching inn. It is now a private house but in the 1980s was one of the few local pubs with some 19th century furnishings. Where the turnpike crosses the Westbury road is a house on a triangular piece of ground with roads on all sides. Formerly this was a blacksmith's forge. The turnpike can be followed, turning to the east climbing the hillside, as a chalk track eventually coming out on top of Coulston Hill, then proceeding south-west to St Joan à Gore Cross.

Part way up the hill from Tinhead are the overgrown remains of an old garden. There is a riot of damson trees and an old apple tree; all that remains of a cottage that once fronted the road where straining teams of horses hauled heavy coaches up the rutted chalk. Further on are two milestones to the right of the track still giving the distances to Bath and Salisbury from these isolated positions.

ENFORD

Enford is a large parish with several early settlements. From the south, there are Fifield, Coombe, Longstreet, Enford, Littlecott, Compton, East Chisenbury and West Chisenbury scattered around the A345, the minor road that runs parallel with it and the River Avon.

The name Enford derives from Old English meaning ford of the ducks, and that ford was close to the present bridge over the Avon. There are still ducks at this point and they are nesting here more than 1,000 years after the first written record of the village name.

Nowadays there are also swans and coots and some good-sized trout that are normally to be seen downstream from the bridge. Man has lived in this area for a very long time. A Neolithic greenstone axe (c2,000 BC) has been found near the bridge, while at Compton various Roman remains have been discovered. On the downs around are Bronze Age barrows, the Iron Age Casterley Camp and Celtic and Roman field systems.

A former pub in the village was The Three Horseshoes, sold to Ushers in 1913, and which had an interesting custom. In this age of instant credit and plastic card payment, we are apt to forget that buying on credit is nothing new. In Wiltshire the word 'ticking' indicated that you would pay for an item later (hence buying 'on tick') and in this pub there was a ticking stool. It was understood that anyone sitting on this required beer but could not produce the money until next pay day and they were thus saved having to ask the landlord to put their drinks on the slate in front of the assembled company.

This fascinating information and a lot more about village life is found in

Enford Days (1986) by Fred Phillimore, whose family have lived in Enford for centuries. He records also that a Flower Show and Carnival were annual events which this village supported; the latter nowadays surviving in only a few Wiltshire villages. A Carnival Queen would be chosen from girls living in the valley between Upavon and Netheravon and she would be crowned on a Friday night while the fair was in full swing. On Saturday morning the Flower Show took place and in the afternoon the judging of the carnival floats. All the local owners of steam engines took part and the sight must have been one which we can now only enjoy at a specialist steam fair.

Between the river and the main road stands the church of All Saints. A fairly large and interesting church of flint and dressed stone with Norman arcades and a chancel arch of the 12th century. Details of its interior, such as the early 20th century parish bier, are well described in a History which is available in the church.

I have kept one of the most astonishing sights of this parish until last. To reach it you must take the lane and track leading east from the bridge along Rainbow Bottom, or for a shorter walk leave your car at the line of Everleigh Ashes (on the A342) between Everleigh and Upavon and walk south-west along the tank track. By either route you cross wild downland with a pattern of trees and scrub, sheep pasture and wheat fields. There are wide horizons but no habitation and there are many wild flowers on the way to Chisenbury Warren. The Warren is covered with small trees and scrub but there is a small dry valley which is mostly clear. On its north-west facing slope you can walk along a Roman street a quarter of a mile long with some 80 rectangular scooped house platforms on either side, an impressive experience. It gives a strange feeling to walk the street of this once busy community in its lonely valley and know that it has been silent for these last 16 centuries. One piece of advice, go in winter or early spring, otherwise long grass and tall flowers will obscure many of the features.

ERLESTOKE

There is an idyllic village street of picturesque cottages set among gracious trees and apparently in a valley. Giving this valley-like impression is a low hill, to the north, which is really an outlier of the higher chalk of Salisbury Plain which curtails the village to the south, rising quickly to over 200 metres. Much of the settlement lies on the east to west road between West

Lavington and Westbury with other farmhouses and cottages on the minor Lower Road to the north. The name was originally Stoke, or Stokes, and the prefix comes from an earl who formerly held the manor, possibly Earl Harold who is likely to have held it before the Norman Conquest.

The village is surrounded on three sides by Erlestoke Park which has been the dominating feature since the late 18th century. The park was laid out in the 1780s when a series of lakes were formed to make seven cascades into the large Long Water. The owner, Joshua Smith, introduced some choice specimen plants and many fine trees. The old house in the park had been removed at some time before 1786 to allow the new mansion to be completed before 1791. At the same time part of the village was pulled down to aid the landscaping of the grounds.

New houses were built in the main street to house the cottagers thus dispossessed. A walk around the village can be quite surprising as figures and carvings from the old mansion have been incorporated into these cottages. You will come across partially draped classical women and grinning faces from pagan-like carvings. There is a good example of the latter on the old village school.

Erlestoke Park is now HM Prison Erlestoke with its entrance above the village on the road to West Lavington. Originally a centre for young offenders, this was upgraded to full prison status a few years ago, in the face of understandable local concern and opposition. The prison seems now to co-exist well with the village and there have been few escapes.

One of the places in the village where the perimeter prison fence is most evident is near the village hall and the Housing Association houses near the Long Water in the park. Also here is the church of St Saviour, built on the site of an earlier church, at the expense of Lady Charlotte Watson-Taylor in 1880. It is in the Perpendicular style but in the porch are two genuine Norman bases and capitals from substantial round piers. There is a third inside the church and Pevsner cites them as evidence for a church with aisles of the period 1130 to 1150. There is a local tradition that says Sir William Brouncker, owner of the manor in the late 16th century, used the tower of this church as a mew for his hawks.

On 26th May 1868 there was a disastrous fire, caused by one Thomas Godden, which destroyed 13 houses. He seems to have been an unpleasant and violent fellow who had received notice to quit his cottage and to revenge himself on his landlord, and his neighbour with whom he had quarrelled, he set fire to his own dwelling. He seems to have been drunk at the time and both his daughter and a bedridden elderly woman were in the house when he set it alight; both were rescued. Messengers were sent for fire engines but at Devizes were told they must supply the horses so only the one from Market Lavington attended, performing sterling work.

The villagers formed a line, three quarters of a mile long, from a pond in the park to the centre of the village and valiantly kept a continuous supply of water arriving in buckets at the scene of the conflagration. The extent of the damage amounted to £3,000 and Thomas Godden was sentenced to ten years penal servitude.

Despite the fire there are still many attractive early houses in this village which is also fortunate in having a post office and store. Opposite this is The George and Dragon where many years ago I learned to play bar billiards, a game which seems to have been largely superseded by the pool table. There is also Turner's Garage which, for many years, has sold Skoda cars and, on the western edge of the village, the much newer Erlestoke Sands Golf Club with an attractive course in pleasant rural surroundings.

ETCHILHAMPTON

Travelling from Devizes to Upavon on the A342 one encounters a monument on the slopes of Etchilhampton Hill where a minor road turns off towards the village. It commemorates James Long, of Urchfont, who in 1768 promoted a new road from Nursteed, in Devizes, to Lydeway, in Urchfont. The gradient on the existing road, turnpiked under the first Wiltshire Turnpike Act in 1707 for the Devizes to Upavon Road, had proved too steep, being on the higher slopes of Etchilhampton Hill. The road of 1768 remains as part of the main road in use today.

It is pleasant to feel that we still remember this road improver who bettered the lot of straining horses and oxen and the men who drove them. One cannot see the promoter of a new motorway being so remembered but then new 18th century roads caused little damage to the countryside, compared with those of the late 20th century. When passing the monument take a look at the stone lion on the top; he has an iron tail. It is said that the lion goes to drink when he hears the clock of St James's church in Devizes strike midnight. At that time when all God-fearing folk were abed he would walk to a farm pond at Stert, quench his thirst and walk back to the monument. Many times over the years has this tale been told by village men as they climbed the hill, when returning to Etchilhampton from the inns of Devizes after closing time. The origin of the belief probably owes much to the potency of the ales brewed by Wadworth's in Devizes and, sad to say, it is unlikely that the striking of the church clock could be heard from Etchilhampton Hill. Although of course lions, being wild animals, will have a much keener sense of hearing than humans.

Etchilhampton itself is a village in two halves. It has been like this since 1885 when it was recorded as being connected by a narrow path, as is the case today. It was not always so as, prior to the mid-19th century, the village stretched continuously for half a mile along a street but somehow the middle section was lost and never became a paved road. Today, if we stand in this section, house platforms are visible to us in the green fields. It would seem that the dwellings in this area became empty, fell down and no one used this section of the village.

At the eastern end of the village, beyond Manor Farm, is a more impressive reminder of vanished settlement. A complete medieval community has disappeared leaving only raised house platforms and eroded trackways as mute reminders of where generations lived and died. The desertion of this community remains a mystery. There are plenty of early buildings, including the church, in the present day village to indicate contemporary existence with the vanished section. It seems likely that there was a gradual decline in population, nothing dramatic, and every few years another house or cottage would fall into ruin. In medieval times the village was often called Ashlington and, until the 19th century, it is referred to thus as often as it is called Etchilhampton. Even in the mid-20th century some villagers still used the old name.

There is a good diversity of houses in the village. Brick is the chief means of construction, although there are a few timber-framed buildings. Several of the brick houses are thatched, including one row which have, what I always think of as, eyes and eyebrows in the upper storey. The deep thatch comes down and envelops the windows, giving the impression of bright eyes staring out from beneath the bushy eyebrows of some of the older inhabitants.

The church of St Andrew has a wide range of unusual features. Of stone, it has a late 14th century nave but the contemporary chancel was rebuilt in 1869. The church is unlocked and inside are splendid box pews dating back to the 17th century. Above the pews, in the blocked north doorway, is a stone carving of the Archangel Gabriel. It is thought to have been part of a reredos, c1400, and was discovered in 1832 buried in the south-east corner of the nave. It is in such excellent condition that at first sight it appears to be only a few years old.

In the graveyard are to be found some very unusual sarcophagus-shaped tombstones. These date to the time of Charles II and were evidently a local fashion. As in many Wiltshire villages the rooks have returned to the churchyard. Although the elms have gone, the rookeries are in lower trees and the cawing associated with village churchyards in the past is once more a part of the scene.

A few years ago the residents of this part of the Vale of Pewsey united to fight proposals for the building of a satellite tracking station. Fortunately for the preservation of beauty in this quiet area, the tracking station has not been built.

EVERLEIGH

This is one of the few remaining downland villages in the county. The whole parish is on the upper chalk with no surface water and until recently deep wells were necessary to the survival of this community. The land was originally in Chute Forest but nothing remained of this in the early 19th century when Cobbett commented on the lack of trees, bushes and hedges in the parish. Some planting took place during that century and there is now a surprising amount of deciduous woodland to be found on this northern part of Salisbury Plain.

The surrounding downs were long used for sport. Hunting and falconry were the chief forms of the chase while the area was still well regarded for hare coursing until well into the 20th century. Horse racing was also popular and there were training stables attached to The Crown. Manifesto, the six to one winner of the 1897 Grand National was trained here.

One of the reasons for concentration of sporting activity in this isolated parish may have been the ease of access to the area, with the village being at the junction of the Devizes to Andover road and the old Salisbury to Marlborough route. The latter now crosses Army land and cannot be followed to the south of the village where there are army ranges. It does, however, remain as a distinctive feature. The modern north to south route follows the valley of the Salisbury Avon.

There were some good inns to provide refreshment and lodging for visiting sportsmen and travellers. The Rose and Crown was first mentioned in 1713, The White Hart in 1815 and The Swan in 1847. The present inn, The Crown, was an inn by 1792 and is housed in a fine early 18th century building which probably began life as a dower house. Sir Richard Colt Hoare stayed here when excavating in the neighbourhood in the early 19th century and its praises were sung by Cobbett in 1826.

Originally the village was in two parts, West Everley and East Everley; the latter is now the present village. Until 1811 the church and some older houses were adjacent to the manor house, all having grown up naturally in the same area. Like so many landowners, Francis Dugdale Astley wanted a little more privacy for his house and so pulled down the church and other buildings, creating a park in front of his manor house. He built the present church of St Peter between the two halves of the village on a pleasant site set among trees. The Norman font and a 1656 memorial to Susanna Tesdale were retained from the old church. Nowadays much of the land in the parish is owned by the Army and is used for non-firing tank training.

FARLEY

Farley lies to the south of its twin village, Pitton, and is built around a triangle of roads with a large empty space in the middle. Here is a surprise - a large brick-built church influenced by Sir Christopher Wren. It was built for Sir Stephen Fox who had been born at Farley and started as a chorister in Salisbury Cathedral. He was a very able and intelligent man who served Charles II in exile as his Clerk of the Kitchen and whose economy and loans greatly helped that monarch. On the triumphant return of the king, Sir Stephen received his knighthood and was given several important posts, including that of Paymaster to the Forces. From his own purse he contributed £13,000 to the building of Chelsea Hospital and, of course, became well acquainted with Sir Christopher.

Sir Stephen bought the manor of Farley and the church was built between 1689 and 1690. The interior is simple but there are fine monuments and most of the furnishings are original. Unfortunately there was a drastic Victorian restoration in 1875 when, amongst other sad occurrences, the box pews were cut down and an over-ornate marble and mosaic reredos was added. Opposite the church are Sir Stephen's Almshouses of 1681, built by Alexander Fort who also worked on the church. The almshouses are in brick and are long and low. In the centre, opposite the churchyard gate, is the two-storey, four-bay school that was incorporated in the structure.

Sir Stephen's wife had died in 1696 and all his children had predeceased him so, at the age of nearly 80, he decided that it was his duty to marry again. He proposed to, and was accepted by Mrs Margaret Hope, the young daughter of a clergyman. Within a year of the marriage the union had been blessed with twins. These boys were to become the 1st Earl of Ilchester and the 1st Earl of Holland. From the latter came Charles James Fox, the Whig reformer and statesman. Sir Stephen died in 1716. There are still families of Foxes in the village and only recently the daughter of one was married in Sir Stephen's church.

FONTHILL GIFFORD

A small village mainly set along the minor road leading from Hindon to Tisbury with estate cottages of different styles and fashions. The settlement on the more major road includes Holy Trinity church built in 1866 by T.H.

Wyatt for the Marquess of Westminster, who at that time owned the Fonthill estate. It is most picturesque with a spire rising from a north-east tower between pyramid pinnacles and with a round tower to the north. It replaced a pretty church of 1748 which had been built for Alderman Beckford.

It is with the name Beckford that Fonthill is forever associated. It had previously been owned by Giffords, who left their name with the manor, Mauduits, Demoleyns, Hungerfords, Werlocks, Mervyns, and Cottingtons. It is a place of vanished mansions and vanished fortunes. A principal house was first built by Sir John Mervyn who had bought the property in 1553. It was bought by Sir Francis Cottingham in 1631 who remodelled the house and erected one of the largest stables in England. Around 1736 the estate was purchased by Alderman Beckford of London who spent huge sums of money improving and furnishing the house and he even constructed a famous water organ which was worked from a reservoir on the hillside.

In 1755 his house was gutted by fire. Beckford was in London at the time and when told of the disaster started scribbling some notes. When asked what he was doing he said that he was calculating the expense of rebuilding and added, 'I have an odd £50,000 in my drawer'. In fact the new house built by Hoare was to cost £130,000. It was a fine Palladian mansion and was so magnificent that neighbours immediately christened it Fonthill Splendens. In the grounds, and still remaining, are a domed flint and stone hermitage, the Dark Walk, a tunnel under the road which is difficult to find, the be-vased landing stage on the far side of the lake, a crypt-like boat house and a grotto.

When Alderman Beckford died his son, William, was nine years old having been born on 29th September 1760. The family were immensely, but newly, rich with their wealth coming from Jamaican sugar and slaves. William's great grandfather, Peter, had been a rumbustious Governor of Jamaica and his father, although a man of refined taste, had an atrocious Jamaican accent and was somewhat uncouth. William's inheritance was the Fonthill estate, £1,500,000 and an annual income from Jamaica of £70,000.

William Beckford was intelligent, romantic, learned and highly discerning but unfortunate in his personal relationships. He is well known as a writer; his first, and greatest work *Vathek* was influenced by his early love of Russian magnificence and the East but is a wholly original work and was to influence many later writers. Beckford wrote it in French, which was natural to him, but was treacherously served by his friend and translator, Samuel Henley, who published it in English under his own name when Beckford was in difficulties abroad.

These difficulties had been brought about by his infatuation for young William Courtenay, a relationship which Beckford probably regarded as similar to those common in ancient Greece. A witness claimed to have observed him in the boy's bedroom and as the 18th century publicly regarded sodomy as a great crime Beckford was turned upon by Society. He issued firm denials and was supported by his mother and his wife, who was pregnant at the time. Apart from one witness there was no further proof and so no prosecution but Beckford had lost his good name and was ostracised. Later, when giving birth to their second daughter, his wife died and a desolate man returned to a lonely life at Fonthill.

He turned his energies to building and in 1796 began what was to be known as Fonthill Abbey, the greatest romantic folly in all England. It was a Gothic building on the hill away from the earlier sites in the valley and when completed was a cruciform building 312 feet long by 270 feet wide with a central tower 276 feet high. There were many setbacks and disputes and sometimes up to 500 workmen were employed at the same time. The Abbey was preposterous, uncomfortable and most inconvenient with many rooms hardly habitable, but as a romantic Gothic statement it was magnificent, it was sublime. It was conceived to be as one with its surroundings and Beckford extensively and exotically planted trees on his large estate to surround his immense creation on the hill.

Beckford was unsatisfied with it and continued to make alterations but by the early 1820s he was in severe financial difficulties with most of his capital gone and his Jamaican revenues misappropriated. In 1822 he put the Abbey up for auction but then astutely sold it for £330,000 by private treaty to an eccentric gunpowder millionaire. He went to live in Bath, building the Lansdowne Tower there and dying in 1844. The quality of workmanship in the Abbey was poor, Beckford often plied the builders with wine and ale, and some of the materials were downright shoddy. In a deathbed confession the foreman told Beckford that the foundations of the tower had not been built according to his specification and the tower was likely to collapse. Beckford passed the warning on to the new owner who decided it would last his lifetime but the tower fell the following year, 1825.

Fragments of the Abbey still remain, cloistered by Beckford's trees and make for an unreal and eerie landscape. Beckford had pulled down his father's house in 1807 and the next house on the estate, that of the Marquess of Westminster built in 1846 to 1852, was demolished in 1955. Yet another house was built on the estate in 1904 by Detmar Blow to the east of the lake.

Called Little Ridge, and later Fonthill House, this 17th century style Wiltshire house was demolished in 1972. It would seem that this landscape is averse to great houses, more have disappeared here than would normally have been built on most estates.

FOVANT

Set at right angles to the A30, London to Exeter road, is Fovant, a long village about six miles to the west of Wilton. The outstanding features of the parish are the badges cut on the chalk downs to the south of the village and its neighbours, Compton Chamberlayne and Sutton Mandeville. It is believed that the first badge, that of the London Rifle Brigade, was cut in 1916 and was so successful that it was soon followed by many more.

Soon after the outbreak of the Great War, much good agricultural land had been taken over for a training camp. Thousands of men from all over Britain, and from the colonies, lived peacefully for a while in the area before going into action on the Western Front, although some were destined to remain in Fovant and their graves in the churchyard, with the badges, are mute reminders of a lost generation. Many of the graves are of men from the Australian Infantry and it seems sad that these soldiers from the far side of the world, who had come to fight for the old country, should die in training, yet good that they did not have to experience the horror and death of trench warfare.

A small military township had grown up with roads, parade grounds, rifle ranges, hospitals, cinema and railway. In the years from 1915 to 1917 well over 30 regiments and battalions passed through Fovant. Many left their mark on the hillside, although some badges are no longer visible and have been replaced by later carvings. It is said that many of the badges were cut in the soldiers' spare time, although local tradition has it that the soldiers found less arduous ways of occupying these hours.

The badge of the 6th City of London Rifles, covering about 4,000 square yards, is at the top of an 800 foot hill and on a one-in-four slope. A member of the regiment recorded that it took three months to complete. After the departure of troops at the end of the war, some of the badges were maintained by local workers, paid by regimental associations and the Australian Government. However, by the Second World War many had almost disappeared and during that war the rest were allowed to become overgrown to avoid their use as landmarks by enemy aircraft.

After 1945 it was members of the Fovant Home Guard Old Comrades Association who began the task of restoration on Sunday, 12th June 1948. During the next three years new badges for the Wiltshire Regiment and the Royal Wiltshire Yeomanry were cut. The Old Comrades Association was succeeded by the Fovant Badges Society whose members have to meet the cost of maintenance with support from local authorities and regimental associations. Since 1950 the Society has organised an annual Drumhead Service on the first Sunday in July; many members of various old comrades associations come to these services.

To see some of the many records and memorabilia of the Society and the regiments, you must pass through the hospitable doors of the Pembroke Arms, the meeting place of the Fovant Badges Society. Many of the walls are decorated with photographs, drawings, badges, documents and records. On the other side of the main road is The Cross Keys and the small commercial centre is sited around here with the post office in a modern house and the Fovant Village Stores. The latter displays an advertisement for 'Colman's Wash Blue for Snow White Linen'.

FROXFIELD

The settlement seems to have been split asunder by the busy A4 Marlborough to Hungerford road, particularly since the road widening of 1932 which brought about the demolition of the old blacksmith's shop. The population has declined considerably since its high point of 622 people in 1841 and in the late 19th and early 20th centuries this resulted in the pulling down of many empty and decaying cottages, leaving gaps which have been filled by modern houses.

The village name is of interest and has caused some disagreement as to its meaning. The standard view is that it means a stream frequented by frogs but there surely must have been a superabundance of frogs on this tiny stream to have distinguished it from other areas. An alternative theory is that it is the 'felde', or forest clearing, belonging to a Saxon called Froga or Frocke. A more daring speculation suggests that the name could come from the Saxon word for a nightingale, 'froecx'; 'the field where nightingales sing'; what could be lovelier than that? I dare say, however, that it is the less musical frogs who are the originators.

Froxfield

Like most settlements in the Marlborough Downs this has an ancient landscape. The chief remains are Roman and the main occupation site was north-west of the village at Rudge, once a manor house, then a farm. A tessellated pavement was uncovered in 1725 by William George, the steward at Littlecote, who also discovered a rubbish-filled well. Among the artefacts here was a brass cup inscribed with stations on Hadrian's Wall and enamelled in red, blue and green. This could have been a votive offering thrown into the well by a retired Roman officer.

Present day Froxfield is clustered on the valley sides overlooking the small stream and the road. The road was the Great Bath Road and for a few decades the great stage coaches, carrying people between London and Bath, were a familiar sight providing news, gossip and income. They pulled up at The Cross Keys, converted to a private house long ago, and villagers could enjoy the bustle and sense of occasion, maybe catching a glimpse of an aristocrat or even Beau Brummel himself. The present inn is The Pelican, which was once a terrace of three 18th century cottages built of red and vitrified blue brick.

In the village, the road to Rudge is named Church Road and at a 90 degree bend is the church of All Saints, standing on an eminence. Most attractive in flint and stone, it is mostly Early English with a wooden bell turret of the 19th century. Inside there is some herringbone work which could date from the 11th century while outside, on the south-east quoins, there are mass dials, dating from a time before church clocks or even sundials, which the priest used for determining the times of services. Nearby is the former school now called Truant House, a reminder of all the children who were kept at home to help their parents or to work on the land at stone picking, bird scaring, leading horses or harvest work. There is a most interesting relief sculpture of a schoolgirl here.

On the other side of the road is a pleasing former vicarage with hanging tiles while Green Farmhouse of the 18th century is of rendered brick and tiles. Back in the centre there is a pleasant area of grass between Church Road and the main road with well grown trees, slide, swings and a climbing frame for the village children, and some inquisitive free range hens. Opposite is Old Brewhouse Hill with interesting cottages from the 17th, 18th and 19th centuries and a former Methodist chapel of 1909.

The architectural glory of Froxfield must be the Somerset Hospital. It was founded in 1686 by Sarah, Duchess of Somerset for the housing and maintenance of 30 poor widows. She was one of the outstanding benefactresses of the 17th century, helping schools and apprentices and providing scholarships at Oxford and Cambridge. Twenty more apartments were added between 1771 and 1773 and the original chapel was replaced by the Rt Hon Thomas Bruce, Earl of Ailesbury in 1813 when it had become dilapidated. There was provision for 29 widows of laymen and 19 widows of clergymen from different parts of England that were within 150 miles of London. Included were nine lay places for widows from the manors of Froxfield, Huish and Shaw, Broad Town, Wootton Rivers and Thornhill in Wiltshire.

I first knew the hospital in 1970 when I was providing a mobile library service there and I received many a welcome cup of tea from residents. At that time the Trust was in need of funds to modernise the hospital and an appeal was launched in November 1973 when Sir John Betjeman, the Poet Laureate, wrote, 'Not only is it a graceful landmark on the old Bath Road but it is also capable of being turned into one of the most charming residential squares in Wiltshire.' In 1986, a total care home for 40 people was built behind the hospital where priority is given to hospital residents who can no longer look after themselves.

GRAFTON

East Grafton is a very pleasant small village which today is set around the A338 Andover to Hungerford road. A large green, dotted with good mature trees, leads south from this road and the church of St Nicholas is sited here. Completely in the Norman style, it was built in 1844 by Benjamin Ferrey. Its tower has a pyramid roof and around the top, jutting out, are the carved symbols of the four Evangelists and, slightly higher, the stone heads of four dogs. Inside, the chancel has a semi-circular eastern end and is highly decorated, mainly in reds and blues set off by gold.

Scattered around the green and the church are many thatched houses but the modern village nucleus is now away from the church on the main road. West Grafton is a small scattered settlement along a minor road which leads only to the large Manor Farm. There are two or three very nice thatched houses here.

Within the parish is Wilton, a small village with a fine duck pond. Most notably it has the only working windmill in Wiltshire. It is a brick tower mill, built in 1821, which worked until the 1920s. It was restored between 1972 and 1976 under the aegis of the Wiltshire Historic Buildings Trust and is a most rewarding place to visit. To the north-west of the village is Wilton Water, a reservoir for the Kennet and Avon Canal.

The Crofton Pumping Station lifts water from this reservoir into the canal and was sited on Wilton Water by John Rennie for the purpose of replenishing the canal. The pumping station has been restored by the Crofton Society who maintain it and organise many weekends when the public can see the engines in steam. One beam engine, the 1812 Boulton & Watt, is believed to be the oldest working steam engine in the world and it is the only engine by those manufacturers still doing the job for which it was installed. Steam is now provided by two Lancashire boilers that were made by the Great Western Railway at Swindon and installed in 1905. Both engines were in regular use until 1952 but after 1958 the British Waterways Board replaced them with electric pumps. Since 1968 the work of the Crofton Society has been hard but also most successful. A combined visit to the pumping station and the windmill makes an excellent day out.

To the north-west of East Grafton is what remains of Wulfhall. From 1427 this was the home of the Seymour family and was held by Sir John Seymour, father of the Jane who married Henry VIII. It is firmly believed that the marriage took place here and the wedding feast was held in the great barn which was 172 feet long by 26 feet wide. The mansion was deserted in the mid-16th century and all that remains is one wing with tall polygonal Tudor chimneys.

GREAT BEDWYN

Great Bedwyn is a much larger settlement than its neighbour, Little Bedwyn, and contains a substantial amount of modern housing. The village was formerly a market town of some importance, and until the Reform Act of 1832, was a rotten borough regularly sending its two members to Parliament. In Saxon times it was important enough to have struck its own coinage. The centre still has the look of a small town and until recently contained a number of shops and small workshops. One craftsman still very much in existence is Ben Lloyd, the stonemason. On and around his premises is a fascinating collection of gravestones and memorials, some with amusing verses. In 1986 the post office moved into one of these buildings and now you go to buy your stamps or collect your pension flanked by gravestones. Another craftsman lives by the twin hump-backed bridges over the canal and railway; he makes baskets which you can buy in the adjoining shop.

Other gravestones are located more normally in the churchyard of St Mary's church. It is built completely of flint and is one of the largest churches in the area with most of its construction dating from the 12th and 13th centuries. Dividing the north transept from the crossing is a screen which was removed from the chancel at the time of the 1853-55 restoration. It then led an adventurous life, first stored behind the vicarage then being moved to the Ailesbury estate at The Warren. In 1919 it was rediscovered as a rare piece of 14th century woodwork and it was displayed in the Victoria and Albert Museum from 1919 to 1946. After being stored in Wivelscombe church it found its way to the Kingsbury Episcopal woodwork restorer, Ralph Fry, where it was rediscovered by the architect Oswald Brakspear. He recommended its restoration to its original church where it was re-dedicated by the Bishop of Ramsbury in 1975.

The village houses are of brick with old tile or thatched roofs. There are businesses here and retailers while services include the village stores, a large garage and the modern building of the British Legion Club. There are two public houses which both serve a variety of food, The Three Tuns and The Cross Keys. This latter is a large inn with an attractive garden and a bar which has hundreds of keys hanging from ceiling beams. Back in 1648 the Quarter Session records show that the people of Great Bedwyn were not happy about the proliferation of alehouses. A petition from 17 people stated that they could not keep their servants at home, 'they go and abide in the alehouses and continue there two or three days'. They also remarked, ' alehouse keepers do buy stolen wood from lewd persons who cut down our young oaks, our quicksett hedges and coppice woods to brew beer to maintain them in their drunkenness'.

On the main street Hillbarn House has an extensive garden which is occasionally open under the National Gardens Scheme. It is an architectural garden very skilfully laid out with good use of large hedges, a hazel pergola and long arcades with prolific pear trees trained over them. There are many box hedged gardens and interesting topiary depicting chairs, baskets, pigs, dogs, rabbits, squirrels, peacocks, ducks, swans and other birds.

There is a small canal wharf at Great Bedwyn and this is a local amenity area and a good place for a picnic. Footpaths are plentiful around the village and good after-lunch exercise can be obtained around Bedwyn Brail and Wilton Brail, across to Chisbury, or by taking the towpath to Crofton or

Little Bedwyn. Near the village are the ruins of a large Romano-British courtyard villa at Castle Copse which has been systematically excavated and studied over a number of years. The result of this was a definitive publication, edited by Eric Hostetter and Thomas Noble Howe, in 1997 which sets the site in its region and considers its associations with other settlements and sites.

GREAT SOMERFORD

The River Avon divides the Somerfords topographically yet links them in name. The name 'Sumresford' in the Domesday Book, seems to indicate the existence of a ford that was only usable during the drier months of the year when the river was low and the surrounding low-lying land had dried out. We find that in 1605 a rector of Great Somerford, Richard Atwood, was drowned while trying to reach the village through the winter floods while as late as 1799 the new rector, the Rev Demainbray had to take a roundabout route to reach the church for his induction. Today the land is better drained and there is much good pasture and many horses, not surprising as Captain Mark Phillips is numbered among the sons of these villages.

Great Somerford is set around a road system in the form of a stylised '8' and is a large village with a good mixture of old and new houses. The oldest is The Mount, built in 1573 but with an early 19th century frontage and iron porch, just to the west of the church.

There are other good houses in the village. One of the best is near the river bridge, Brook Farm, a 17th century house with a Georgian facade and new houses built alongside, while nearby in Frog Lane is 'Bevis', a house name that indicates we are near Richard Jefferies' country. The Methodist chapel was built in 1872 as a village reading room and was purchased by the Methodists in 1881. In the main street is Mills Farm, c1600, a fine building but not improved by its historic rendering, and next door The Bartons, an almshouse for elderly women in the early 19th century.

In the chancel of the church of St Peter and St Paul is a memorial tablet to the Rev Stephen Demainbray (rector from 1799 to 1854) who was nearly 95 when he died. It records that he was 'best remembered as the poor man's friend' and the story behind this is most interesting. During the time of the Enclosure Acts, from 1700 to 1845, about six million acres of land were enclosed in the country at a heavy cost to small farmers and cottagers. As well as the cost of fencing land, men lost their rights of grazing on the common fields, access to the enclosed waste and often fuel gathering. This caused great distress amongst the cottagers and labourers who could no longer keep their cow and pig and lost what small stake they once had in the land.

Of course, the larger farmers and landowners benefited and the parson, who had his glebeland and his tithes, probably preached that misfortune was the poor man's lot. Not so the Rev Demainbray, for when the 1806 Enclosure Bill for Somerford was introduced, he managed to insert a clause whereby half an acre of land was attached to each cottage. He also reserved eight acres of his glebe for annual allotment among the villagers. He then succeeded in obtaining the same terms for several neighbouring villages. Most definitely an enlightened man who had the well-being of all his parishioners at heart.

The church is separated from the winding road by a small field grazed by ponies. Walk the path leading to the church and you will discover a tablet commemorating the gift of an orchard from Colonel and Lady Alexander Palmer in memory of their two sons who died in the Second World War. The large Mount House, near the church, has what appears to be a timber-framed barn alongside the path. The windows are still glassless and on the upper floor are divided by wooden bars.

GRITTLETON

A small village very much dominated by the massive Grittleton House. The manor had belonged to Glastonbury Abbey for 600 years until the Dissolution, after which it descended through various marriages to the clothier, Joseph Houlton, of Trowbridge, in 1707. In 1828 his descendants sold the property, which included a 17th century manor house, to Joseph Neeld of Hendon. Aged 39, he had recently inherited £900,000, a vast fortune at that time. Very little is known about Neeld as a person but he became MP for Chippenham in 1830 and in 1831 he married Lady Caroline Ashley, the daughter of Lord Shaftesbury. The marriage fell apart after a two week honeymoon and the couple spent much time in suing and counter suing one another. Publicly much dismay was expressed by the establishment concerning all the newspaper publicity but I am sure that privately the public appetite for voyeuristic details was as great in 1831 as it is today. One of the facts that emerged was that Neeld had an illegitimate daughter from before his marriage whose mother was a French woman of great beauty. The child was living in the house which doubtless affronted Lady Caroline but seems to show that Neeld had a paternal sense of duty even if he was insensitive to his wife's feelings.

Architecturally, Neeld altered and enlarged the manor house and built new cottages in the village. A few years before he died he embarked upon a grand rebuilding of Grittleton House. Started by 1842 to the design of Henry Clutton, there was an hiatus when Neeld quarrelled with him and James Thompson took over. Clutton then seems to have behaved very badly to Thompson and with other delays the house was unfinished when Neeld died in 1856. It was completed by his brother. To quote Sir Nikolaus Pevsner, 'It really is a monstrosity', with Jacobean, Venetian and Byzantine features.

Walking around the village one is conscious of the presence of the house in the background. Particularly in the churchyard, it is a dominating influence as is the dark green foliage of the trees lining the manor boundary on the far side of the road. I am sure that I am being somewhat fanciful as the house now contains Grittleton House School and must be full of youthful enthusiasms.

The church of St Mary was somewhat over-restored by Arthur Blomfield between 1865 and 1867. There is a nice Perpendicular west tower but all exterior features are those of the restoration. The churchyard is pleasant with springy turf and some wild flowers while over the wall, to the north of the church, is the old Rectory. Of the late 18th century, with a big fanlight over the door, it has a dummy owl high on the ridge of the roof which one imagines is designed to keep pigeons away.

In the village Neeld's stone estate cottages are attractive and very obvious, giving an ordered appearance which was probably not there earlier. Eighteenth century houses on the road include the very attractive symmetrical The Barton, formerly Old Laundry Cottage as it states on its name plate, and another further along the road dated 1789. Behind the very pleasant former school is an attached, seemingly earlier house and, along School Lane, other cottages at various angles to one another. This then would appear to be the earlier form of settlement, scattered cottages and farms around the church before the 19th century brought some order to the development.

There are still two farmyards in the village while other buildings include The Neeld Arms, the village reading room and the attached Reading Room Cottage, now The Old Reading Room, and a meeting house to the south of the village school which must date from the early 18th century. The pleasant rural surroundings contain a good cricket ground with pavilion and, on the same site, a most attractive new village hall built in stone to match the rest of the village.

 HAM

Soon after leaving the Hungerford to Salisbury road you are confronted by a finger post suggesting that if you turned left you would be Prosperous in two miles. Set your mind against worldly goods and continue along the road to Ham and Buttermere where you will find tranquillity and spiritual refreshment. Drive carefully into Ham for, as the notice warns, there are children on bicycles and no pavements. Ham nestles in a slight hollow and has Ham Hill as a backdrop in a range which rises to the eminence of Inkpen Beacon to the north-east.

Much of the village is comfortably set around a triangular green - Ham Cross, of brick with hanging tiles; brick and thatched Ham Green Cottage; Dove's House of 18th century ashlar with a central gable clad in hanging tiles and an old tile roof; Dove's Farm Cottage, mostly of the 17th century. There are other pleasant cottages wearing a hat of thatch or tile while at the bottom of the green is the hospitable Crown and Anchor where you can sit outside and peacefully enjoy a drink in pleasant surroundings. Just along the road is the delightful Rose Cottage dating from the 16th and 17th centuries. Timber framed with brick and wattle and daub infill this single storey building, set at a right angle to the road, has an attic jettied out over that road. The thatched cottage next door has a hanging bird house made of the same straw as the thatch.

Opposite, a short road leads to the church of All Saints and Ham Manor. The church is attractively simple and typically Early English (1200-1275) with a 14th century tower on which a carved date, 1349, was still visible in the first quarter of this century. Most of the outer walls now have rendering over flint, sarsen ironstone and greensand. There is evidence that the church was once thatched and it has been fortunate in its restorers of the early 18th century and of 1849. Inside are plain white walls and ceilings with black painted roof timbers. There is a pleasant 18th century west gallery which is illuminated by dormer windows of a most secular appearance in the roof of the nave. From the same century come the box pews, altar rail, oak communion table and rectangular manorial pew and, most probably, the

Biblical texts below the balustrading of the gallery. Outside is a splendid yew, over 18 feet in circumference, which must date from the mid 16th century. The churchyard is large and, in one corner, most pleasantly wooded. Interestingly, the old vicarage is on the far side of the village set on the Inkpen road.

The neighbouring Manor House is of the 17th century with a late 18th century wing. Like many local houses it is of brick with tile hangings although remains found in the left wing indicate an earlier house with 16th century timber framing. In the grounds is a dovecote of red brick with blue panels and dated 1793. On the first floor there are about 300 nest boxes.

That the village was once even more compact than it is today is shown on an Inclosure Award map of 1828 and the 1773 map of Andrews and Dury. This is fitting for a village which grew up in Savernake Forest and is even now very isolated. One of the farther flung dwellings is Ham Spray House on Spray Road; a house which has seen tragedy, literature, art and love.

Built around 1830, it was bought by Ralph Partridge and Lytton Strachey, in 1924, who established a bizarre Bloomsbury menage. The homosexual Strachey had had a long-standing relationship with the artist Dora Carrington since 1915 and they had already set up home in several houses. Carrington, as she was called in the style she herself set, was greatly in love with Strachey, despite affairs on both sides and the fact that she married Ralph Partridge in 1921. In 1931 Lytton Strachey died of cancer and the heartbroken Carrington shot herself in Hungerford shortly afterwards.

After spending some time in Europe, Ralph Partridge and his second wife, Frances, returned to Ham Spray which became a literary and artistic centre for many in the 1930s. In the 1940s it became a centre of pacifism. Ralph's experiences as a major in the First World War had turned him completely against the call of arms while Frances was a pacifist by nature and upbringing. Literary associations continued at the house until the 1960s and one feels that if houses had the power to write, this one could produce many interesting books, including one on most of the Bloomsbury Group. The house has had a most able biographer in Frances Partridge. One of the early women students at the Slade, she turned to writing and photography and has produced delightful diaries and a published photographic album which recall a lost world in one of the most literary houses in Wiltshire.

HEDDINGTON

The village of Heddington, with the hamlets of Stockley, Broad's Green and Heddington Wick, lie to the south of Calne and to the north-east of Roundway Hill, in an area that is even now seldom visited. Since the early 1800s no one has needed to pass through Heddington in order to reach any destination; those who come either live here or have business with those who do. This has enabled the village to remain pleasantly rural with houses from most periods, but with no signs of any great expansion in any particular one. The attractive arc of hills to the south and east create an impression of an encircling green arm and also provide romantic, though bloody, associations, for it was on Roundway Down that Sir William Waller was defeated by Royalist forces in 1643. Not too bloody a battle however, as it is believed that only about 50 Parliamentarians were killed while only one Royalist fatality is recorded, a Mr Bartlett of Rowde.

At one time the villagers were engaged in the weaving trade and in the 18th century were supplying the clothiers of Trowbridge. The powered machinery of the factory brought this occupation to an end although the remoteness of Heddington and the poor roads probably had a greater, and earlier impact. Today, as has always been the case, this is an area devoted to farming. Farmhouses and yards are mixed with cottages and small houses along the roads and much of the traffic consists of tractors and cattle. Mixed farming predominates here, mainly cattle and sheep with a little arable, while the area is also well known for its horses. The latter interest was also apparent in the 19th century when stables for racehorse training were situated within the parish. It was only in the middle of the 19th century that Heddington's own form of rough music died out. Instead of targeting adulterous couples, the boys and young men of the village banged on pots and pans for most of the night outside the window of a newly married couple.

The settlements are built around an oval of roads and this has led to a very scattered pattern of habitation. In the south-eastern arc is the church of St Andrew, which is approached by a cobbled path leading through a neat graveyard set with stone benches. Above the church porch is an old niche whose statue was probably destroyed during the Civil War. In recent years a replacement has been provided, which I believe depicts Samson having just pulled down the pillars of the Temple. There is no stained glass in the windows of the nave, which might indicate the poverty of the parish in the 19th century, but lack of Victorian glass does not detract from the quality of a small simple village church performing the function for which it was founded 700 years ago.

Francis Child was born in 1642 in a house on the site of the present Splatts House. After being apprenticed to a London goldsmith he prospered and went on to found Child's Bank, the first bank in the country to be controlled by an Englishman. He later became Lord Mayor of London and was knighted. Near the church is a good large thatched timber-framed house while the later Home Farm is nicely built of brick with a brick extension. It was in Heddington that I found the only inn sign I know which shows three Latin phrases. On the sign of The Ivy Inn are pictured three species of ivy with their botanical names, a pleasing contrast of the classics with the homely timber framing and thatch of the house.

HEYTESBURY

After surviving the First World War, the poet Siegfried Sassoon made Heytesbury his home. Like many officers in both wars, he was stationed in this area for training on Salisbury Plain and would have been familiar with local villages. In the late 1920s he bought Heytesbury House and lived there until his death in 1967. Nowadays, although he is perhaps best known as one of the war poets, his chief fame is as an autobiographer, with his posthumously published Diaries, and as a novelist with such works as *Sherston's Progress* and *The Diary of a Foxhunting Man*. Apart from his *War Poems* of 1919 he published a further eight volumes of verse in his life time. A few years ago the house was sold by the Sassoon family and has now been converted into luxury apartments with further conversions of stable blocks and other outbuildings into individual dwellings

The village itself had the misfortune to be sited on the busy A36 road and in summer villagers used to have great difficulty crossing from one side of the village to the other. A bypass was built in 1986 and has restored peace to the community although it has taken the road across parkland to the front of Heytesbury House, thus providing motorists with an excellent view of the building until recent landscaping partially blocked it. Though now of village status, Heytesbury was once a borough and was the prosperous centre of the sheep rearing interests of the Hungerford family who, by the 14th century, had already been granted the right to hold markets and fairs. By the late 18th century the water power from the river had attracted a series of cloth mills along its course but full industrialisation failed to materialise and Heytesbury never rivalled its neighbour Warminster.

When Cobbett rode through in 1826 it was a rotten borough still returning its two members. He commented that 'what was formerly a considerable town, is now but a very miserable affair'. In 1831 the population was 1,412 people but in the Great Reform Act of the following year, borough status was lost and numbers gradually declined to a 'low' of 454 by 1931. Today the village is thriving, although there are now few residents employed within the community.

William Cunnington (1754-1810) is one of the fathers of British archaeology and became the partner of Sir Richard Colt Hoare whose *Ancient Wiltshire* was published in 1812. The first volume is dedicated to Cunnington whose letters and reports provided the material for the publication. Cunnington was a wool merchant whose doctors, for the sake of his health, had advised him to 'ride out or die'. This pronouncement was probably the original driving force behind his archaeological work. More than most he turned the antiquary into the archaeologist and in later life was ably assisted by his wife and three daughters. The latter also wrote many of his letters and reports. There is a fairly complete set of these in Devizes Museum.

The Hungerford Hospital of St John and St Katherine was founded by the second Lord Hungerford in 1442 for the housing of twelve men and two poor women. It was provided with both a chapel and accommodation for the local schoolmaster. The present structure dates from after the village fire of 1765 and is to the design of the Trowbridge architect Esau Reynolds.

Also rebuilt in the 18th century was The Angel Inn, situated in the High Street. A sign of the earlier structure is a rainwater hopper head, dated 1695. It was here that the Parliamentary 'elections' were held, although from as early as 1689 the only candidates were the two nominees of the Lord of the Manor. The Burgesses who elected the Members lived in properties owned by the major landowner; these were concentrated in an area known as Little London from at least 1773. It is believed that the name derives from those electors who sent the nominees to Parliament in London, although in other villages the term was often jokingly used for a small or outlying part of the community.

HILPERTON

The village centre is quite distinct but when on the outskirts you are uncertain as to whether you are in Hilperton or an adjacent parish. Adjoining to the north-west is Hilperton Marsh, now more populous than the main village, which is partly in Trowbridge parish. To the south-west there is only a field before the houses of Trowbridge begin, while if you take the little road north to Whaddon you pass into Semington parish without realising it. The village has grown around a long S bend of the road. An 's' from the 18th century that was written like an '*f*' without the cross.

Little is known of the early history of Hilperton but in recent centuries its fortunes must have been linked with the town of Trowbridge. Certainly before the powered mills centralised the cloth industry in the towns the village must have contained large numbers of handloom weavers; there is still some evidence in a few large weavers' windows in older cottages. At the time of the first census, in 1801, there was a working population of 708 with 688 employed in 'trade, manufactures, or handicrafts' and only 20 in agriculture. A survey of 1840 into the conditions of 36 families found that 90 adults and children were employed in weaving in their own homes while only one adult worked in a mill in Trowbridge. The livestock farmers employed little labour or, maybe, attracted labourers from bordering parishes.

A bypass now takes through traffic away from the old A361 which has mainly recent houses on its northern side, and long raised sections have been placed on the old road to discourage traffic. As there are eight of these, plus two other areas at a roundabout and a junction, on a short stretch of road, some residents feel it is a little excessive. Around the bypass is being built Paxcroft Mead, a new 'village' of 1,100 houses. Only now it seems is the impact of this being realised in local villages. It extends from Trowbridge nearly to Paxcroft Farm whose houses, fields and farm shop will have new houses for neighbours.

The new road, where rabbits are often seen on the newly grassed verges, has its forerunners. The Kennet and Avon Canal brought a new form of transportation to the parish in 1810 and Hilperton Wharf was the nearest port for industrial Trowbridge. Here Welsh slates for roofs and Somerset coal to fuel the steam-powered factories were unloaded and carted into the town. The turnpiking of the road has left a reminder in the turnpike house, opposite The Lion and Fiddle. Originally of one storey, its white gates were set across the main road to the pub to stop travellers so that they paid their dues. The house is now occupied by Rod Naylor, a wood carver who specialises in antique restoration and keeps a set of stocks outside his window.

Today there is but one shop and one pub in the village. The latter is the only pub with this name in England. Its origin is uncertain but one can guess that an innkeeper disdaining the commonplace and nursery Cat and Fiddle decided that his house would have a more regal sign. In recent years two shops have been reduced to one, the post office and stores, although 50 years ago, in 1939, there were only four; doubtless the result of the close proximity of Trowbridge.

Much of the older village dates from the 18th and 19th centuries. In the centre is a nice row of stone houses, 232 to 234 Church Street, which are believed to be a mid-17th century house which was turned into weavers' cottages. At the northern end is an 18th century brick range built so as to form a letter T. Nearby is the empty Wesleyan Methodist chapel of 1891 which had replaced an earlier chapel built in 1819. The Baptist chapel of 1806 has been amazingly reconstructed as a house. It did have a plain interior, box pews and a west gallery. There is a nice terrace between the chapel and Whaddon Lane with coloured glass above the doorways and wrought ironwork on the window sills of one. Around the corner in Church Street is an older and interestingly angled terrace.

Like many local villages Hilperton has a blind house, or lock up. In this case small, with a very small doorway through which it might have been difficult to push a large man who didn't want to be locked up. It is probably of the mid-18th century and was restored a few years ago. The war memorial is alongside, recording that Hilperton lost 25 men in the First World War and eight in the Second. On the opposite side of the road is an old public water pump set in an alcove in the stone wall.

There are farm houses on the street with Church Farm and Rookery Farm prominent. There is an interesting architectural mix and worthy of mention among the older houses are Yew Cottage, Pantiles of the late 17th century, and Little Ashton. In Hilperton Marsh, set back from Horse Road, there are also some interesting older houses with the 17th century Pound Farm the most notable.

The church of St Michael and All Angels is not in Church Street but is approached from it via The Knap. To your left is the early 18th century Hilperton House with a late 18th century extension and very fine cast iron gates with a wheel design. On the gate pillar is a notice, 'Warning - This house is protected by an attack bird'. In the churchyard one is surprised by views across fields to Hilperton Marsh, Staverton, Holt and Trowbridge as, until now, one has been enclosed by houses.

The church itself is well hidden from casual visitors and only its tower is old, medieval with a broach spire. The rest was built to a design of T.H. Wyatt in 1852. The Old Rectory is early 19th century but had lost its original function by 1880. Some distance away, in Whaddon Lane, is the village hall, a little reminiscent of a barracks, with a sports field beyond.

Today a most respectable village and a far cry from the time in 1838 when a Chartist meeting attracted 500 people and the villagers were called 'Tie Downs', possibly a reference to their weaving and spreading cloth on tenter hooks.

HINDON

Set high and remote on the downs, with its High Street declining to a tiny stream, is Hindon. In this village, with a little imagination, you can believe yourself to have travelled back several centuries. For Hindon has remained faithful to the plan on which it was constructed in the early 13th century. Up to 1218 this was empty downland, populated by sheep and shepherds and the wild downland birds and animals, with the only sounds being sheep bells and bird song. In 1219 Bishop des Roches of Winchester with, it must be admitted, an eye to commercial gain, set out a borough around the Salisbury to Taunton Road. The settlement was fairly close to the productive villages of the Nadder and Wylye valleys yet far from the established centres of Mere and Shaftesbury, so it was hoped that it would act as a market for these villages.

The tenements of the town, for town it was, were set out in narrow burgage plots on either side of the main street. The intention was for the dwellings to be occupied by artisans and craftsmen rather than farmers; more than 700 years later traces of these plots survive. In 1250 there were 150 houses and over the centuries there were many craftsmen and tradesmen but the concentration of a major industry never developed. The market was busy and rated by John Aubrey, in 1650, as being second only to Warminster as a corn market, when Warminster was considered the largest corn market in southern England. A Michaelmas Fair had been granted in 1219 and by 1332 there were two fairs lasting three days each. Naturally the dues from both markets and fairs went to the church.

Up to the mid-18th century there was considerable development as a centre for travellers which, with the market, probably accounts for the 14 inns and alehouses that existed in 1754. That year is an inauspicious one in the history of Hindon for it marks the first of its major setbacks when fire, that scourge of all thatched and timbered properties, was a most unwelcome guest. It began at about three o'clock on 2nd July when sparks from the forge of Mr Tyler, a cutler, ignited the thatch of his house which was on the western side of the High Street to the north of the church. The fire spread rapidly with wind blowing the flames from one side of the street to the other.

With houses packed tightly against one another and wooden outbuildings containing hay and corn, there was little the townspeople could do. They were not aided by the fact that having been built on high land, the town wells were deep and it was impossible to obtain any large quantity of water. In the fierce heat and acrid billowing smoke it was amazing that only one person was killed and another seriously injured but, after four hours of the conflagration, 140 houses had been destroyed and numerous outbuildings, barns and stables lost. Of the 14 inns only one survived and it is recorded that vast quantities of beer, as well as the supplies of hay and corn, had perished.

Hindon quickly recovered and rebuilt. Relief funds were started in many towns and cities (including one as far afield as Canterbury) and some of this money would have found its way to the inhabitants who used Chilmark and Tisbury stone in their reconstruction. For a new era of prosperity was ahead and its beginning was marked when the first mail coach stopped on its journey from London to Exeter on 2nd August 1784. The coaching era brought many jobs for, in 1800, The Lamb was said to have kept 300 post horses. The Lamb, first mentioned in 1755, still exists on the coaching road as an inn, hotel and restaurant; in the early years of the 20th century W. H. Hudson stayed at the inn when writing his acclaimed *A Shepherd's Life* (1910). The other present hotel and inn, The Grosvenor Arms, was first mentioned as The Angel in 1752.

Population peaked in 1831 and then gradually declined. The market also declined when the railway came to Tisbury in 1859 and had ended by 1882. The fair had been reduced to a single day by 1790 but lasted until the First World War. After the railway had ended Hindon's importance as a centre for travellers, the town also lost its Petty Sessions and police station to Tisbury. Six centuries of town-life were at an end and Hindon sank gracefully to village status. I, for one, am pleased for it has escaped the depredations of the 19th and 20th centuries and we are able to cherish this medieval-based small Georgian town.

HOLT

An industrial Wiltshire village is a rarity nowadays but Holt is one in which a long established firm survives, although another has recently closed, while newer ones are moving in. Appropriately this industrial area is in The Midlands, so called from its position in the middle of the village, where it is mixed up with 18th and 19th century houses in both stone and brick. J. & T. Beaven have their origins in the 17th century and their tannery was founded in 1783. Their office building is extremely pleasant, having been converted from brick cottages which date back to 1758, while a nice touch is the 'B' on their wrought-iron gates. The main three-storey factory building is in stone while the chimney is brick. A tiny stream is channelled alongside and eventually finds its way into the River Avon.

The bed manufacturers, John Sawtell & Co Ltd, were established in 1830 and for over a century was run as a family firm. Their older building was of brick and stone and used to turn out the 'Sleepline' beds. It was on this site that the Holt Spa flourished but the only visible remains today are an arch, pump handle and stone tablet on the end wall of the factory. The tablet is inscribed: 'Sacred to the Memory of Lady Lisle and The Revd. James Lewis. The persons who patronised this Spring and rendered it famous in the year 1720.'

A house for visitors was built in 1730 (now demolished) and bottled spa water from Holt was on sale in London. Although famous in its day the spa declined in the face of competition from Bath and the well is now sealed.

New companies are settling in Holt and the 20-unit Midlands Light Industrial Estate has been set up to provide accommodation. The Midlands is also home to a building supplies company, the Holt Joinery and a nursery school in the Old Orchard. However, much of this large village is home for people working in Bradford on Avon, Melksham and Trowbridge and this is reflected in the decline of local shops. Until quite recently there was a fair range but recently the Co-op grocery shop closed, leaving only a hair stylist, the post office and a garage. Fortunately the Co-op building has now been opened as an independent shop, Holt Superstore, while a large equestrian centre and a nursery have opened on the eastern outskirts of the village near the turning to Broughton Gifford.

Just off the main road is The Courts, a National Trust property with excellent gardens. Originally an old house on this site was bought by John Phelps in 1703; by 1731 he had rebuilt it. Being a clothier he also built workshops and a dye house and by 1797 it had passed to John Davis who is thought to have built the factory. The factory was originally water-powered but had changed to steam by 1822. It continued in use until 1885 and was demolished about 1890.

The church of St Katherine is not immediately evident from the main street. Built in 1891 it contains early work in the south porch (c1300) and the Perpendicular tower. The church is close to open fields through which run a network of footpaths which eventually encompass the whole village. An interesting feature of these paths are the iron stiles in an individual local style. Back on the main road are the Congregational churches. Most obvious is the rather florid new one of 1880 obscuring the pleasant plain one of 1810.

Until quite recently Holt had three public houses but one, The Three Lions, has now been converted to housing. This still leaves the beflowered Toll Gate, formerly The White Hart, at the western approach to the village, strategically placed near three incoming roads, and The Ham Tree. This latter in its 18th century building, with raised garden at the back, faces the pleasant triangular Ham Green and the site of the long gone tree from which the name was taken.

Holt was once a junction on the Great Western Railway where the now vanished line led off to Devizes. In more recent times the Royal train was seen on a stretch of line near here and there is a strong local belief that meetings prior to a royal engagement took place just outside Holt.

HORNINGSHAM

Little Horningsham, in its fan-shaped valley surrounded by wooded hills, has long been dominated by Longleat. It was created out of the great Forest of Selwood and for many centuries remained relatively poor and unimportant. Today it exhibits no cohesive pattern, although there are some concentrations of houses around The Green, the church and at Meeting House Batch. Elsewhere the dwellings are very scattered, being set in large gardens or former smallholdings. The whole presents a delightful picture with snug cottages set amid verdant pastures and multi-coloured gardens.

The best known building is the Old Meeting House, which claims to be the oldest non-conformist chapel in the country, being founded for the Presbyterian workmen who built Longleat. The Presbyterians were, of course, Scots and the area to the west of The Bath Arms is still known as

Scotland, being the area in which they were housed four centuries ago. The Bath Arms itself is a stone rubble building of the 17th and 18th centuries and faces a group of twelve interlacing lime trees planted in 1783 and known as 'The Apostles'. The church of St John the Baptist was rebuilt in both 1783 and 1844 but despite this has managed to retain its 14th century tower.

In an area which still specialises in dairying, there are naturally many farms. Manor Farm was erected in the 17th century as a new manor house; its extensive outbuildings include a roundhouse for a horse mill. The 18th century Woodhouse Farmhouse contains masonry from the old Woodhouse Castle of the Arundells. The castle was to the north of the present house, an area marked by undulating ground and masonry. Mill Farm, beautifully situated at the end of its long mill pond was originally Lower Mill and was worked as a grist mill until 1909. One other mill remains only as low ruins at the southern end of Church Street. These and the drying shed, indicated by a conical roof at No 82, were the complex of Upper Mill. The destruction of this mill was recorded in *Das Kapital* (1867) from the confines of the British Museum by Karl Marx thus: 'In 1758 Everet constructed the first woolshearing machine to be driven by water. It was burned down by 100,000 workpeople who had been thrown out of work.' The mill had actually been smashed in 1767 by a maximum of 500 rioters but apparently Marx was prepared to sacrifice strict adherence to the truth in favour of a better copy for his political message.

Longleat itself is an Elizabethan palace. The present house was started by John Thynne in 1568 and continued by him for the rest of his life. To maintain such a house the late Lord Bath installed a Safari Park, Garden Centre, railway and numerous other attractions. There are also many special events held here, such as mammoth Teddy Bears' Picnics. This entertainment industry, with forestry and timber products on the estate, has enabled many villagers to continue to work locally. The present Lord Bath, well known for his paintings, writing, mazes and Wessex politics, has presided over the creation of a Center Parcs holiday village in the woodlands which attracts large numbers of people for both holidays and weekend breaks and has provided many more jobs in the area.

HULLAVINGTON

A fair sized village which has developed around the south-west to north-east axis of a route which once ran from Grittleton to Corston. There are good older houses along this route, now called The Street, and many of the houses have large gardens. The original village seems to have developed as a street village with just a few lanes, such as Gibb's Lane, providing alternative areas for house building.

The manor, with Clatford near Marlborough, once belonged to an alien priory, St Victor's in Normandy, but after the confiscation of alien priories Henry VI gave both to Eton College. The church of St Mary Magdalene contains a fine 13th century north chapel. The bench ends are Perpendicular while there is a 17th century panel depicting the Sacrifice of Isaac. The church suffered a poor restoration in 1871 and an oak rood screen, from the 14th and 15th centuries, which had survived that was taken down in 1917 and later replaced with a new screen as a memorial to the men of Hullavington who had died in the First World War. Canon Jackson, of Leigh Delamere, mentions a 'curious piece' of medieval embroidery which was originally a cope and, in the 19th century, was used as a pulpit cloth. He described it as being a brown satin ground with embellishments in silver and gold. In the centre was Christ on the cross with an angel either side receiving blood in a chalice.

Between the church and the road is a large open churchyard. There are many monuments but one of the more interesting is to be found on the east exterior wall of the church. To the memory of the vicar, John Jackson, and his wife who both died in 1739, it is a metal cross with engraved inscription and a skull and crossbones underneath. Slightly earlier, at the end of the 17th century, Quakers had been numerous here and, in 1684, three men of Hullavington had been sent to prison for their religious beliefs.

In the village is Lawn Farm, at the corner of Watt's Lane. There is a one and a half storey building which seems to be the old farmhouse with integral barn. Nearby the substantial Queen's Head is attached to an earlier stone building and has outbuildings and a yard. There are still shops serving the village including the newsagent's and stores and the post office in London House. On the corner of Frog Lane, the garage has a shop attached while farther north The Star provides food and drink for those approaching from that direction. This building seems to date from the 1910 to 1920 period with three very substantial brick chimney stacks, but has an older stable or coach house to the side.

Opposite The Star are two rows of good houses with the date 1935 on a hopper head. Seemingly local authority housing, these blend well with the older dwellings. Elsewhere in the village are The Old Surgery and The Old School, both now residential with the present school set among modern housing.

Within the parish is Bradfield, once a manor house, then a farm house. It is a rare survival of a 15th century hall described by John Aubrey as 'in the old Gothic fashion'. A tall three-storey range was added in the 17th century. Further west is Surrendell, once a manor and now represented by a 17th century farmhouse. There was once a Tudor 'Mansion House' here and it was probably the site of a small village.

IMBER

One day in 1956 an eight year old boy was taken by car over rough roads to a shattered village on Salisbury Plain. To begin with he didn't really understand what it was all about. Groups of people including grandparents, parents and men and women in their early twenties were lovingly examining ruined walls and roofless houses. Voices were muted and there was a catch in the throat when many spoke. Unashamed tears were in many eyes yet there were exclamations of joy when plants and shrubs were discovered in overgrown and neglected gardens.

There seemed to be no walls or hedges around these gardens, which appeared strange to the eyes of this town-bred boy; the only fence was a very high one around the churchyard. Inside the church a service was taking place but the boy did not go in for he had been told that this was for the people who had once lived in this village. After the service the people came out and walked around the churchyard, pausing before a tomb, or gravestone. It was very quiet and an air of sadness enveloped everyone; although the boy did not know the meaning of the word, he understood that these people were on a pilgrimage.

Later he walked around the streets and lanes with his father, being very careful not to stray for he had been told all about possible unexploded shells. Everywhere were people who seemed unwilling to leave. They would return again and again to the ruin of a certain cottage or would walk from person to person quietly speaking or pointing to things. Later, when many photographs were taken and much cine film exposed, the boy left, but still the people walked around the remains of their village.

Of course, I was that small boy in 1956 and this remains one of my earliest and strongest memories of any Wiltshire village. I am most grateful to have been there on the first return of the Imber villagers and I must be one of the few members of my post-war generation to have any knowledge of what Imber looked like when its people were given six weeks to pack up and get out in December 1943. For Imber the writing had been on their thatched walls from 1932 when the War Office bought all the village, except the church, the school, the chapel and the pub, and from 1939 carried out intensive and dangerous training in the area.

The villagers always believed that they would be allowed back after the war but it seems that Imber was too important a training ground and, after a long public enquiry at Trowbridge in 1961, the Crown closed off the entire area and all its rights of way. Each year on the first Sunday in September the village is open and a service conducted in the church of St Giles by the vicar of Edington. Over the years numbers of villagers attending have naturally dwindled and can now be counted on the fingers of one hand. The area and its roads are also open at other public holidays; details appear in local newspapers beforehand.

INGLESHAM

Inglesham parish is a little peninsula of Wiltshire stretching into Gloucestershire in the far north-eastern corner of the county. The road from Highworth to Stow on the Wold passes through Lower Inglesham where there is a scattered settlement of farmhouses and cottages. There is little recent development. Further north a tiny signpost invites you to turn left and visit Inglesham church.

It is a small structure with a nave, two arcades and a small chancel; a belfry with two bells is at the western end. To the east of the porch is the base and shaft of an old preaching cross. The exterior of the church shows signs of repair but basically appears to have been unaltered for many centuries. Go inside and I doubt if you will have seen the like of this church before. It has remained virtually unaltered since the early 16th century; you are looking at the way your ancestors worshipped 400 years ago.

William Morris loved this church and through him and his Society for the

Protection of Ancient Buildings it was beautifully restored in 1888-89. A further careful restoration took place in 1933 by Percival Hartland Thomas when the remains of a reredos of c1330 were re-placed in the chancel. The church was declared redundant in 1979 and vested in the Redundant Churches Fund in 1981 who now sensitively look after it. Do visit it and see how a church evolved and what one looked like before being tidied up and 'beautified' in the 19th century. Contributions are welcome for its upkeep for it is only thus that churches like this can be preserved for future generations.

Outside in the fields can be seen the house platforms of the village which once surrounded the church. It declined with the Cotswold wool trade and all that remains is Church Farm, the 18th century Inglesham House and a nicely gabled cottage.

KEEVIL

About four miles due east of Trowbridge, set amid green pastures and pleasant mature trees, lies the village of Keevil. Within living memory most inhabitants were dependent upon farming for their livelihood but now it is chiefly a dormitory village for the nearby towns. That is not to say that community spirit has gone, for there is a new village hall and when the local landmark of Stocks Tree Elm, at the end of Martins Road, needed replacing, the village made it their commemoration for the Silver Jubilee of Queen Elizabeth II. They obtained an oak from the nearby ancient Biss Wood and planted it where their descendants would know its shade for centuries to come.

I have great affection for Keevil, for it was here, at the age of twelve or thirteen, that I photographed the church seen through the spring foliage of its lych gate trees. That picture won me a competition and I have to reflect that I have still not taken many better photographs than that one.

Many years on, the trees, taller now, still stand at the gate; two lime trees, flanked by two chestnuts, flanked by two more limes. It is a splendid approach to a village church and inside the churchyard, which is at the highest point of the village, there are excellent views towards Salisbury Plain. A new section has been added to this churchyard and it is interesting to note that centuries of burials have raised the old part about three feet above the new.

The church of St Leonard was rebuilt in the late 14th century or early 15th century and remodelled in the early 16th century when the tower was added or rebuilt. The Sanctus bell is one of the oldest in the country, dating from the

12th century and, unlike later bells, it was not cast but moulded on a lathe.

Keevil has some really splendid houses dating from the 15th century. At the western end of the village there are several pleasant timber-framed houses of the 17th century and the early 18th century brick Beach House, formerly the Beach Arms. Moving into the village along a raised pavement is the line of a high stone wall; behind this lies Keevil Manor House.

Beach House and the Manor House are associated with an 18th century love story. The Manor of Keevil was owned by William Beach whose daughter, Anne, fell in love with the humble curate, William Wainhouse. Her father was greatly shocked for he was wealthy and had doubtless contemplated an alliance with a local landed family and curates, though often well educated, were notoriously poor and had few prospects. To prevent an elopement and, he hoped, bring his daughter to her senses he locked Anne in her bedroom for two years. This bedroom was over the porch of the Manor House and it is likely that Anne saw her love walking to the church opposite on most days.

Using her diamond ring on the glass of her window, she scratched their two names which remain to this day. Eventually, realising that his daughter was as stubborn as himself, William issued an ultimatum; she could marry the curate and give up her inheritance or forsake him and keep the family fortune. True to the traditions of romantic tales she chose love and happiness above gold and silver. Sadly though, they did not follow tradition to live 'happy ever after'. After only three months of married bliss, tragically Anne died.

On the other side of the street, in front of the church, is Tallboys, perhaps the most striking house in the village. It is a beautiful symmetrical timber-framed house apparently of the 15th century but appearances can be deceptive. The eastern part is a careful copy of the 15th century centre and western cross gable made in 1876. Inside the roofs are extremely fine with three tiers of wind braces in the hall. Beyond Tallboys is Blagden House, c1600, and said to have been once much larger, although what remains seems a very large house. The gardens are most attractive and can sometimes be visited under the National Gardens Scheme. Further along is Field Head, formerly the vicarage, built in 1842 with shaped Jacobean-type gables. Then a nice touch of humour. After all these grand houses, The Small House, was built of brick with stone quoins and not particularly small.

For many years Keevil was the village without a pub; now it no longer even has an off-licence and thirsty folk must drive to Great Hinton or Bulkington or walk across the fields to The Lamb on The Strand. The latter has been revamped at great cost in recent years from the homely, but probably unprofitable, traditional old pub that it had been for generations.

South of the village lies a legacy of the Second World War, Keevil Airfield. From here Spitfires, made and assembled locally were flown to operational airfields while many airmen from home and abroad made a temporary home in this quiet corner of England. Nowadays it is used by the local gliding club, although part of it is retained for military use and Hercules aircraft are a common sight over the village as they practise dropping supplies and equipment.

Within the parish lies the village of Bulkington and this is approached by means of a minor road leading east from Keevil. The road crosses the Semington Brook by means of the 18th century Pantry Bridge. Just beyond the bridge, on the right-hand side of the road, stands 'Turpin's Stone' in the hedgerow. The inscription is badly eroded and only a few words can be made out but it is believed to have said:

'Dick Turpin's dead and gone
This stone's put here to think upon.'

Maybe a warning to local youths who thought of becoming highwaymen.

KINGSTON DEVERILL

It is likely that the Deverill Valley has seen continuous farming for more than 5,000 years and today it is still given over entirely to agriculture. Now, though, it exhibits large rolling fields of grain yielding three tons per acre, rather than the upland pastures that were the norm for some millennia. The valley once played its part in national events when Wessex, and therefore England, was on the brink of complete foreign domination. For it is believed that on Court Hill, west of Kingston Deverill, King Alfred held his court two days before the battle of Edington and one day later positioned his men at Iley Oak, a place which could be the present Robin Hood's Bower, north of Longbridge Deverill.

It is likely that this gathering of the men of Wessex remained long in local memory. Certainly a hatred of the Danes could have been transmuted into the tall Viking warriors becoming bogeymen to be used to instil obedience into miscreant children or to frighten young wenches. Centuries of oral tradition retain this type of knowledge and it comes as little surprise to find that up to the end of the 19th century a red-haired boy in the Deverill valley would often be called a Dane or Daner by his fellows. It is possible that the facts about the red-haired invaders were imparted by a Victorian schoolmaster but it is more likely to my mind that a thousand years of stories told on winter evenings kept fresh the memory of that threat to the peace of Wessex.

At the top of the valley is Kingston Deverill, a scattered village of attractive farms and cottages spread along several roads and lanes tucked under the hillside. The church of St Mary the Virgin was restored and partly rebuilt in 1846. There are some splendid gargoyles on the short 15th century tower with matching carved heads on the top of the walls of the 1846 nave and south aisle. The church is unlocked but has a bolt on the outside of the door, maybe a device to prevent early exits during a long sermon. Inside it is a good church with a priest's chair of 1688, a battered stone figure from a tomb of the 13th or 14th century, and a fine 14th century wood carving of the Madonna and Child presented to the church in 1970. A Saxon font was discovered buried in the churchyard in the mid-9th century. This was renovated in 1982 and has been in use since; doubtless it is a relic of the Saxon chapel of St Andrew recorded in about 1099.

Elsewhere is a large and turreted old rectory and a farm called Marvins on a site mentioned in the Domesday Book of 1086. The handsome Pope's Farmhouse, which has a 15th century doorway and some contemporary windows, stands by the bridge across the clear and swift flowing little river. There is another small decorative bridge by Bell House while overhead, as you walk around, is the sound of cawing rooks who nest in trees around the churchyard yews, and the noiseless shadow of a glider from the nearby gliding club. On a recent visit we encountered a white goat and a Shetland pony, both very inquisitive and friendly.

KINGTON LANGLEY

Kington Langley and Kington St Michael now lie either side of a north to south dual carriageway from junction 17, on the M4, to Chippenham. Villages that are now split asunder by heavy traffic had already followed separate patterns of development since the times of the land enclosures. The Plough Inn which now lies on the Kington St Michael side of the dual carriageway gave its name to Plough Lane, and the more recent Plough Corner, leading into Kington Langley.

Kington Langley is a prosperous looking village scattered around its three commons, Upper, Middle and Lower, and has a network of house-lined lanes around the top of Fitzurse Hill. Langley Fitzurse was once the village name when the Fitzurse family owned the manor. One family member was one of the three murderers of Thomas Becket. The present church is comparatively modern, 1855-6 and is predated by the Union Chapel of 1835 on Middle Common. Also here is Langley School, serving both villages. One of the finest houses is the Greathouse. Built around 1700 it has a grand, even, nine-bay front and the doorway has a good shell hood.

There are many open spaces which doubtless were once used for producing small amounts of potatoes, beans and corn. The commons were used for pasturing animals, cattle, sheep and geese; the pigs would have been allowed pannage in nearby woods. There is still a pond, now covered with yellow flowering water lilies, on Middle Common, once used for watering all these beasts. One building which appears quite early and is of painted rubble construction is the village pub. Named The Hit and Miss, its sign shows a batsman attempting a big hit and being bowled.

Tucked away in this village is Langley Wild Animal Rescue Centre. Also run from here, by the Stinchcombe family, is Greywolf Film Productions. They are making a series of films, available on video using animals, local people and local locations. Profits are being put towards building studio facilities to help train disabled and special needs students in all aspects of the film and television industry, and to the Centre, where those students have work experience in caring for wild animals.

KINGTON ST MICHAEL

Kington St Michael was the birthplace of two of Wiltshire's most celebrated historians. John Aubrey was born at the tiny settlement of Easton Piercy in the year 1626. In 1648 he brought the monument of Avebury to the notice of the Court and the scientific establishment and further publicised his native county by writing *The Natural History of Wiltshire* and *Wiltshire, the Topographical Collections*. Nationally his best known work was, and still is, *Brief Lives*. A further discovery, and one that is named after him, was the holes at Stonehenge that are still an enigma.

In 1771 John Britton, the son of a baker and maltster, was born in the village. As his father died when John was 14, he was apprenticed to his uncle, a London lawyer. His uncle was unhelpful and apprenticed him to a wine merchant. But during six fairly miserable years, he read a great deal before emerging to write the many volumes of his *Beauties of England and Wales* between 1801 and 1825. The first two volumes of his *Beauties of Wiltshire* were published in 1801 and the third in 1825. Between them they describe most of the great houses of the county. He was also well known and respected for his numerous architectural works which included many volumes on English cathedrals. Britton was one of the founder members of the Wiltshire Archaeological Society in 1853 and much of his collections are in their library in Devizes. There is a stained glass window of 1857 commemorating both men in the church of St Michael while a plaque in the outer wall of the village hall records the birth of Britton.

It is a street village with many of the older houses having a step or two from the street to the front door; a wise precaution to keep them free from the mud of an unmade road. Lytes Almshouses were founded in 1675 and still fulfil their original function. Their gables and stone mullions face No 23, built only slightly later on the other side of the street. Behind the almshouses are allotments, pleasingly still used by villagers. The church of St Michael was somewhat over restored by J. H. Hakewill in 1858 although he could not greatly affect the very wide Norman chancel arch and the contemporary south doorway. Some other features date from the 13th century but the tower, often the oldest part of a church, dates from 1725 and is in the Gothic style. The sporting theme for licensed premises, set in Kington Langley is continued here with The Jolly Huntsmen, a name which seemingly dates from the 18th century.

At the end of the village, where a slanting crossroads takes one either to Stanton St Quintin or Easton Piercy, there appears to be a separate older settlement. This has now been joined to the main part by modern housing and small closes while the chapel, which once lay between the two early settlements, is now a house. Take the narrow lane to Easton Piercy between summer verges of meadowsweet and you will find a peaceful isolated, scattered settlement. The beautiful Manor Farmhouse has a nice range of impressive stone barns.

LACOCK

My association with Lacock began when I was aged two and I have photographic evidence to prove it. At a celebration of William Henry Fox Talbot, the 'father of modern photography', Trowbridge Camera Club took part in the re-enactments of many of his early photographs. A cine film of the activities was produced and, when watching this, I suddenly saw myself listening, with apparent understanding, as my father guided a group of people around the Abbey. I was fortunate in the link between our Camera Club and the Abbey for it enabled me to meet Miss Matilda Talbot who, until her death in 1958, invited us annually to the Abbey; a tradition that was maintained by Mr and Mrs Burnett-Brown after 1958.

It was Matilda Talbot who presented Lacock Abbey to the National Trust in 1944 and who recorded her life and work in *My Life and Lacock Abbey*. With the Abbey she gave the rest of her property, which was the medieval village around its rectangle of streets at the Abbey Gates. The village has remained virtually unchanged since the 18th century.

The dominating influence on the village has been the Abbey. Founded in 1229 by Ela, Countess of Salisbury, for Augustinian canonesses, it prospered during the Middle Ages enjoying various grants and endowments. At the Dissolution in 1539 its lands and buildings were bought by Sir William Sharington for £783. In converting the Abbey to a private residence he retained much of the medieval architecture while building the octagonal three-storey Sharington tower and the Stable Court which houses the bakehouse and brewery besides the stables. Within the Abbey there is much to see, including the peaceful cloisters, a 16th century brewery, the impressive 14th century dormitory roof, the refectory, the nuns' kitchen with its superb cauldron and much, much more.

The Abbey passed by marriage to the Talbot family, the best known member of whom was William Henry Fox Talbot (1800-1877). He was the inventor of the negative-positive process upon which all modern photographs are based. His earliest surviving negative, of 1835, is of the oriel window in the South Gallery of the Abbey. You may take the same photograph yourself and count the 200 small panes of glass which Fox Talbot was able to count with the aid of a lens on what he called his 'photogenic drawing'.

The story of Fox Talbot's life and works are told on the ground floor of the Fox Talbot Museum in the 16th century barn at the Abbey gates, converted to

a museum in 1975. It also has displays on photography of all periods and from many countries.

Despite in some ways being a fossilised village, Lacock is still fully alive. The National Trust encourages craftsmen to settle here and there have been a goldsmith and silversmith and a potter working for several years. The village school remains open and there is a post office and shops while the cricket team is one of the better village sides in the county. The descendant of the medieval fair is now held on August Bank Holiday while every Boxing Day hundreds of people flock to the village to see the meet of the local foxhounds in a most traditional 'Christmas Card' setting.

LANDFORD

Landford is a far flung parish reaching deep into Hampshire, and with many of that county's characteristics. The village itself is very scattered. In the original part is Landford Manor, now the home of Cartographical Services Ltd and Cartographic Engineering Ltd.

To the west of the Manor lies the rebuilt church of St. Andrew. Of 1858, it is constructed of brick with bands of stone and vitrified blue brick. Outside the churchyard grass is kept short by the grazing of three sheep. Some distance away are Landford Lodge, c1776, and the Tudor-style Hamptworth Lodge of 1910-1912, a large house genuinely constructed of timber framing with

brick infill - no 'Stockbroker's Tudor' here - with some original Elizabethan or Jacobean overmantels, from Herefordshire, inside.

This is a very rural agricultural parish and certain local events were important in bringing people together. One of these was the annual cider making of which there is an account in the *Landford and Hamptworth Women's Institute Scrapbook* (1956). The practice continued until about 1925 when the cider press was drawn by a lorry around the orchards rather than the patient horse of a few years earlier. The press was set up near to the cider apple trees, which had curious and now largely forgotten names, although cooking and dessert apples as well as the small bright cider apples would be used. The fruit was pulped in the grinder, which required two men to operate it, and the juice which ran off at this stage was caught in all sorts of domestic containers.

The pulp was shovelled onto the press in layers between felt (in my own part of Wiltshire straw was more often used) and a heavy wooden slab screwed down on top. The latter task was completed by everyone available walking around with capstan type bars leading into the centre of the press. The apple juice ran into a vat below from whence it was transferred into old wine casks. Some people would add wheat, molasses or meat to the casks, holding that it improved the flavouring or that the cider 'fed on meat'. There are many stories, from all parts of the county, which centre on the fact that the best cider turned out to be that in which rats had accidentally drowned. They are most probably apocryphal. At least we hope so!

So the cider was made for another year and a most important commodity it was when each farm made its own. Although the traditional memory is cider at harvest time, for many farm labourers it was available for much of the year. It certainly helped with many a hard day's work behind the horse-drawn plough and some of the older ploughmen and carters could absorb a tremendous quantity each day. This farm cider tended to be stronger than most modern cider and local names such as 'Tanglefoot' and 'Stunnen' were indicative of its potency.

LIMPLEY STOKE

The village poses many questions. Why is it built on a steep hillside? Where does Limpley Stoke end and Freshford begin? Where is the church? How do the villagers negotiate the narrow roads in their large cars? The answers to the first three questions must lie in the early history of the community and a study of this would be most worthwhile.

Houses cascade down the valley side and are planted on less steep, or levelled, pieces of ground. Indeed the original name was Hanging Stoke and is far more appropriate than is the 'Hanging' added to Langford further south in the Wylye valley. Why Limpley supplanted Hanging is a mystery but by 1585 it was recorded by both names and after that only the new one was used.

The valley itself has always been popular with tourists and I well remember being told, as a boy travelling on the steam train to visit a great aunt or go shopping in Bath, that many people came here to journey on that railway line just to see the autumnal colours in the valley. At that time I was more interested in the railway engines than the trees but I did appreciate the changing colours of September and October, while in the spring there was one bluebell wood with such mists of slatey blue flowers that I was driven to try to find it on my bicycle, but I could never discover the right road. Perhaps it was only meant to be seen by train passengers who could not dismount and violate it with their feet and hands.

Back to the village, which should really be traversed on foot leaving the residents to negotiate the roads which only they can truly know. It is in three parts, Lower, Middle and Upper but only Lower is obvious. Much of it is set along the road near the bottom of the valley which joins the Winsley to Bath road. The railway line runs parallel with this road but the railway station is now closed. It was here that many scenes from *The Titfield Thunderbolt* were filmed and the area has been a place of pilgrimage for devotees of the splendid British film. Now the Titfield Thunderbolt Shop has moved to Brassknocker Basin, on the Kennet and Avon Canal, just below the A36 Bath road and The Viaduct Inn.

Moving into the village you come to a large welcoming porch leading to the Avon Bar and Valley Bar of the hospitable Hop Pole Inn. The stone building itself is seemingly low when viewed from the road and has good stone mullions, smaller on the first floor than on the ground floor. Opposite is the entrance to the imposing multi-windowed and multi-dormered Limpley Stoke Hotel with a large extension to the rear. Hospitality is obviously big business in the village for there is also the Cliffe Hotel while on the main Bath road above the village is The Rose and Crown which has long had a good reputation for its food.

On the other side of the road to The Hop Pole is the Post Office and General

Stores. Right on the road, it is bedecked with flower pots and window troughs while flowers from tubs attempt to pollinate passing cars. The Manor House shows its Georgian frontage to the river but the back is gabled 17th century with mullioned windows. By the house called The Cottage is a pole for electricity cables. Eleven wires radiate from it and around most of them clematis has rampaged, crossing gardens and the road. Whilst I was admiring this a grey squirrel nonchalantly leapt from one of the cables into a tall conifer nearby.

Just before the road ascends Crowe Hill a footpath leads off to the left under a brick railway arch to the river. From here it is a pleasant valley walk to Freshford and its New Inn one and a half miles away. There are also steep footpaths and steps to the right by which you can get to Upper and Middle Stoke, coming across houses both old and new tucked away in secluded spots on the hillside on your way. If you climb Crowe Hill you can look above houses with stepped and terraced gardens to the other side of the valley. The trees on Murhill display a wide range in shades of green interspersed with the brown of copper beeches.

The road shrugs off most of the houses, turns to the right and makes a T junction with another minor road. Turn left and you will find yourself in Freshford and Somerset but turn right and you will return to Limpley Stoke and find the church of St Mary, for this is Church Lane. At the junction with the road to Middle Stoke is the church but you might not notice it if you were driving instead of walking. Set a little above the road, it is small and untouched by Georgians or Victorians. It has a stumpy west tower and a short nave and chancel and inside you will find work of the 13th century. The arcading in the 20th century aisle includes the early south doorway of narrow and undecorated Saxon work. The west gallery has some nice Jacobean panels.

My personal theory is that the village has slipped down the hillside from its church, which is right on the Somerset border. So close as to make it the only Wiltshire church in the Diocese of Bath and Wells. Along with the three roads, three footpaths converge at the church, one from Crowe Hill and two from the south. These six routes might be an indication of an early street pattern although one of the southern footpaths does ascend a fairly steep hill.

The road through Middle Stoke to The Rose and Crown has a good mixture of houses with some quite early. Along here is the village hall, formerly the village school, and the tops of those routes from the lower village. Off Wood's Hill is a well equipped play area for children which, as to be expected here, is on a slope which must lead to some interesting games. If you are now tired by exploring and climbing you can make your way down Wood's Hill to The Hop Pole where, hopefully, it is opening time.

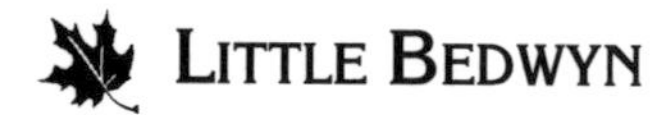

LITTLE BEDWYN

Wherever you find chalk or limestone in Wiltshire you will find the wild clematis. Rampaging through the hedgerows, it is called Traveller's Joy in summer, from a time when its flowers gave delight to wayfarers on England's green roads. In autumn it becomes Old Man's Beard, when its straggly appearance suggests a particularly thin and elderly beard. One authority believes that it is from this plant that the village was named; *bedwine* or *bedwind* in Old English, indicating a place where wild clematis grew in profusion. A more prosaic explanation is that the name of the Bedwyn stream is likely to be Celtic and means the stream by the white birch. However, the old Wiltshire name for wild clematis is bithywine so let's keep to the more poetic origin.

Little Bedwyn lies to the north of Great Bedwyn and is still the smaller of the two. Attractively set around the Kennet and Avon Canal, it possesses several pleasant houses much older than the waterway. Best of these is the 18th century Manor Farmhouse in chequered brickwork and with a rare octagonal game larder. The farmyard is most attractive with timber and brick barns in the middle of the village. A footbridge takes you across the canal and the adjoining railway line into the western part of the village. A pause on the bridge will provide good views of a straight stretch of canal in both directions.

The church of St Michael is of several periods, the earliest being of the 12th and 13th centuries, and is of flint interspersed with limestone. In Church Street there are examples of the typical local style of 19th century building, of red and blue brick, in the estate cottages of 1860. Other cottages are from the 17th century and are of timber framing refaced in brick. Around the village keep a look out for three 18th century milestones of painted stone.

School Lane, with its delightful Old Manor Cottage of timber framing set on flint sills, reminds us of a famous son of the village. Felix Pole, born in 1877, was the second son of the village schoolmaster. The family moved to Ramsbury when Felix was eight and the highly regarded schoolmaster also taught in Great Bedwyn. The 14 year old Felix entered the Great Western

Railway in the Telegraph Department at Swindon in 1891. His rise was rapid and in 1921 he became one of the youngest ever General Managers of the GWR at Paddington and later acted as advisor and consultant to various overseas projects after he left the General Manager's post in 1929.

LITTLE SOMERFORD

Little Somerford is the smaller village, to the north of Great Somerford, straggling along the four roads that radiate from its crossroads. The oldest buildings are in The Street and The Hill while newer development is concentrated off Clay Street (the Swindon Road) and from the crossroads towards Dauntsey. Around are small well kept and well hedged fields while to the west the slightly rising ground and some trees provide a most pleasant outlook.

Farms and farming permeate the village with most of the surrounding land being pasture. There are handsome farmhouses and former farmhouses, stone built with stone tiles. Manor Farm is of six bays, is symmetrical and has walled gardens and good barns and outbuildings. Most buildings are of stone but there is one good thatched, timber-framed house with brick infill.

The church of St John the Baptist is fairly simple with lots of tie beams through the walls of the nave and chancel, which are combined in one. There is a narrow Perpendicular west tower but most of the treasures are inside. A grand Perpendicular screen still has a tympanum above on which are painted the Royal Arms of Elizabeth I. On the walls are late 17th century texts in cartouches while the pulpit and reader's desk are of 1626 and the benches are cut down Jacobean box pews. Outside, the churchyard is full of some remembered but mostly forgotten villagers and a new graveyard has been opened to the south by Meadow Lane.

By the church there are two interesting buildings. Mills Farm with an undulating roof indicating early roof timbers and the very pleasant brick Georgian Old Rectory. Opposite the church is 'Bob Shepherd, Motor Engineer' in an old stone house with a workshop at the rear. The filling station is bedecked with flowers in spring, summer and autumn and there is a lovely hand-painted sign. This is the sort of garage where I would like to take my car to be repaired; the sort of garage which I thought had long since disappeared.

LOCKERIDGE

Lockeridge cannot really be classed as a village as it has no church, being a hamlet in the parish of West Overton, while Lockeridge House is in Fyfield parish. However, the settlement must be at least as big as West Overton and is much bigger than Fyfield, so I am going to include it. The name would seem to mean, 'the ridge marked by enclosures' and if this is right it could refer to the higher land to the south-east. The manor belonged to the Knights Templar from the mid-12th century until the suppression of the order in 1308. After that many families held the manor and the frequent changes must have destroyed the continuity and growth that was the lot of most manors.

The hamlet is to be found along the bottom of a small valley running south-west from the River Kennet. On the other side of the Kennet is Lockeridge House. It is a handsome brick house of c1740 with good stone and brick gate piers with very large pineapples atop. Along the road are some cottages from the 17th century, Myrtle Cottage of colour-washed sarsen stone, and Jay's Cottage of sarsen with some timber framing. Two more sarsen buildings from the late 17th or early 18th centuries are Hillside Cottage and Castle Cottage but most of the other houses are from the later 18th or early 19th century.

The sarsen stones used for building were just lying around and were the southernmost extension of the great flocks of stones to be found on Fyfield and Overton Downs. The more massive of these were used at Avebury while some were transported south across Salisbury Plain for the more recent monument of Stonehenge. There are still some stones in Lockeridge Dene and in 1907 the National Trust bought this part of Lockeridge Green to preserve them in their original state. In the Dene are 18th and 19th century cottages and Dene Farmhouse, of the 17th century, all built from sarsen stones. It was here, in the house called The Lachet, that Carrington is said to have stayed when visiting this part of Wiltshire although her main local connection will be found under the village of Ham.

There are many attractive estate cottages of brick on a stone plinth, which were built by the Meux family in the 1870s. They were also instrumental in the National School of 1872, which is from a design by C. E. Ponting. It is also believed that the public house is one of their buildings. Its name is Who'd 'a Thought It? and, like others in the country, the name expresses the surprise of landlord Percy Long and his neighbours when the hard hearted justices allowed him a license around 1930. The neighbouring hamlet of Manton also has an unusual pub name, Up the Garden Path. Not the one up which farm labourers might have led young ladies but a literal meaning in that the house is well set back from the road and is approached by a long garden path.

The hamlet is most attractive with the sarsen cottages giving the appearance of having grown from the ground. There remains a small green, with play equipment, in Lockeridge Dene while the main street is lined by pollarded lime trees by the school. To the south are West Woods, an outlier of Savernake Forest, through which runs part of Wansdyke. In 1564 there was said to have been a windmill here and it may have been on White Hill, to the west, but as the hamlet is enclosed by hills on three sides there are many windy places to be found here on higher ground.

LONGBRIDGE DEVERILL

The name Deverill is given to the upper part of the River Wylye and it is the long bridge here that gives this village its distinguishing name, which in the 13th century was in the French form of Longepont. In the early 10th century the manor was granted to the Abbot of Glastonbury who held it until the dissolution in 1539. This was one of the manors acquired by Sir John Thynne, the builder of Longleat House, which once stood within the parish. His manor house was sited to the north of the church but all that now remains is a stone wall between the road and the river.

Sir John is buried in the church of St Peter and St Paul which has some early Norman features and bits and pieces from most other centuries. There is a tradition that the altar stone was used by Thomas Becket when he consecrated the church. The stone was discovered, buried under a path, when the chancel was rebuilt in 1858 and it is believed that it was buried by the vicar for safety, when Cromwellian soldiers were advancing on the village. The magnificent altar stone came from the church at Hill Deverill when it was closed in 1984. The three medieval shields on it commemorate marriages of the Ludlow family.

Near the church are the Thynne Almshouses, founded in 1655, while on the other side of the road is Longbridge House, of around 1840, which is now a nursing home. Also on the main road is The George Inn and a little further south is the gate used to close the road when it is blocked by snow on higher ground.

If you are travelling by car and you blink you may miss Hill Deverill altogether. From the road can be seen a few houses and some earlier cottages which now appear attached to Longbridge Deverill. The tiny church was rebuilt in 1843 and has the rarity of being one of the few Church of England churches with a Roman Catholic dedication, to The Assumption. The late 17th century Manor Farmhouse has a very long barn attached; some 15 bays with three porches. The 'lost' village is visible as earthworks to the south and west of the church. In 1894 it was recorded that people would go to the churchyard on Midsummer Night to look for ghosts. One informant remembered that he went as a boy in 1833 to see them come in and out and reported that many fearsome things had been seen. One such ghost was that of Sir Henry Coker who had lived at the Manor Farm and died in 1736. He was reputed to be a smuggler and a robber and tradition says that many entered his house never to reappear. He is still said to gallop around the parish with his hounds but this may be a faint echo of the Wild Hunt.

From Hill Deverill to Longbridge Deverill the river has been widened for watercress beds, where Hurds grow organic watercress, to which a trout farm has been added in recent years. In the parish is the village of Crockerton, where the manufacture of pots (crocks) on an area of clay in the Shearwater Valley has been recorded since the 13th century and only ended in 1954. There is also sufficient water power here to drive a mill suitable for textiles. Bull Mill is mentioned in the Domesday Book, although the present building is 16th century. Originally a woollen cloth mill, it was converted to silk spinning in 1824 and greatly expanded until it was closed in 1894. The large factory buildings have now disappeared leaving only the house. On the road to Shearwater and its sailing club is The Bath Arms, at Shear Cross, part of which is late 17th century.

LYDIARD MILLICENT

Both the Lydiards now suffer from the same affliction: the expansion of Swindon Borough Council, or the Borough of Thamesdown as it was known between 1974 and 1997. The westward growth of this once unpretentious but pleasant 19th century railway town is swallowing up many square miles of fields, hedgerows, trees and villages. Toothill and Mannington have gone and the scattered houses and farms of Shaw have been engulfed. The development is not far from the pleasant little village of Lydiard Millicent which has several early brick houses, some of them very small. There are also some quite fine larger houses, both of brick and stone, and an increasing number of modern houses with one or two really fine new dwellings. The village must be seen as a very desirable place to live but I feel that the number of new houses have lessened the attraction that I experienced in the 1980s.

The church of All Saints is a mixture of Decorated and Perpendicular styles which suffered a thorough restoration in 1871. The font is Norman but the pulpit is heavy Victorian Gothic carved in 1862 by local boys under the instruction of the then curate. The Jacobean pulpit was given to the little church at Braydon. Structurally, however, the church is much as it was in the mid-15th century and there is a nice medieval squint which gave the part of the congregation in the south aisle a view of the altar so that they could observe mass. There is a fine Renaissance weather vane on top of the tower while three scratch dials are to be found on the walls of the south porch and the south aisle. In the churchyard is a cross, the shaft of which probably dates from Saxon times although the cross itself was added in 1854, replacing one which had been destroyed by Puritans.

An elementary school had been established here in 1840 by the Lord of the Manor. In 1870, after Forster's Education Act, the first head teacher, Hannah Shore was appointed. Her problems are typical of those encountered in rural areas at this time. Inadequate schoolroom, many children kept at home or called out of school for seasonal work on the land, epidemics of infectious diseases and deaths of children in these. Parents also had to pay for children to attend school and in 1871 the fees were one penny halfpenny a week per child. Also in that year the headmistress opened a night school three evenings a week for twelve young men and boys at threepence each per week.

In the 1990s children from the present Lydiard Millicent School helped the Butt's Pond Group, founded in 1990, to restore Butt's Pond. In 1992 they again helped to plant native woodland trees around the pond and thus a nature reserve for plants, birds, amphibians and insects has been created which the school is able to use for field study projects.

LYDIARD TREGOZE

The most splendidly furnished church, probably in the whole of Wiltshire, is to be found at Lydiard Tregoze. There is no village here but next to the church is the mansion of Lydiard Park and there are a scatter of farms around the parish. The village was once close to the church while the Rectory House stood at the eastern end of the church until 1830. Nowadays the only village in the parish is Hook, two miles away. The mansion, which is now owned by Swindon Borough Council, was rebuilt in 1743 by John Lord Viscount St John who retained some features of an earlier building in the north-east side.

Quite peaceful it was a few years ago but that has now changed. Swindon has taken it over and, having built houses on the surrounding fields, they have created a countryside park for the people who live on those housing estates. Here there are sports fields, a restaurant, a visitor centre, much parking space and still pleasant walks through the woods of the park. The Friends of Lydiard Tregoze have carried out a great deal of interesting research into the estate and there is a wealth of publications available.

Behind the mansion is the medium size Perpendicular church of St Mary. Inside it is superb. Nikolaus Pevsner says it is 'richer than any other of similar size in the county', while for monuments John Aubrey said 'it exceeds all the churches of this countie'. The first church was on this site by the year 1100 but the present church has 13th century origins in the nave, some arches of the north arcade and the eastern threequarters of the north aisle. A scheme of improvement and enlargement in the 15th century gives an impression of a church of that date but the spectacular internal change came about in 1633.

The south chapel was the burial place of the St John family and was extensively remodelled by John St John who died in 1648. In memory of his parents there is an highly elaborate painted triptych, twelve feet wide by fifteen feet high, which has been described as the most splendid monument of its kind surviving in England. Sir John was responsible for the installation of Flemish glass, in the east window of the chancel, which shows the descent of the manor to him. All these monuments and others are remarkably well preserved and the whole gives the impression of a private chapel rather than a parish church. The family is also remarkable in having owned the estate from the early 15th to the 20th century. No mean feat when land could be forfeited for many transgressions.

Outside the gates Park Farm is worth a mention for it is being engulfed by the houses creeping towards it. But for the moment at least Friesian cattle still graze the fields in what remains of this once important part of the north Wiltshire dairy and cheese-making industry.

LYNEHAM

Lyneham is the home of RAF Transport Command, a fact it is difficult to forget if you live in the area. There are times when the skies seem full of lumbering, unwieldy Hercules aircraft which, like the bumble bee, appear to fly in direct contradiction to the laws of nature. The perimeter fence of the airfield and its ancillary buildings now abut the churchyard. The church of St Michael is largely Perpendicular, although much restored in 1862-1865, and within is a Perpendicular rood screen and a Jacobean tower screen. Unfortunately the church is locked but outside can be seen a splendid large yew tree and the beautifully kept RAF cemetery with uniform headstones from the Second World War to date.

The village has grown greatly with the coming of the RAF and can boast many shops that other villages might envy. To me, however, it has the appearance of a town suburb and a further blight is cast by the thunder of speeding traffic on the A3102; I let my mind wander wistfully to more halcyon days. In 1927 Ernest Walls wrote, 'Here are delightful cottages that call for your admiration, surrounded by a gladsome green, where a few cows are grazing and children are playing.'

There are still some nice old thatched houses and while the remains of old farmyards stand derelict by the roadside there is still one working farm in the middle of the village. The old farmhouses are mainly of stone, with stone tiles, and have been well renovated. But much of the older property, and most especially the church, now finds itself in an alien landscape.

To me the most pleasant area is the small village of Bradenstoke lying to the north of the airfield. Here was an Augustinian Priory founded in 1142, of which little now remains, although it was only in the 1930s that the great barn and guest house were taken down and moved to St Donat's Castle by William Randolph Hearst. The existing remains consist of a 14th century tower and part of a 14th century undercroft.

MAIDEN BRADLEY

Close to the Somerset border and astride the B3092 that joins Frome to Mere is the compact village of Maiden Bradley. The 'Bradley' part of the name is likely to mean a wide open space in woodland but the later prefix 'Maiden' comes from the period when there was a leper hospital here for maidens afflicted by the disease, originally founded c1152 by the powerful baron Manser Bisset. He appointed a Proctor and Assistants to look after the maidens (all of whom were of high birth) and administer their dowries that had been paid on admission. In 1184 the foundation was converted to a Priory of the Black Canons or Augustinians. The unmarried daughter of Manser, Margaret Bisset, took a great interest in the hospital, providing gifts and building a house nearby in 1180. From this it was often assumed that Margaret was a leper girl who had founded the hospital, but this was not the case.

By the end of the 13th century it seems likely that there were no lepers in residence and mention is only made of the Brethren and Sisters. The Priory was rebuilt around 1380 and continued to prosper. The last Prior before the Dissolution was Richard Jennings (1506-1536) whose life provides a very good reason for this suppression. He claimed to have a Papal licence to keep a mistress and took 'maidens, the fairest that could be got' and 'married them off right well' when they became pregnant. By the time of the Dissolution in 1536 he had fathered six sons and several daughters and had quarrelled violently with many of his neighbours.

Today the village is most decorous. It still enjoys a fairly isolated situation and has many pleasant stone houses. The remains of the Priory are to the north where an 'L' shaped medieval building remains at Priory Farm, while odd pieces of masonry are to be found in field and bramble thicket. The church of All Saints is in the south of the village and is basically 14th century, having been restored in the 19th century. Inside is a Jacobean pulpit and stalls, 17th century box pews and some fragments of stained glass from the 14th to 16th centuries.

The present Bradley House is but a small part of the mansion of the powerful Seymour family who became the Dukes of Somerset. The present Duke of Somerset still owns it. In this lively village there is the large square-built Somerset Arms which is a friendly pub with good food, a skittle alley in a stone outbuilding for winter and boule in the beer garden in summer. There is a good village stores, a post office in a barn behind the fine stone house opposite the pub, a village hall and much evidence of community spirit.

There are excellent walks in the parish through woodland, over hills and through level pastures. It is possible to walk through the deserted village of Yarnfield, one and a half miles south-west of Maiden Bradley, and in your mind populate again its green hollow-ways and platforms with the farmers and labourers who once lived and worked here. In the south a footpath takes you along the high ridge of Long Knoll while to the north and north-west Little Bradley Wood, Great Bradley Wood, Renstones Wood and Tyning Wood provide a very different environment on the Somerset border.

THE MANNINGFORDS

The Manningfords - Abbots, Bruce and Bohune - lie along two miles of the Salisbury Avon, on the southern edge of the Vale of Pewsey. I have known these villages for nearly 30 years. Despite this, I can still get lost when walking or driving around their footpaths and lanes without the aid of an Ordnance Survey map. I was pleased to discover that H.W. Timperley, writing on the Manningfords in *The Vale of Pewsey* (1954), confessed that he, too, found them puzzling. He also reminded me that Edward Thomas, the poet who loved walking in Wiltshire, remembered them in his poem *Lob*:

> 'Their churches, graveyards, farms and byres,
> Lurking to one side up the paths and lanes,
> Seldom well seen except by aeroplanes.'

Alphabetically first, and easternmost, is Manningford Abbots, a small and very scattered village with little modern development. The church which was rebuilt in 1861-64 stands among fields, the lane having been re-routed. It is approached by a track, doubtless on the route of the original lane, and now presents a forlorn appearance. This view is strengthened when you learn that this is one of the few churches with no recorded dedication. When the church was rebuilt by S. B. Gabriel he followed the original medieval plan and provided a nave, chancel and double bellcote in the Early English style. The manor house was originally late 16th century or early 17th century and of timber-framed construction but this was encased in brick and enlarged by a parallel range in the early 19th century.

Next, to the west, is Manningford Bruce built around a rectangle of lanes in a pattern that dates back to the 18th century. Buried in the churchyard is Mary Nicholas (died 1686), the first wife of Edward Nicholas, the Lord of the Manor of Manningford Bruce. She and her sister Jane were the daughters of Thomas Lane of Bentley, Staffordshire, and are believed to have had some part in the escape of Charles II after the Battle of Worcester in 1651. Mary is also reputed to be the original of Alice Lee in Sir Walter Scott's *Woodstock*.

The church itself is a well preserved Norman structure dedicated to St Peter.

The parish was originally called Manningford St Peter but the name was changed in 1291 when the manor was given to William de Breowse. The church is sited near the main Pewsey road and close to the village of Manningford Bohune.

Manningford Bohune, so called from the 13th century when it was owned by the Bohunes who were Earls of Hereford, is the most compact village of the three. Settlement is around a semi-circular lane off the Pewsey road and has been little changed for the last 200 years. Most of the cottages date from the 17th and 18th centuries but the thatched cottages at Townsend were built in the 19th century, probably for estate workers. Also at Townsend is the Providence Chapel of 1869 which has a small graveyard to the east. The Manor Farm is a two-storey brick building of the late 18th century or early 19th century.

To the north-west lies Manningford Bohune Common, an area of greensand and alluvium which is well suited to market gardening. Further west, but still within the parish, is the small hamlet of Bottlesford, a development along a minor road to the bridge across the railway line. The Seven Stars inn at Bottlesford was first mentioned in 1822.

Within the parish of Manningford Abbots lie the inconspicuous remains of Swanborough Tump, just to the south of the road from Pewsey to Woodborough and to the east of Frith Copse. Until recently it was tree covered with its explanatory sign partially obscured but, for the Saxons, it was the meeting place of the Hundred Moot of Swanborough. In the famous will of King Alfred, written when the Danes were assailing Wessex from their base at Reading in AD 871, he writes of assembling at Swanborough with his brother Ethelred. When I revisited the Tump at the end of September 1998 I was most surprised to find the Chairman of the Parish Council working there. For a millennium project they have installed a sarsen stone and commissioned a new commemorative plaque. The undergrowth has been cleared but the impressive ash trees remain. A most worthy project.

This small, and now revived, corner of Wiltshire once loomed large in affairs of state when a future King sat there and drew up a document which contained his forebodings for the lands of the West Saxons and his future provision for those same lands.

MARKET LAVINGTON

Market Lavington has the appearance and feel of a small country town but with a population of around 1,500 is village sized. As the name indicates it once possessed a market, held on Wednesdays, but the fact that the town of Devizes is only four miles distant was always likely to be detrimental to commercial expansion. As it now stands, Market Lavington shows just how a small town would begin to develop.

Although commercial growth passed to nearby towns, Market Lavington is still the centre for several surrounding villages. The old market place may now be a car park but it is filled with the cars of shoppers. There are around ten shops providing a wide range of merchandise and there are also various services such as a bank, post office, library, estate agent and garage. Industry is represented by a manufacturer of electronic equipment while further evidence of this technical age is evinced by a computer programming consultant who can operate equally as well from here as from a town.

There are three pubs and two have a military ring to them. The King's Arms and especially The Drummer Boy bring an echo of marching boots and the sound of fife and drum from a time when recruiting parties marched through the villages to persuade labourers to take the King's shilling. Today the names are still somewhat apt, for the largest landowner in the parish is the Army. The remaining pub is The Green Dragon, whose name is likely to have originated in a much earlier age.

On the highest ground in the village stands the church of St Mary. A mixture of Decorated and Perpendicular styles, it also has a late 13th century Early English chancel and includes some small Norman pieces in the south porch and the east wall. These latter had been found during the 1862 restoration and incorporated in the structure at that time. The church as a whole looks solid but weather-beaten. The latter is only to be expected as it has been situated on an eminence at the foot of Salisbury Plain for so many centuries.

In 1674 a son, Thomas Tanner, was born to the vicar. He was educated at Queen's College, Cambridge; a college which gave special advantages to Wiltshiremen in scholarships and fellowships. When barely 20 he wrote *Notitia Monastica; or a Short notice of the Religious Houses in England and Wales* (published 1695) and went on to become a learned, if laborious, writer and antiquary. In 1731, four years before his death, he was consecrated Bishop of St Asaphs. In his will he left £200 to his native town. Amongst other items the interest from this was to be used to teach poor children to read and write, to provide for a friendly meeting in the evening to promote peace and good neighbourhood, and to buy four Bibles with Common Prayer for four poor persons.

Descending the steep cobbled path from the church back to the village, a glance to the left shows that early headstones have been put to a new use providing a retaining wall for the graveyard. Nearby the early Georgian vicarage is of brick with stone dressings under a slate roof. In Parsonage Lane are more cobbles where an old narrow pavement leads past houses of brick and thatch to The Old House which incorporates the remains of a 14th century hall and a late medieval cross wing.

Lack of urban development has ensured the retention of farmyards in and around the central area and there is now a small area of market gardening to the south-east lying between the village gardens and the slopes of the Plain. Mixed with the agricultural buildings and small workshops are some very nice town houses.

Also to the west is the modern (1962) comprehensive school which takes pupils from many villages including West Lavington, The Cheverells and Urchfont. Other modern developments have taken place and there is recent housing in a small valley to the north-west and more on the eastern side of the village whilst most recently new houses have been built to the west and south.

MILDENHALL

The roads the Roman legions built ran through the Kennet Valley. At the junction of three of these, from Bath, Winchester and Cirencester, lies the settlement that is today called Mildenhall. It is possible that two other roads, from Old Sarum and Silchester (Hampshire) also converged at this place. It is not, therefore, surprising that a thriving trading centre grew up here. When viewed from the air this Roman community of Cunetio reveals a villa and street system within a rectangular enclosure.

When the Romans withdrew, Cunetio survived as a small market town into Anglo-Saxon times. Before this withdrawal one local Roman had hidden a hoard of coins in a lead coffin. This survived intact into the 1980s when it was illegally dug up by a treasure hunter. Unfortunately, the lead coffin, far more valuable than the whole hoard of coins, was smashed through greed and ignorance.

The Roman road which runs north, north-east towards Wanborough (Roman Durocornovium) can be followed from the telephone kiosk at the bottom of Thicket Road. It begins as a road, then changes to a track beyond Woodlands Farm, finally joining the Marlborough to Swindon Road at Ogbourne St George. The major present-day road runs from west to east through the village connecting Marlborough with Ramsbury. The parish is networked with other small roads and lanes. One leading into Savernake Forest to the south is called Cock-a-troop Lane. A place name in the north-east of the parish has the rather amusing name of Sound Bottom.

The village has a pleasant situation, being in the attractive Kennet valley with an alluvium plain over 400 yards wide. In the past this has given rise to rich water meadows, which were worked into the 1930s but which have now been ploughed out. In the 14th century Mildenhall was one of the manors, owned by the Hungerford family, which were linked in a very large sheep rearing operation. More modern times have seen tomatoes grown under glass, until the market gardener, Ken Messenger, took to flying and manufacturing hang-gliders. During the 1980s at Grove Farm, in Stitchcombe, a vineyard was planted but had closed down by the end of the decade; it has recently been opened as a plant nursery.

Living in the village is Jack Ainslie who, in 1985, became the first Liberal Chairman of the hitherto Conservative Wiltshire County Council. In the 1970s the parish was distinguished by having the oldest Anglican vicar in the country. When he retired in 1978 the Rev Courtman was aged 94. One of his acts during his rectorship was to introduce the spelling of the village name in the form used orally by local people. This is 'Minal' and if you are in the vicinity, make sure that you pronounce it that way or you will immediately be labelled a 'vurriner'. One idiosyncrasy of the rector that I must record, having encountered it personally when driving, was his habit of stopping his car in the middle of the village street whenever he saw a parishioner with whom he wished to converse. Definitely a habit from a bygone age.

At the junction with Thicket Road is an interesting building, the school of 1824. It has a two-storey octagonal central block and lantern roof with single-storey wings radiating from alternate sides, all in the Perpendicular style. It is the result of a bequest of £4,000 and a piece of land in 1821 by Charles Francis, the rector. The school closed in 1969 and the building has now been converted into a most unusual house. At the far end of Thicket Road lived a colony of gypsies until well into the 1970s. Living in caravans, they continued their traditional practices and after one matriarch had been buried in the gorgio way, the family returned and burned her caravan in the time honoured fashion.

MILTON LILBOURNE

The neighbouring villages of Milton Lilbourne and Easton Royal sound as though they have been given both Christian names and surnames. As with so many places that have names composed of two words the Lilbourne refers to a family who owned the manor, William de Lilebone in 1236. Milton means middle farm, maybe midway between Pewsey and Easton Royal.

It was to Milton that William Cobbett came when he descended from Milton Hill after viewing the valley of the Avon which so impressed him. This was in August 1826 when he calculated that the parish produced 3,000 quarters (750 cwt) of wheat, 6,000 quarters (1,500 cwt) of barley, the wool of 7,000 sheep, plus pigs, poultry, green vegetables, milk and butter. He estimated (and Cobbett's rates allowed three times as much food as a labourer could normally afford) that the parish could provide bread for 800 families, mutton for 500 and bacon and beer for 207, allowing five people per family. Naturally, as he was quick to point out much of this was used for the city dwellers and most especially those in London.

The modern village is pleasantly positioned along a tiny road, leading from the Pewsey to Burbage road, which eventually loses itself near the summit of Milton Hill. There are many nicely restored thatched cottages and farmhouses which date from the 17th century and they go to make up a most attractive street village which deserves more visitors than find their way here. One of the more recent buildings is the early Georgian Manor House of red and blue bricks in a chequerwork pattern.

The church of St Peter was restored in 1875. It is small but soundly built and stands high on the west side of the street. It has examples of both Early English and Decorated styles while the tower is Perpendicular. Inside are some very nice box pews of the 17th century while both the pulpit and the reader's desk contain Jacobean sections. Looking over the village, on Milton Hill, is Giant's Grave, an unchambered long barrow. A footpath leads here from the village and one can enjoy the same superb views of both the valley of the Avon and the Vale of Pewsey that pleased Cobbett.

MINETY

Minety is a large scattered village, seemingly without a centre. It has grown up out of the clearings in Braydon Forest and probably owes its origins to early charcoal burners and woodcutters; Sawyer's Hill is still one local name. The church of St Leonard is in the area now called Upper Minety, to the west of Minety itself. Perpendicular in style, the church appears to have been little altered architecturally since the 15th century.

The greatest material treasures of the church are the richly carved items of 17th century woodwork. The pulpit of 1627 has a back panel and tester and is most impressive. In the chancel is a contemporary reader's desk and front of one choir stall while in the nave are Jacobean pews with knobs on each corner. The chancel screen is the earliest piece of carving, being 15th century, and is lovingly polished to a state that belies its antiquity. There are more chandeliers here than I have found in most village churches. One large brass chandelier dates from 1748.

Minety parish is a low lying area falling away in the north to the valley of the infant River Thames. Much of this part of the valley has been obliterated by flooded gravel pits but the Swill Brook still maintains its west to east course. This brook flows into the Thames to the north of Cricklade, though it would be more accurate to say that the Thames flows into the Swill Brook for it is the brook that has the greater volume of water. In fact most of the headwaters of the Thames come from Wiltshire. It is interesting to speculate that if the topographers had paid more attention to this fact both Oxford and London might today be standing on the River Swill.

The clays in this area have long been used for pottery. There are medieval kilns while to the west is evidence that the Romans made good use of this local raw material. Here were found the remains of tile kilns which doubtless supplied their Cotswold villas.

Minety

NETHERAVON

On the elevated and exposed eastern side of Salisbury Plain, just halfway between Amesbury and Upavon, is the parish of Netheravon. The village is sited in the river valley and forms part of a line of nearly continuous settlement between the two larger places. Today, the village has a substantial military presence and this has been the position for most of the 20th century. In 1898 almost the entire parish was purchased by the War Department and since that time virtually all development has been connected with military establishments. In 1904 a cavalry training school, with an indoor riding school, was set up in the grounds of Netheravon House. The house, which dates from the 18th century, and is of red brick, was already the local military headquarters.

In 1922 a machine gun school was established and a glance at a present day map will show that the Plain to the west of the village is largely composed of red-printed Danger Areas, with the Larkhill Artillery Range being prominent. The camp at Larkhill is about three miles to the south, while the other large military establishment, Bulford Camp, is a little over four miles to the south-east. The military presence has provided benefits for the village. There are several shops, a post office and store, a garage and a library. The infants' school, built in 1846 is still open. The concentration of young couples with children, albeit a changing population, is fairly rare in villages and it has helped Netheravon to retain many amenities that other villages have lost.

It was in The Fox and Hounds that, in 1840, a local friendly benefit society was formed. It was popularly called 'The Top Hat Club' from the headgear affected by many of its members. Evidence of local industry is found on the eastern side of Mill Road. The former mill buildings were converted into an electricity generating station by 1926 but now they house Bunces Brewery, brewing Stonehenge Ales; a recent independent concern which is open for off-licence sales at the brewery door.

If we return to a time before the Army bought the parish, we find that Netheravon was best known for its sport. Around 1734 the Dukes of Beaufort based a large sporting estate, which survived intact until 1898, on the village because of the excellent hawking and coursing that was to be found on the downs. There was, and still is, excellent trout fishing on the Avon which flows placidly through and around the village.

An idea of the abundance of game can be gained from William Cobbett. In one of his journeys, described in *Rural Rides*, he writes on 22nd October 1822:

> 'Not far above Amesbury is a little village called Netherhaven, where I once saw an acre of hares. We were coursing at Everly, a few miles off, and one of the party, happening to say that he had seen an acre of hares at Mr Hicks Beech's at Netherhaven, we, who wanted to see the same, or to detect our informant, sent a messenger to beg a day's coursing which, being granted, we went over the next day. Mr Beech received us very politely. He took us into a wheat stubble close by his paddock; his son took a gallop round, cracking his whip at the same time; the hares (which were very thickly in sight before) started all over the field, ran into a flock like sheep; and we all agreed that the flock did cover an acre of ground.'

I make no apology for quoting at length for Cobbett loved this valley of the Avon with its abundant farms.

An attractive feature at 116 High Street is a clock, over the door, covered by a canopy and showing two faces so that a traveller approaching from either direction could see the time. The church of All Saints is at the southernmost end of the village next to Netheravon House and its stables, with their strange oval and half oval windows and its square dovecote. The west end of the church dates from the late 11th century and illustrates the overlap of Saxon and Norman styles.

NORTH BRADLEY

The parish of North Bradley contains two substantial villages: North Bradley itself and Southwick. Both lie within two miles of Trowbridge and have been dependent upon that town for a very long time. Both were important as centres of domestic clothworking for Trowbridge clothiers in the days before steam power drove the villagers to work in the factories. In both villages it is likely that handloom weavers built houses on the common land and created enclosures for their animals. Although the early local Baptist movement originated at Southwick, both villages were deeply involved.

In the early 19th century nearly every cottage had at least one loom at work while many had three or four. Children learned to spin at an early age and many were apprenticed to weavers. So closely were the villages tied to the local cloth industry that their populations fluctuated within the pattern of prosperity and decline of that industry. After the concentration of spinning and weaving in the Trowbridge factories many of the inhabitants walked daily to and from the town to work at the machines.

Historically North Bradley is built around a rectangle of roads with an outlier at Woodmarsh on the Trowbridge road. Many of the older houses are, or were, farms, including Manor Farm and Pound Farm of the early 19th century. There are a very few timber-framed houses, probably of the 17th century. Most of the cottages are brick, of the 18th and 19th centuries and were built for clothworkers. A common feature is a dentilled string course at the first floor level. There were a few farm labourers' cottages but as much of the farming had long been devoted to livestock there were not too many men employed on the land.

There are several outlying settlements, including Scotland and Ireland, on the Southwick road. These were originally settlements on common land and doubtless derived their name from the fact that villagers considered them to be in the back of beyond. They have been the subject of many local jokes, and you could always claim to have been on a long walk or cycle ride if you included them in your journey! Today there are still only a few houses in each. Cutteridge Farm, in the south of the parish, marks the site of a mansion which was said to have been second in size only to Longleat in the whole of Wiltshire. It was pulled down c1800. A poignant reminder remains in the avenues of graceful trees that lead up a gentle slope to an empty space. The only one of these settlements to have increased in size in the 20th century is Yarnbrook. In this hamlet, Bridge Mill was built in 1773 and has recently been restored. In 1803 the Longs Arms inn was built by a butcher who already held the most appropriately named Axe and Cleaver in North Bradley. There is an interesting scatter of cottages dating from the 18th century and much modern ribbon development. Between Yarnbrook and North Bradley the White Horse Park Business Park was built in 1986.

Back in the village, mention must be made of the Daubeny Almshouses. Built in 1808-1810 by the vicar, Charles Daubeny, they were to be 'an Asylum for the accommodation of four aged people of good character and rather above the lowest classes'. Some of my ancestors came from North Bradley and I suspect that they would not have qualified for admittance but would have been accommodated in the row of three cottages built in 1818 to provide homes for twelve poor people. There are still two pubs: The Mash Tun, licensed as the New Inn in 1881 on Woodmarsh and the earlier Rising

Sun. In the early 20th century the landlord of the latter used to put up a barrel of beer at Easter, as a prize in a football match between the married and single men of the village.

NORTON

The village is a small scatter of about 20 houses set in a hollow. The small stream, which joins the Malmesbury Avon, must flood the road some winters as there is a raised wooden footbridge and nearby is Splash Cottage. The settlement has never been large or populous, the known peak being reached in 1851 when 123 people lived in the parish. This figure was only attained again by 1981.

Norton Manor, whose park is to the south-east of the village, is the home of the Countess June Badeni who has researched widely and well on the families and villages of north-western Wiltshire. I admit to having mined her books for some of the facts which I have used in this book and recommend them to the reader for far more detailed histories than I am able to give. From one of her books is a succinct piece concerning a former curate: 'Mr Jones, sometime curate of Norton, lived in the inn at Hullavington and served Hullavington Church, Foxley and Norton - the latter once a fortnight... He was fond of his glass and was often overtaken. His sad end was to be found dead in a field by Pig Lane between Farleaze and Hullavington.'

The Manor itself has been owned by the Lords Chandos, the Estcourts, Chollertons, Workmans, Jacobs and Lord Holland, who altered and restored the house around 1856. Walter Long of Rood Ashton spent four winters at the manor, for the sport and country pursuits available in the area, after his marriage. The manor house is dated 1623 when it was rebuilt with parts of an older building retained. Also of the 17th century is Buckland Farm.

The size of the nave and chancel of the church of All Saints has been little altered since the 12th century and it is a small and simple church. It does have, what Pevsner calls, 'a presumptuous bell-turret of 1858', but this was intended for the extravagant Grittleton House and does therefore look out of place. Inside, the font is from the 12th century and the pulpit is Jacobean but there is evidence of work from most centuries here. In this quiet spot the Quakers flourished in the 17th century and several names are recorded. On the road to Foxley, in the opposite direction in which the curate was travelling when finally overtaken, is The Vine Tree, a free house of painted stone brightly adorned with geraniums in window boxes. The building is 18th century and the house was first licensed in 1890.

OAKSEY

Oaksey, or 'Wuxey', as older residents often pronounce it, is strung out along its village street with most new building at the western end. Among its residents this village can number a well known lord. Lord Oaksey was a National Hunt jockey and since his retirement has become a popular speaker, writer and broadcaster. His father, created the first Lord Oaksey, as Lord Chief Justice Lawrence, presided over the Nuremberg trials at the end of the Second World War. The internationally known writer Elspeth Huxley came to the village in the early 1940s and among her many published works is a diary which she kept from April 1974 to March 1975. Called *Gallipot Eyes*, it documents the daily happenings of the village and contains much genealogical and historical research showing the village set against the backcloth of its past. I am indebted to her for some interesting information about this village and, like many, mourn her passing.

That great medieval family of landowners, the de Bohuns, had an estate here and to the north-east of Dean Farm is Norwood Castle, a Norman motte and bailey earthwork. To the south of the church are earthworks on a site noted by John Aubrey (c.1670) as 'the ruins of an old seat of the Duke of Lancaster's and a Chapell'. By the beginning of the 19th century the building was gone but John Britton noted a deep moat and a large mount. That the early house was quarried to provide stone for local cottages is still evident. No 8 has stones with carved foliage decorations in its walls and three stone mullioned windows that most obviously came from an earlier house.

The church of All Saints is largely of the 13th to 15th centuries but with some possible Norman features. Outside, to the left of the Decorated porch, is a carved sheela-na-gig. Quite rare in England, this one is an explicit and well-endowed hermaphrodite figure whose origins are from an earlier time than the Christian church in this country. Maybe at a time when many people still preferred the old religion of these islands it was an action by the church to associate the new form of worship with its predecessor.

There are farms and farmyards along the village street and horses are much in evidence. This is most appropriate, not only with the Lord Oaksey connection but because until 1914 the village held its own well attended race meeting.

THE OGBOURNES

The little valley of the River Og is aligned north to south and the river joins the Kennet between Marlborough and Mildenhall. There is always water in this lower part but for much of the year the upper reaches are dry, like those of many other chalkland streams. The valley is followed by the present Marlborough to Swindon Road and was previously used by a railway line, the old Roman road from Mildenhall and possibly by the Saxon army when they were attacked by King Arthur from Liddington Hill.

The southernmost village is Ogbourne Maizey, or St Michael, although it has no church. The Jacobean Manor House has bands of sarsen stone and knapped flint with later additions in brick. The central doorway is dated '1636' and there are some original stone mullions, although in places tall arched Georgian windows have been inserted. The little lane to Rockley has some cottages of the 17th century. There have been racing stables here since 1903 with gallops on the downs to the north-west.

Ogbourne St Andrew is slightly larger and does have a church of St Andrew. It is to the west on slightly higher ground, which was probably the site of the original settlement. The church is of flint with a stone tower; much of the structure is Norman with 14th century and Perpendicular additions and the whole was restored in 1847-49. In the churchyard is a bowl barrow of which succeeding ages have made good use. Besides the Bronze Age burial it was re-used for interments in Roman, Pagan Saxon and medieval times.

The largest village, Ogbourne St George, has its older buildings at the western end. Here is the 17th century timber-framed 'Kemms' while east of the bridge are cottages of the 16th and 17th centuries high on the banks. Along the main street are farms, houses and cottages of the 18th and 19th centuries; Rectory Farm House of 1742, Rectory House of 1755 and The Park, built in the 18th century but much extended in the 19th century. The Manor House is on the site of a Benedictine priory, founded c1149, and is little changed in design since 1659. The date '1619' on the eastern chimneystack probably indicates the original construction. The little settlement of Southend with its houses of timber framing and sarsen stone is of the 17th century and has remained virtually unchanged since the late 18th century. In 1940 an army camp was built to the north-west of the village and was used as a transit camp for British and American forces until about 1957. A late example of rough music was recorded here around 1840 when an 'ooset hunt' was held. Men and boys with frying pans, old kettles filled with stones,

sheep's horns and cracked cow bells created the noise to penalise a couple's infidelity.

The small settlement of Rockley, to the west of the Ogbournes, was once more important than it is now. It is enclosed by folds of the downs in a lonely setting, although it is only just over two miles from Marlborough. The Rockley White Horse was probably cut in the early 19th century but became overgrown and was only re-discovered in 1947. The flint and stone chequerwork church of All Saints was built in 1872, closed in 1961 and sold in 1973. It became a highly regarded restaurant, appropriately called The Loaves and Fishes, but was a victim of the uniform business rate and closed in 1990.

In the north is the Iron Age hill fort of Barbary Castle. There are superb views to the north and west and within the 111 acre site a chariot burial has been found. Unfortunately the castle has been somewhat wrecked by the US Army driving a road through the middle of it in the past but it is now a Wiltshire County Council Countryside Park. To the east of the castle, on Burderop Down, is an enormous sarsen stone with memorials to Richard Jefferies (1848-1887) and Alfred Williams (1877-1930), both writers and naturalists who loved to roam across the open downs.

There is a well documented ghost story concerning Ogbourne that can be found in James Waylen's *A History Of Marlborough* (1854). It concerns a deposition made on 23rd November 1674 by Thomas Goddard, a weaver, to the Mayor and Town Clerk of Marlborough and the Rector of St Peter's church. On his way to Ogbourne in the morning of Monday 9th November he met the apparition of his father in law, Edward Avon, who had died the previous May. A conversation about the family ensued but when Thomas refused to take money to send to his sister in law, Sarah, the apparition disappeared. It returned at Thomas's workshop on Tuesday and Wednesday and again near Axford on Thursday. This time it asked Thomas to get William Avon (Edward's son) to take his father's sword to the wood on the Alton Barnes road and also to repay a debt about which Thomas had known nothing.

On the orders of the Mayor, Thomas and William took the sword to the wood where Thomas again saw the apparition which confessed to the following: In the year 1635 Edward Avon had murdered a man from whom he had stolen money and buried him in the wood. His purpose in returning from the grave was to let the world know about his evil deed. The dead did not lie easy in the 17th century!

PEWSEY

The best way to approach Pewsey is from the west, along the road from Devizes. Rising above the road, to the south, is the scarp slope of Salisbury Plain while to the north stretches the broad flat floor of the Vale until the land raises itself up into the Marlborough Downs. Just before Pewsey is reached the white horse appears to the south on a hillside that does not really seem steep enough for it. First cut in 1785, it had disappeared by 1900 and was re-cut by Mr Marples in 1937 to commemorate the coronation of King George VI.

A series of double bends takes the road over the River Avon and around the earliest settlement site where Saxon remains have been found. A cemetery of these early Saxons lies on the slopes of the Plain at Black Patch and excavations have shown it to be pre-Christian. The earliest visible period of the present church, on the site of the Saxon village, is late Norman. The church of St John the Baptist was restored in 1861 and 1889-90 but much of it dates from the 13th, 14th and 15th centuries. The early medieval village was around the church but the village later shifted to the north leaving the church on the southern fringe of the village.

In the centre of Pewsey three roads meet, from Devizes and Salisbury, Marlborough and Burbage, at a point where the young Avon provides accommodation for the resident ducks and, for the carnival in 1998, a large model of the *Titanic*. Also at this junction is the slightly incongruous statue of King Alfred, unveiled on 25th June 1913 to commemorate the coronation of King George V on 22nd June 1911. The inscription mentions that this illustrious ancestor of George V owned many estates around Pewsey. I do feel though that there are other places in the county associated with Alfred the Great in matters of national importance, that would have greater justification for a statue.

Although Pewsey is called a village it has all the importance of a small town and has a population of nearly 3,000 with many shops and services. Including national chains and local concerns which have a branch in the village, there are over 100 businesses here. That really is an amazing number and must ensure that many people are able to work in the village in which they live; a rare event nowadays. To me there is always something a little old fashioned about Pewsey and I hope that this will always remain. Too frequently have large villages and small towns that once served a rural area, become emasculated and standardised so that the chief businesses remaining are supermarkets and for anything other than the basic necessities of life one has to travel into a large town.

There are two interesting pieces of cast iron in the village. The recently closed Phoenix Inn has a locally made cast iron inn sign while at the junction of High Street and Ball Road, where there is an early timber-framed cruck house, is a splendid combined sign post and lamp standard. The lamp, once gas lit, is now electric but the sign post retains its three early fingers pointing to 'Pewsey and Salisbury', 'Milton and Burbage' and to 'Southcott'. These have seen many processions of the well known Pewsey Carnival which began in 1898. A group of prominent villagers got together to raise money for Savernake Hospital and the first carnival was made up of bicycles decorated with flowers, Chinese lanterns and fairy lights. Within a few years horse-drawn carts and steam lorries were included. In the 1920s the event achieved national prominence with special trains laid on from Bristol, Paddington and Birmingham. The carnival lost momentum in the 1930s but was revived in 1947 and has attracted many people to Pewsey each September. In 1998 there were 80 floats in the procession.

It was at an earlier Phoenix Inn that a murder plot was hatched in 1798. A farmer by the name of Dyke, from Manningford Abbots, was drinking there after a successful sale of some of his livestock. After a few drinks he could not resist telling the assembled company how well he had done and doubtless boasted of the gold coins that he was taking home to Manningford. He never reached his farm for he was murdered on the way and his gold and his pocket watch taken from him.

The crime lay heavy upon the parish for it was evident that a local man must have committed the act. The Rector, the Reverend Joseph Townsend, was an unorthodox character and he found a novel way to unmask the murderer. Playing upon the superstition that the corpse of a murdered man will always know its assailant, he had the body brought into the church the following Sunday. Each person was required to place their hand upon the dead man's face and declare their innocence! A man called Amor was afraid to take the test; he was subsequently charged with the crime and hanged in 1799.

A recent development has been the opening of the Pewsey Heritage Centre in a former foundry. The collections include photographs, machinery and a wide range of small artefacts. Future plans are for educational facilities and a full visitor centre. On 23rd October 1993 a local community project opened its doors; Pewsey Crafts and Tea Room is entirely run by volunteers and sells locally made items and provides refreshments at very reasonable prices. Proceeds go to the local community and the venture is one greatly deserving of its success.

PITTON

The parish of Pitton and Farley has two villages that have developed along different lines. Pitton is a substantial little village nestling on and below a north-east facing hillside. In a crescent to the south of the village lies much woodland. As in most places, this was once much more extensive than it is today and many inhabitants obtained their living from the woods. Along the small roads and tracks to the south, the Slateway, Cold Harbour and Dunley, were the small cottages of woodmen living as close to their work as possible.

Having considered the situation of Pitton, it seems a little strange that most houses face north-west instead of being on the other side of the tiny valley facing to the sunnier south-east. The position of the church, at the north of the village and just on the south-facing slope gives a clue that all was not once as it appears today. In 1861 a fire had raged through the village and wiped out the northern part; of six farmhouses destroyed, only one was rebuilt. Many of the earlier cottages were of cob construction and a few still survive today. The foundations were of flint and the cob (chalk rubble, horse hair and wheat chaff) was mixed into a paste by men trampling it underfoot in a similar way to the crushing of grapes in a sunnier clime. The cob was then put onto the flint with special forks, to a height of 18 inches and allowed to dry; any higher and the whole section would have collapsed. The wall was gradually built up to the required height and then the wooden joints of the bedroom floor were laid. The walls normally only continued about two or three feet above this, for building with cob was heavy back-breaking work, and then the roof was put on and thatched. The requirement for cob is a good hat and a good pair of boots; these the thatch and flint provided, for otherwise rain and frost will destroy the walls in a few winters.

One of the woods on which the people of Pitton were dependent was that of Clarendon Park to the south-west. Within its bounds are the remains of the once magnificent Clarendon Palace. Beginning its life as a Saxon hunting lodge it was added to by various monarchs until, in the 14th century, it ranked as second only to the Palace of Westminster in size and importance. Henry II and Henry III were responsible for creating such a fine palace with its great hall, apartments for the king and queen, council chambers, chapels, kitchen, pantries, etc decorated with wall paintings, floor tiles and screens and boasting glazed windows in some apartments. Here Thomas Becket and Henry II quarrelled, the captive kings, John of France and David of Scotland hunted with their captor, Edward III and, after 1453, Henry VI was confined during periods of insanity.

The site was excavated in 1933-1935 by Dr Tancred Borenius, who wished to match extensive documentary evidence with the information on the ground. Today one can visit the Palace, although with difficulty and no helpful signposting. East of Salisbury take the road to Laverstock and Milford, off Churchill Way and through Milford take the small road that leads to Sangers Lodge Farm. From here on foot take the track and the marked footpath that branches off from the right. After about three-quarters of a mile on this path you are above the Palace and can reach it through the woods. The other end of this path starts from Pitton, opposite the entrance to Bove Hedges, and involves a walk of just over two miles. The Palace is embosked in trees but ruined walls still stand to a height of two feet, broken floors show through the vegetation and the remains of pottery and roof tiles are everywhere. A most neglected ruin from the time of the Wars of the Roses and one whose history and glory surely deserves better preservation and recognition.

Before we leave the village, mention must be made of another well-known man. Ralph Whitlock, the writer and farmer was born at Pitton and for the full flavour of village life, before outside modern influences had rendered it bland, you must read his *A Family and a Village* (1969). Ralph himself was greatly influenced by his family and his farming background writing many, many thousands of articles on farming, natural history and folklore for national newspapers and magazines. He also wrote over 100 books for both adults and children. After the Second World War he created the series *Cowleaze Farm* for BBC radio and played the main character himself. He was also largely responsible for setting up and maintaining the nature reserve, Bentley Wood. A real countryman whose instincts were for good farming, preserving wildlife and keeping the land in good heart.

POTTERNE

Potterne – the house, or place, of the potter. Sure enough there has been much pottery found here and some of it dates back to the transitional period between the Bronze Age and the Iron Age. Recent excavations have also uncovered much evidence of metal working from this period and a wealth of bronze and iron objects, some of them most unusual.

There is still much that is old in Potterne. The most famous late 15th century timber-framed house in all Wiltshire is here. Indeed, it is one of the most famous in all England. The superbly preserved Porch House has upright timbering, a two-storey great hall with hammerbeam roof, a solar and largely original windows, which are but a few of the noteworthy features of this beautiful house. In 1876 the house was restored for George Richmond, the portrait painter, who added the mosaic floor in the hall. This provides a striking contrast with the 15th century stained glass.

The nickname for Potterne folk was 'Potterne Lambs', a name generated by the same sense of humour that makes Englishmen call the shortest person in the community 'Lofty'. In the 1830s an Assistant Poor Law Commissioner said that the village was 'filled with a very discontented and turbulent race'. In 1816-17 there had been outbreaks of cattle maiming which resulted in rewards of between 16 guineas and £100 being offered but without result. A result of the remarks of the Commissioner, however, had been the purchase of a 'Burn's Justice' from a subscription raised by the paupers so that they could outwit the overseers and magistrates.

Potterne men were famous for work, drinking and fighting; many of them found their way into the army and navy. In those days there were six pubs, three having skittle alleys. Now there are only two, The Bell and The George and Dragon but the latter still has a seemingly semi-subterranean skittle alley. The greatest event in the village calendar was the Potterne Feast held on the first Sunday after 19th September. Besides being a massive bout of eating and drinking, the activities comprised skittling, quarrelling and fighting in equal parts. Various vicars tried to make the Feast more respectable with the natural result that it declined and finally ceased. The second most important event was the King's Arms Club Feast on Whit Tuesdays. The Club was a friendly society founded in 1793. It is now long gone as, more recently, is The King's Arms, although it was a thriving pub when I drank beer, played bar billiards and listened to folk music there in the early 1970s.

Gone are pastimes such as 'scrigging', the knocking down of small apples that were left after the main crop had been picked, with squailers, or throwing sticks; gambling for beer; bandy (a type of hockey); a game of rounders that was so rough that broken bones and heads resulted; and visiting entertainers, such as hurdy gurdy men and German bands. Gone too are the days in the early years of the 20th century when people walking between Easterton and Devizes took the roundabout way over One Tree Hill to avoid this rowdy village. The turbulent village has at last been tamed by the dehumanised late 20th century. Or has it?

POULSHOT

The village of Poulshot stretches for nearly two miles along a minor road which leaves the A361 west of Devizes at the bottom of Caen Hill. The church of St Peter has become isolated at the southern end of the village with only a few farms and cottages around it, although visual evidence in adjacent fields indicates that there was once a more substantial settlement here. This area is now appropriately called Townsend.

The old rectory lies to the south, beyond the churchyard wall, and is connected by a well-trodden path about 18 inches below the level of the graveyard. This rectory is mainly of brick, with a frontage of brick and lath and plaster rough-cast and was built in 1781, being the successor to that occupied by Isaac Walton from 1680 to 1719. This Isaac was the son of Isaak Walton, the ironmonger who was the friend of many of the most learned men of his day and has left us his masterpiece, *The Compleat Angler*. The rectory is now a farm with some nice outbuildings, including a brick barn with hayloft. To the south-west, at the bottom of Mill Lane, was the watermill that once ground snuff for the Devizes industry.

There is a scatter of houses between here and the Green. Belle Vue Farm must be named for its panoramic view of the Vale of Pewsey spilling out into the lowlands of western Wiltshire with the stern slopes of Salisbury Plain behind. The house has a rough cast rendering which probably hides an early building, as does that of the nearby Yew Tree Cottage. At Manor Farm there is a very good large brick house, with timber framing at the back, and a newer good brick house. On the roadside is the remains of an overgrown farm pond with fair sized willows growing out of it. There are some large 20th century houses here and, just before we reach the green, is Stansfield Cottage, thatched with timber framing and rendering. Over the porch is the date '1656' in wrought iron work; this seems right for the building.

Entering the green one is amazed at the apparent vast open space and the distance of many of the houses, several of which were formerly farms, from the road. It seems likely that many of the predecessors of these buildings were constructed at the edge of the common land. There is good variety here with timber framing, brick, thatch, tile and slate. The chapel of ease of St Paul was built in 1897 to serve this area of the village, which is about a mile from the church. Of brick and timber-framed construction, it contained 100 seats but is now disused.

Just beyond the northern edge of the green stands Poulshot's only pub, The Raven. Inside, a welcome sight awaits one behind the bar: seven wooden barrels from which the beer is served direct. The interior is traditional Wadworth's with no modern re-vamping but a bar that would have looked much the same 60 years ago.

Apart from Isaac Walton, there is one other well-known person connected with Poulshot. In the 18th century the son of the miller was Thomas Boulter who, scorning the family trade, became a highwayman and was most notorious in the neighbourhood and throughout England. He began his career in 1775 when his father was sentenced to 14 years transportation for stealing a horse at Trowbridge. First he robbed the Salisbury stagecoach, and continued to hold up coaches, farmers returning from market and travellers of all kinds for the next three years. At times he did qualify for the romantic appellation 'gentleman of the road', for after robbing a farmer of £90 he returned his watch because it was of great sentimental value and when a lady burst into tears on the theft of her ring it was returned.

In 1776 Boulter stole a famous mare, called Black Bess (like Dick Turpin's horse) from Peter Delme of Erlestoke. In May he set out on his own long ride, emulating Turpin's legendary ride to York earlier in the century. Leaving Devizes he reached Staines on the second night and on the third day robbed several carriages whilst riding to Maidenhead. In Maidenhead he had the audacity to stop and feed his horse shortly before his most recent victims arrived there. A hue and cry was raised and Boulter and Black Bess set out to return to Wiltshire where he could go to ground in the Poulshot neighbourhood. Stopping only at Hartley Row, Whitchurch and Everley, both horse and rider consuming a bottle of wine at each halt, he reached Poulshot in seven hours, a rate of eleven miles an hour.

Boulter was eventually taken at Bridport, whilst trying to reach France, on 14th July 1778 when he was aged 30. He was executed at Winchester on 19th August 1778 at noon with an accomplice, James Caldwell. Boulter was said to have been very penitent and made little remark except for saying that he had left an account of his transactions which he desired should be printed for the information of the public. Although he robbed numerous people he shrank from shedding blood, even when fired upon, but for many decades after his death Boulter was the name of the bogeyman used to subdue unruly children in Wiltshire and Hampshire.

PURTON

A large village, with a population of 4,000, which for employment looks towards Swindon. Purton is built around the Wootton Bassett to Cricklade road. Most modern houses here are constructed with bricks supplied by the London Brick Company, a sad comment upon the fact that the Purton Brickworks only closed in 1977. Some of the last of their bricks were used in the sheltered accommodation at Hooks Hill, off the High Street.

In the High Street, on the higher ground, are some good houses of the 18th century. Two early inns faced each other across the road. Dated 1673 was the now closed The Maltster, in stone but at some stage the walls have been heightened using brick, while The Angel, dated 1704, is built of stone rubble.

In College Road is the large school, of stone with a clay tile roof. Further west was the former North View Hospital, once the workhouse of 1840, built in brick and with two storeys but demolished in 1999. At the eastern end of the High Street is the Workmen's Institute of 1879 which incorporates a stone on which are carved the dates 1779 and 1873. It is a fine stone building of some character and now houses the library.

From here Station Road leads downhill. On the lower part of the hill is Collin's Lane Gate, opposite the entrance to Collin's Lane and the Elmgrove Saddlery. This is a very nice turnpike toll house which still has its board of tolls on the front of the building. The fee for wagons and carts with nine or six inch wheels was fivepence halfpenny, oxen, goats and cattle were tenpence a score while calves, sheep, lambs and pigs were fivepence a score.

The railway station which gave its name to the road has now gone so the adjacent pub has been appropriately renamed The Ghost Train. The road leads through the surrounding farms to Purton Stoke where Bentham House is a good example of early Victorian Tudor. Another product of the Victorians is the small octagonal pavilion built in 1859 as the pump room of Purton Spa, all that now remains of a 19th century attempt to attract visitors to the area. From the mid-16th century the saline spring water had been used by local people for a variety of ailments. In the 1850s the property was bought by Dr Sadler who, as he did not believe in the curative properties of the water, filled in the well to the dismay of the villagers. However, when he became seriously ill Dr Sadler did try the water and was cured. Whether it really was the water that cured him of course we do not know but that the doctor was converted we do know because he re-opened the well and built the pump room in 1859.

It was soon being reported that the waters would cure liver and kidney disorders, gout, rheumatism and arthritis, and ulcers of the leg. Orders came from both home and abroad and while the water was sold for a penny a pint at Purton it was 6d a pint, carriage paid, elsewhere. After a record year for sales in 1874 the spa declined in the face of competition with patent medicines and the growth of a greater critical examination of the claims of 'cure-alls'. A revival was attempted in 1927 by the then owner, Mr Neville, who travelled the country in his pony and trap selling bottles of the water. He later changed his mode of transport to a car and was selling water at 8d a bottle up to 1952. Only a little dearer than 90 years earlier!

RAMSBURY

Near the Berkshire border, in the beautiful Kennet valley is Ramsbury; a large village which, in the 15th century, probably had the appearance of a small town with markets, fairs and a number of tradesmen and artisans but, for various reasons, development was not sustained. The local towns are Marlborough and Hungerford and Ramsbury, lying midway between them, no longer challenges them in status. The village is set in a large parish that includes many small settlements such as Knighton, Littlecote, Whittonditch and Marridge Hill and the villages of Baydon and Axford. Axford is a linear village following the Ramsbury to Marlborough road with its oldest buildings, to the south of the road, dating to the 17th century. In 1856 a chapel of ease dedicated to St Michael was built and served from Ramsbury. Until 1940 there was no right of marriage here and village brides and bridegrooms had to make a wedding day journey into Ramsbury.

The church of the Holy Cross at Ramsbury is an early foundation with a 13th century chancel and much 14th century work including the tower. It was an important religious foundation and in the early 10th century a bishopric of Ramsbury had been created; this was united with the See of Sherborne, Dorset, in 1058. It seems likely that the church was served by a small cathedral establishment and by the 13th century a bishop's palace existed to the west of the village near the present Ramsbury Manor. In recent years the title has been recreated and Ramsbury once more has its Bishop.

Much of the medieval street pattern remains; High Street, Oxford Street and Crows (later Crowood) Lane are medieval, while Tankard Lane was so called from 1677. The predominant building material is red brick, often used in bands or as dressings with flint in the smaller houses. There are also timber-framed cottages in parts of the High Street, Back Lane, Burdett Street and Oxford Street; many of these are thatched. There were once many more early thatched buildings but these were lost in two serious fires; one in 1648 and another in 1781, the latter being said to have destroyed 40 dwellings; several of these were in Back Lane and were not replaced. The problem of fire still remains and only recently a thatched cottage was gutted and has been replaced by a modern bungalow.

The village is now only served by three public houses: The Burdett Arms, which had a brief recent existence as the Ramsbury Village Inn but has now reverted to its original name and dates from the early 19th century, The Crown and Anchor and The Bell which was established as an inn by the mid-

18th century. The Bell also has a substantial restaurant. There is still much social and community life with many events during the year, including the beating of the bounds - all 26 miles of them through river, marsh and hill which many villagers, both adults and children, undertake.

The most notable architectural feature is Ramsbury Manor, described by Sir Nikolaus Pevsner as, 'A perfect example of the moderate-sized brick mansion of about 1680'. The present building is of brick with stone dressings and decorations of carved and painted wood designed by the architect Robert Mitchell. The best view can be obtained from the bridge at the end of the lake, approached by a lane to the south of the gate house. The house was probably started for Sir William Jones in 1681 on the site of a 'fair square stone house' owned by the Pembrokes. Sir William died in 1682 but he had directed his executors to finish the house.

In 1800 the Manor passed to the Burdett family, in whose hands it remained until 1951 when Sir Francis Burdett died. By his will, much of the 18th century furniture from the Manor was held in trust during the lifetime of his daughter. After her death a final link was broken on 21st May 1986, when this furniture realised about one million pounds at auction. The Manor was purchased by Lord Wilton who, in 1958, sold it to Baron Rootes. In 1964/65 it was bought by Harry Hyams for a then record price for a private house. An even greater sum was spent on restoration.

The area is rich in wildlife and a wide range of birds will be encountered while walking any of the local footpaths. Much of this is centred upon the river, for Ramsbury is a very watery place and the Kennet has played an important role in its development. There is still visible evidence of the water meadows, noted by John Aubrey in 1646, best seen between the river and the road to the east of the Manor lake. The river has been noted for trout since the late 17th century and the fishing rights are expensive and carefully protected. From the 1890s watercress was grown and in the 1930s up to 15,000 lbs a week were sent by train to London, via Hungerford, from beds at Ramsbury, Froxfield and Shalbourne.

Surprises await the nature lover on this part of the Kennet. On a casual springtime walk you may pass a nesting native swan and then chance upon a pair of black swans on the river. A little further and there are Canada and Brent geese nesting. These come from the grounds of Ramsbury Manor and a programme of wildlife conservation.

Before leaving Ramsbury one must mention the Building Society which proudly bore its name for 57 years. Starting as the Provident Union and

Investment Society in 1846, it became Ramsbury Building Society in 1928. It was then taken over and became the Regency and West of England Building Society, and in recent years more corporate activity has seen it become the Portman Building Society. The head office remained in Ramsbury until 1982. The symbol of the 'great tree' was adopted on the Society's incorporation in 1893. This tree in front of The Bell was one of the best known features of the village and, since its death some years ago, there was much controversy as to whether it should be replaced or left standing. After a village referendum the tree was removed in October 1986 and an oak tree, sponsored by the Building Society, was planted in November. The original was certainly of great age for in 1751 mention was made of a wych elm growing in the Square.

In the far east of the parish, one mile west of Chilton Foliat, stands the only major brick mansion in Wiltshire, Littlecote House. The house looks very Elizabethan, although it is much older and the earliest recognisable part is 15th century. The house was the home of the Popham family from 1589 to 1929 when it was sold to the Wills family. More recently the mansion was bought by Peter de Savery and a public appeal, launched by the Tower of London, successfully purchased a unique assemblage of Cromwellian armour that had originally been left at the house by hastily departing Roundheads. When the house was sold more of the contents went and you can now visit it in its new incarnation as the Littlecote House Hotel.

In the park near the river can be seen the ground plan of a Roman villa. Excavations were initiated by the Wills family on the site where a mosaic pavement had been found in 1730 and then reburied. The villa was found with the mosaic, although the latter had suffered much damage through tree roots. Fortunately, the wife of the 18th century steward had incorporated the mosaic design into a piece of embroidery and restoration was able to be undertaken. Recent archaeological reinterpretation has assigned several sites, previously believed to be villas, as pre-Christian religious centres dedicated to the worship of Bacchus. A fine Roman bronze bust of Zagreus-Bacchus, a pagan deity whose suffering and rebirth has much in common with the story of Christ, was found. This son of the supreme god Zeus was murdered by his enemies and born again as Bacchus; death and resurrection with strong overtones of the oneness of the Father and Son are here. It is quite likely that Littlecote was the Bacchic forerunner of a monastery.

REDLYNCH

I find the settlements of Redlynch very confusing. It is quite a large parish with substantial wooded areas stretching through Hamptworth and Nomansland to the Hampshire border and the New Forest. This wooded part of the parish is the New Forest but it lies outside the accepted modern forest boundaries, although Nomansland, which is written of below, is a forest village. Most of the houses lie in the western part of the parish above the valley of the Salisbury Avon and it is here that I get confused. Morgan's Vale, Woodfalls and Redlynch itself all join together and it is difficult for the visitor to know when you leave one and enter another. At least the settlement at Lover is distinct from the others but it does merge into Bohemia. On the Ordnance Survey map it looks easy but it is not so on the ground.

The earliest settlement was probably at Pensworth, first recorded in 1227, but all that remains here now is Lower Pensworth Farm. Redlynch, meaning the red ridge or rising ground, is first mentioned in the early 13th century as was Hamptworth. Woodfalls, meaning fold by the wood, is recorded first in 1258 but Morgan's Vale is a modern residential area. On Greenwood's map of 1826 it is marked as Morgan's Bottom but this was obviously too impolite a name for incoming householders. The name Lover probably derives from Lower Redlynch although its earlier name was Warminster Green. It is set amid attractive country but does not, alas, live up to its name, being a fairly unromantic collection of houses. But on one day of the year it is known throughout the land for the post office here then uses a handstamp, bearing the place-name, on envelopes containing Valentine cards.

The strangely named Bohemia first saw houses in the 18th century. Its name is said to have derived from gypsy encampments there; a supposition which is quite likely considering the extent of woodland. Also in the 18th century we find iron working in the parish with some iron ore found locally. At the end of the century there was a foundry on the site of Foundry Farm. Three families were involved in the industry and the Shelley family cast a two hundredweight bronze bell for Downton church but the foundry closed around 1850. As this was closing so production of cast iron items, including troughs and firebacks, began at Lover. The local clay was good for brick making and from the 18th century good quality bricks were produced for use in the local area. In the late 19th century a potter from the well known potteries at Verwood moved to the parish and produced an orange coloured ware with a yellow to green glaze on one side.

The proximity of Downton meant that there were a number of cottagers making lace. In the 1841 census there were 77 lace makers working but ten years later this had decreased to 14. In the mid-19th century a New Forest industry took root when some families engaged in broom making.

There are pleasant walks to be found in the woods but little of interest in the mainly modern settlements. Redlynch lies at both ends of a lane from The King's Head and I noted a house called The Old Reading Rooms. In Woodfalls there is the attractive long building of The Apple Tree Inn while Morgan's Vale has both the school and the main church dedicated to St Birinus. Built between 1894 and 1896, from a design of C. E. Ponting, it is of brick, most appropriately, with stone windows under brick arches and is surmounted by a low shingled bell tower. A slightly earlier church, that of St Mary, was built in 1837 in yellow brick. In 1912 St Mary's Hall Institute was built for the church. As with many forest areas extensive settlement and the established church came late.

Unknown to many people from northern Wiltshire, there is a small part of the New Forest in Redlynch parish and therefore in Wiltshire. This is at Nomansland, originally the home of 18th century squatters on the waste. Around the middle of the century a gypsy named Willett settled here finding the site convenient for the New Forest and its game but outside the Forest boundary and its laws. He was joined by eleven settlers from the Redlynch, Landford and Salisbury areas. These were single men who built cabins made of clods or sods of earth, called clotten houses, broke up the ground for cultivation and soon married and raised families.

The early houses, 'mud houses', were built with a mixture of pressed clay and heather for the walls with a thatched roof. In 1910 there were 67 houses; 22 all of clay, seven of clay and brick, 36 all brick and two corrugated iron bungalows. There are still a few 'mud houses' remaining. Much of the present village runs along the county border with the trees of the New Forest ever-present and with the New Forest ponies roaming free around the roads and houses.

ROWDE

This compact brick-built village is set around the Devizes to Chippenham road. There is much modern development, mainly on the southern side, but all the older houses line the main road. There is a good timber-framed house, with brick infill, and a stone tile roof that dates from 1600. Close by is The George and Dragon which can't be very much later. The other early pub was a timber framed building of c1600 which was thatched. It was destroyed by fire in 1938 and shortly afterwards the replacement Cross Keys was built.

The earlier cottages may well have been connected with workers in the woollen trade for there is evidence for the industry from the 17th century. In 1700 only half the working men were employed on the land, the rest were cloth workers or were engaged in other industries. One trade in which the people of Rowde, like those in other Wiltshire villages, engaged was that of smuggling. One such man, Robert Trotman, has a memorial in a Dorset churchyard for on 24th April 1765 he died in a fight with customs officers. The sympathetic inscription says that he was 'barbarously murdered on the shore near Poole' and continues in verse:

'Put tea in one scale, human blood in t'other
And think what 'tis to slay a harmless brother.'

I like that t'other; it has the authentic ring of Wiltshire but, as a fellow Wiltshireman, I hope that he was not only smuggling tea. How scornful William Cobbett would have been for he detested tea drinking, holding it to be responsible for many of the ills of the early 19th century,

The church of St Matthew is all but hidden from the old village, only the top of the slender Perpendicular tower is visible from the western part. Apart from the tower the rest of the church was rebuilt by H.E. Goodridge in 1831-32 and is embattled with numerous pinnacles. The principle secular building is Rowdeford House. Built in 1812 it is now a school.

There is much slate in the village used for roofing material and I suspect that this came from South Wales via the Kennet and Avon Canal. The canal is just under a mile south of the village and from the bridge, on the Poulshot road, one can view the splendidly restored set of Caen Hill locks. There are 29 locks, with 17 in one impressive flight between the bridge and Devizes. The total rise is 237 feet in two and a half miles and there is only one longer flight, of 30 locks, in the country. Apart from being good healthy exercise, it is a stimulating walk to ascend the flight and, especially for the less willing, there is the prospect of a drink in The Black Horse when you reach the top on the outskirts of Devizes.

RUSHALL

Rushall is a tiny and seemingly little known village largely sited on a minor road between the A342 and A345, just to the north of Upavon. Yet this place became known throughout the country as the venue for the Rushall Horse Trials. This three-day event, early in the year, gave riders an opportunity to bring on young and inexperienced horses.

I think of Rushall as the village that has abandoned its church, for the latter now stands in isolation by the river while the former hugs the life-giving artery of the road. The divorce started when the land around the church was imparked in the 18th century by Edward Poore, whose formal grounds then encompassed the church. From 1803 to 1838 the nearby farm buildings were taken down and the farmhouse converted into three cottages, to be replaced by France Farm in 1842. In 1840 the manor house was demolished, its only remains being a large mound on what was the front lawn. The cottagers, whose forebears had been driven out in the 18th century, did not return in the 19th century and the area remains pastureland.

The church of St Matthew (the original dedication was to St Andrew) was largely rebuilt in 1812 leaving only the Perpendicular west tower unchanged. Other early work remains in the east and north walls of the chancel which are likely to date from a new church recorded as being built in 1332. There was also an extensive restoration in 1905. Go inside and you will find an octagonal Norman font and two small, coloured 15th century panels in the south-east window of the chancel. The church and churchyard, which has a ha-ha on the western side, are on a high point with sheep grazing on three sides.

A walk towards the Avon brings us to a pleasant three-arched bridge, now flat but probably once with a slight hump-back. Upstream is a stand of willow, once coppiced but now grown out, and over the bridge the road changes to a private road and continues through a farmyard where ornamental free range hens and bantams are everywhere. France Farm, pleasantly whitewashed with stone chimneys and louvered pots stands by the river, while the outbuildings include a substantial stone rubble and weatherboard barn.

Returning to the church, we pass an imposing clump of trees to the south. There are now 16 but some seem to have grown from the roots of others while some have decayed and it is a pleasing fancy to imagine that the original number may have been twelve, representing the Apostles. Near the church is one of the most ingenious stiles I have encountered. It is new and consists of three uprights and four horizontal bars. The bars are set in slots in the uprights and lifting the topmost bar at one end depresses all the bars at the other, so that there is only a low obstacle to be surmounted. A thoroughly good piece of work that seems less prone to damage than traditional types and looks most attractive as well.

An interesting local development is the Rushall Flour Mill which was set up in 1973 to process the produce of experiments in growing chemical-free wheat on Rushall Farm which had started in 1969. In 1973, 30 acres were in production and the wheat was stone ground in an electrically powered mill and baked into bread at Upavon. By 1986 the whole farm was chemical free and 569 acres of winter wheat were sown for harvesting in 1987. The average yield in 1986 was 1.8 tonnes per acre and everything is grown to the Soil Association's standards for organic produce. Flour is produced from 'hard' varieties of wheat using a Simon Barron Stone Mill. Barley is also grown and processed in a Pearling machine. Wheat, flour and barley can all be purchased at the mill which is open to visitors during working hours while in recent years a shop has opened and sells bread and other organic produce.

SANDY LANE

As its name indicates there is a light sandy soil here, similar to that of Bromham and eminently suited to growing market garden crops. It is a tiny village, hugging the sides of the Devizes to Chippenham road and not encroaching into the fields. Sandy Lane has a slightly synthetic air probably caused by the pretty thatched estate houses which are nearly too good to be true. The unusually coloured stone is ironstone boulders from the sandstone quarries at Naish Hill and elsewhere. Being estate houses they all have good sized gardens where the employee could not only grow his potatoes and greens but have space for a pig and a few hens as well.

Sandy Lane has a long history. Here was Roman Verlocio on the road between Bath and Mildenhall. The site has been difficult to trace but has recently been identified to the south-east behind Bell Farm and Bear Farm. While the settlement was grouped around the Roman road it is evident that there were many surrounding villas, possibly the country retreats of the citizens of Aquae Sulis. One, at Nuthills, has been partly excavated and wall plaster decorated with red, blue and black in geometric patterns was found. In a large room a fountain was discovered and the pottery included fine red

Samian ware besides coarser local work.

The charming little church of St Nicholas was built as a private chapel in 1892. It is of timber with deep thatch on its roof. On the main road is an earlier former chapel, in stone and flint, which has now been converted into a house; the traditional yew tree is still growing by the gate. A little further along the road is the village pump, canopied with a timber framework and roofed by stone tiles. In the north of the village is The George Inn, early 18th century with a substantial doorway of that period.

A short walk along the lane that leads north from in front of The George provides excellent views across the downs. Looking east we see the Cherhill Monument, Morgan's Hill and Beacon Hill.

SEEND

It is difficult to imagine today but for more than 30 years in the middle of the 19th century the extraction of iron ore and its smelting was carried out at Seend. The ore had been mentioned by John Aubrey in the 17th century as being of such a quality as could be smelted on a blacksmith's forge, far more easily than that of the Forest of Dean. Commercial extraction began in 1856 when 20,000 tonnes of ore were taken from land near The Bell Inn and sold most profitably. In 1857 a tramway was constructed to the nearby Kennet and Avon Canal and the ore exported to iron works in South Wales and Staffordshire.

Later it was decided that it would be more profitable to smelt at Seend and two blast furnaces were in operation by 1862, producing 300 tonnes per week. However, the history of Seend iron is littered with companies going bankrupt or being wound up and the works finally closed in 1889, owing to very high freight charges. It seems that the ore at Seend was particularly pure and there is still doubtless much of it remaining in the ferruginous sands of the lower greensand below ground. What remains above ground are a few quarries, slight evidence of the tramway and the ironmaster's house called 'Ferrum Towers'.

A much longer lasting industry was that of cloth, although Seend was probably more used for country homes of the clothiers than for their working operations in later years. Weaving prospered greatly in the 16th century but the main later visual evidence is the misnamed 'Weavers' Cottages'. By The Bell, at the west end of the village, these were built as a factory and recorded as being used as such from 1818-1827 after which they were converted into houses as was allowed for by their design. The earlier name of 'Factory Row' is more honest but much less romantic. Other industrialists followed the clothiers to the fine houses of the village, notably the Ushers, brewers of Trowbridge.

There are many fine houses in the village and naturally most of the better ones are those from earlier centuries. But not all. One of the best houses was built only a few years ago and Wiltshire House shows what can be done when someone is prepared to invest time and money in building a good house in a village.

If you drive through Seend you may miss the church of the Holy Cross. It has a pleasant approach between the garden walls of the Manor House and Seend House and is all but invisible from the road. It is basically 15th century, Perpendicular and was rebuilt in 1876. Inside there is a fine monument to the clothier John Stokes (died 1498) and his wife in the north aisle which he built. On the other side of the main road from the church, and down another lane is the village hall. For many years Seend WI has been famous for serving breakfasts here to early rising holidaying motorists.

To the west of the village are three mills: Baldham, Seend Head and Littleton. Baldham is first mentioned as a fulling mill in 1371 and a mill on this site was operated by J. & J. Noad & Co who produced flour here and at Littleton Mill until 1976. I visited these mills shortly before they closed when they were still using a water turbine installed in 1926. It was an idyllic setting for one of the last water-powered corn mills in Wiltshire but that very setting was its doom. Being some distance from large centres of population entailed high transport costs which were to prove too much for the business.

SEMINGTON

The village itself is quite compact but with several outlying small settlements and farms in the parish. It lies around the north to south road between Melksham to Steeple Ashton and Westbury. This in itself is a slight puzzle as you might have expected it to grow around the crossroads, now a roundabout, where the Trowbridge to Devizes road runs east to west. Doubtless the proximity of the Semington Brook, to the north, providing a supply of drinking water was a greater incentive. Standing at the eastern end of a low ridge of Cornbrash, providing lighter soils, it is in the Hundred of

Whorellsdown which contains no towns, only villages.

The outlying settlements include one at Littleton, where there was a turnpike gate, and others at Little Marsh, Outmarsh and the optimistically named Newtown. On the edge of the parish is the ancient settlement of Paxcroft, where a house probably stood by 1254, while in the north-west is the now isolated community of Whaddon.

The church of St George, an unusual dedication in Wiltshire where we seem to have given the name to inns not churches, stands at the eastern edge of the village. Although the dedication is mentioned in 1470 the church is mostly of 1860 with a 16th century structure. It is now both an Anglican and Methodist parish church. Inside are monuments to the Bisse family who took their name from the river that flows past Westbury and through nearby Trowbridge. There is also a large coloured marble monument to William Blagdon of Littleton, who died in 1697, and outside there are chest tombs of the late 17th to early 19th centuries. The workhouse of the Trowbridge and Melksham Union was built in the parish and later became St George's Hospital although its workhouse reputation was still apparent among older people in the 1950s and 1960s.

Near the church is the stone rubble Manor Farmhouse which could have been the capital house of the manor. It is a former hall house, probably late medieval, which has been altered in the 17th and 19th centuries. Standing on staddle stones, the brick granary is inscribed 'CP 1711'. Church Farmhouse is late 16th century timber framing which has been altered, expanded and refronted in rubble stone in later centuries.

In the early 19th century Semington became an important canal junction as it was here, by the bridge, that the Wilts and Berks canal struck out northwards from the Kennet and Avon. Work on the former had begun in 1795 with a regulating lock, then two local contractors and their labourers excavated a three mile section to the north and prepared the foundation pits for eight arch and four lift bridges. The local businesses of John Smith and John Bosville were then responsible for the bricklaying and masonry. While the Kennet and Avon allowed the easy importation of Somerset coal and Welsh slate into central Wiltshire, the Wilts and Berks performed the same service for several of the towns of the northern part of the county. In fact it was the canal in Swindon which allowed easy access to materials for the construction of the Great Western Railway Works, whose railway lines killed off the canal trade.

The present day village does not seem to have capitalised on its remaining canal attractions although The Somerset Arms may get a little trade from the canal to augment the usual motor-borne customer. This mid to late 18th century building could well have housed The Bell inn which existed in 1810. There is still a post office and stores and a garage in the centre along with some good 18th century houses and the Manor House which has a datestone of 1698. Some of the outlying farmhouses are early. Littleton Wood Farmhouse has origins around 1500, while both Littleton Green Farmhouse and Mill Farmhouse, the latter in Littleton Mill Lane, date from the late 16th century. Littleton Mill itself was a water mill and is now a dwelling standing alongside the late 18th century mill owners' house. It was here, in 1802, that a party of men fired the mill and threatened the occupiers with a pistol in one of the riots against newly introduced machinery. From identifying features of red hair and protruding teeth, Thomas Hilliker was convicted of this and hanged at Salisbury. His body was brought back to Trowbridge in a long procession with weavers from the West of England and Yorkshire present. The rector being conveniently absent, the curate buried the hanged man in the churchyard and Hilliker later became one of the martyrs of trade union history. At the time there were many who believed him to be innocent.

Finds at Whaddon indicate that there were temporary camps here in Mesolithic times. The later, now lost, village was around the church of St Mary where there is still some evidence for it on the ground. There had been a connection with the Long family from at least 1544 and the mansion of Whaddon House was probably built in the 16th century, but was unfortunately destroyed by fire in 1830. It is well worth driving, or preferably walking, along an attractive little road to Whaddon from Hilperton. At the church, which has features dating back to the 1160s, there is a tombstone to the Rev Edward Cooper who was uncle to Jane Austen.

SEMLEY

The south-western corner of Wiltshire is the butter country, as opposed to the chalk and the cheese, and although butter was made elsewhere in the county it was this area that specialised in its production. Although poorly drained, the parish of Semley has good pasture lands on clay soils and is most suitable for dairy farming. There has never been much arable land here. The River Sem, from which the village takes its name, rises in the parish and once fed three large pools while other smaller pools are also much in evidence.

The village now lies just east of the Warminster to Shaftesbury road and has the hills of Dorset as a backdrop to its green fields. The minor road to the village has swards of unenclosed land alongside it; an unusual sight in lowland Wiltshire. In fact out of nearly 3,000 acres about 300 were never enclosed because there was more land than people to farm it. On the lower ground it has been left in grassy strips and verges but on the southern hills it is covered by bracken and woodland. The settlements too are scattered around the parish. The small village of Semley and its church is in the centre while in the late 17th and early 18th century cottages were built on the waste at St Bartholomew's Hill and the Wild West-sounding Gutch Common below Tittle Path Hill. Both have remained small settlements which were joined by buildings at Huggler's Hole in the early 19th century and at Sem Hill, which had previously only been occupied by two farmhouses, in the late 19th century.

The church of St Leonard itself was built on common land at the crossroads and Church Green is still open land. The church, which had a chancel of the 13th century and a nave and tower of the 14th, suffered more than most at the hands of the Victorians. It was restored in 1846 and later demolished to be replaced by a building in the Perpendicular style, designed by T.H. Wyatt for the Marchioness of Westminster, who then owned Fonthill. Remaining inside is a late 13th century effigy of a priest at rest while outside in the churchyard is a bronze equestrian monument, only about four feet high, to Lt Gen Armstrong, died 1916, and a memorial cross, in Cornish granite, to the men of the parish who fell in the Great War.

The oldest building is probably Church Farm, of the 17th century, as most buildings in the village have been replaced within the last 200 years. They are scattered somewhat randomly and are often set well back from the road and separated from it by wide verges. Of note are the Old Rectory of dressed limestone of the early 18th century and The Bennett Arms, of painted dressed limestone from the 17th century but altered in the 19th. The village pound is probably a remodelling of that of the 19th century. Semley CE First School has a school and schoolhouse of 1866, probably designed by Wyatt. It is a good example of a little altered village church school and forms a good group with the contemporary church.

In 1859 the Salisbury to Gillingham railway line was opened through the parish and in the same year Semley was provided with a railway station. By 1865 The Railway Hotel was open although in 1935 its name was changed to The Kingsettle Hotel. The railway provided the means of export for the chief produce of the area and from 1871 there was a milk depot near the station which was the first in Wiltshire mainly serving the London market. Founded by Thomas Kirby, the company grew, opening other depots, until taken over by the Wilts United Dairies in 1920. There was a factory by 1924 and by 1928 milk was being pasteurised and cheeses stored here. This was an important business in a small place but unfortunately economies of scale forced the closure of the factory by 1985.

Semley is an attractive place to live with rail and road links nearby and a surrounding pattern of small villages. The internationally acclaimed guitarist Julian Bream has found it so and for many years he led his own cricket team from the village.

SEVINGTON

Sevington should not really be in this book as it is not a village, only a hamlet in the parish of Grittleton. There is no church, no shops, only a few houses and a farm, but there is something special here. The hamlet has a lovely setting, surrounded by pastureland with cattle and sheep grazing. No matter that the M4 is barely a stone's throw away, this is a very peaceful place.

The few houses are set either side of a short street. To the south-west is the creeper-clad Sevington Farm House with its farmyard and a big stone tiled barn. On the other side of the road is the attractive Sevington House, of one and a half stories, with gables in the roof and pleasant gardens on the road. There are typical Neeld estate cottages here with triangular bay windows and good sized gardens. Both Rose Cottage and its next door neighbour have traditional vegetable gardens, a most welcome sight.

At the south-eastern end of the street is an estate lodge and then our special building. A school of 1847 which incorporates parts of the old church of Leigh Delamare, also in the parish of Grittleton. This includes the tremendous bell turret, a 14th century chancel arch reused as the porch doorway with a Madonna and Child above. The school is a most unusual building but its present use is also unusual.

It is still a Victorian school. Or rather it has been recreated as a Victorian school in which a modern school class can spend the day being taught in Victorian fashion and dressed in Victorian-style clothes. The children use dip pens, are separated into boys and girls, sit at desks and are taught by the present incarnation of Miss Squire; the original one was a strict disciplinarian. The Sevington School Project began in 1991 and welcomed its first official school group on 12th November in that year. It is a charity set up by a small group of people working in the field of education. The group is still fairly small but they are dedicated and very enthusiastic. As well as school visits there are open days and special events plus many publications. A book, *The Victorian Schoolday* by Wynne Frankum and Jo Lawrie, features much material from Sevington.

A recent project has been the garden. There is a pincushion flower bed, a herb bed, a bee hive and a kitchen garden. All are Victorian in style and contain only trees and plants of the period. Outside the garden walls are elder bushes, covered with berries in autumn and most suitable for making a cordial to be sweetened with honey from the hive. There is a small green between the school and the lodge where a splendidly architectural cedar makes a fitting counterpoint to the rustic buildings. Also outside the school garden is a substantial tree stump which makes a good platform on which to stand and view a green rural scene, albeit with your back to the motorway.

SHERRINGTON

Sherrington is one of the most attractive small villages in Wiltshire which, considering its name, is most surprising. In AD 968 the name was Scearntune and in Old English scearn was dung and so the settlement was mud or dung farm. The village has long outgrown this name although if you are walking the roads after horses have recently passed that way you may not be so certain.

It is a quiet village lying on a loop of road off the minor road that traverses the southern edge of the Wylye valley. The parish is typical of the chalk streams with meadows and houses in the valley and a broad strip of land on the higher ground to the south and south-west. This allowed typical Wylye valley sheep and corn farming with the sheep folded on the higher ground each night, fertilising it with their dung so that crops of corn could be grown. There has never been a large population. A peak of 194 people was reached in 1841 but in the 1991 census there were only 70 people here.

Two streams flow from the spring line on the southern slopes, north into the Wylye, and this is a very watery place. Alongside the road are broad, shallow pools on which there are numerous ducks, moorhens and, beneath them, very small fish. Across the main pool is a bridge of railway sleepers leading to a footpath by which one can get up on to Sherrington Down and enjoy grand walks above Boyton and Stockton. The pools are old watercress beds and are very much the central attraction of the village. They were made when the Warren family, who grew cress on the River Wandle, near Mitcham in Surrey, expanded their operations in the 1870s and sent Elias Case to work the beds.

The water from the chalk springs keeps a constant temperature of 51 degrees Fahrenheit which is important as cress is sensitive to the cold. During frosty weather covers were put over the cress to push it under water and thus protect it. The cutting season was autumn and winter and Sherrington never produced less than ten tons a year, which was packed in locally made withy baskets. Watercress growing ended in 1976 and the beds became overgrown and very smelly in summer. After much discussion the upper beds have been cleared leaving the lower part, which is a flooded sunken lane, as a nature reserve and the haunt of the shy water rail.

Near the River Wylye is the oldest man-made structure. A tree-covered mound near the old rectory is a Norman motte which was raised in the late 11th or early 12th century. In the 1970s evidence of a west bailey was found and this must have been a good defensive site controlling the valley and the local English although, later, buildings connected with the site spread to lower ground in the field to the west of the mound. This mound is almost surrounded by water, a feature created by landscape gardening, which is home to more ducks.

By the water, and alongside the road, is the churchyard and church of the village. The road here is one of the few places where you may be able to park, the village being best visited on foot leaving your car elsewhere. It is a simple, homely church with an unusual dedication to SS Cosmos and Damian. These were twin Arabian doctors who were martyred for their Christian faith in AD 301. They became the guardian spirits of healing and safe travelling, having been known when alive as the 'silverless physicians' as they performed their work without reward. There is a picture of them in the chancel reproduced from a 15th century choir book.

For many years this information was lost and the dedication was thought to be to St Michael. Then, in 1907, a will of 1554 was found in the Muniment Room of Salisbury Cathedral which indicated the true dedication. The cathedral is thought to have possessed their relics in 1536 and there are figures representing them on the west front over the central door. Inside the church are an almost complete set of Elizabethan and Jacobean wall texts, one dated 1636, which had been whitewashed over but which were fortunately uncovered when Janet Becker, an expert on religious wall paintings was staying in the neighbourhood. She stayed on to restore and treat them and we can benefit from her work today.

Walk around the attractive churchyard and you will see more recent signs quoting Biblical texts. On the chancel wall is 'Remember the Sabbath Day to keep it Holy. Ex.28.8', while on the gable wall of the thatched Rectory Cottage is, 'Prepare to meet thy God. Amos 4.12' and 'I was glad when they said unto me, let us go into the House of the Lord. Psal. 122.1'. At least the latter is cheerful and not from the hellfire and brimstone school of preaching. From 1965 simple wooden crosses have been used to mark new graves while In Memoriam stones have been placed in the porch wall.

The village contains stone thatched cottages in a beautiful, peaceful setting. In the small fields are Jacob's sheep while from a garden wall a local cat will mew for some attention. The most attractive cottages are probably those around the old watercress beds, cottages which were cleverly sited some centuries ago to be out of reach of any flood waters. There is a causeway across the lower end of the flooded sunken lane and near here the road turns to cross the River Wylye where one of Sherrington's streams enters it. I say cross but it is actually a ford now used by equestrians, as the sign board says, while pedestrians are directed to the wooden footbridge and so to the path across the railway line and into Codford. If you wish to learn more of Sherrington read Rosamund Willoughby's book, *Sherrington: a Wiltshire village*, published in 1998.

SHERSTON

Free, independent and prosperous are adjectives that spring to mind when visiting Sherston. On the edge of the Cotswolds, it is far enough from any town to have escaped becoming a dormitory village and, as a result, it is a thriving busy community. A new planted town, away from the early settlement by the church, was set around its wide High Street, once used for a market; Sherston was a borough by the 15th century. It still has the feel of a small market town about it with back streets and lots of small lanes and alleys, while there are still early passages leading through houses into courts and gardens to the rear.

An early legend concerns John Rattlebone, a sturdy yeoman who, for some reason, was promised land by Edmund Ironside if he fought against King

Canute in 1016. Rattlebone was mortally wounded and although he staunched the flow of blood with a stone tile (a nice touch of the Cotswolds that) and continued fighting, he died as the Danes withdrew. Still current in the 17th century and recorded by John Aubrey was the following doggerel:

Fight well, Rattlebone,
Thou shalt have Sherston.
What shall I with Sherston do
Without I have all belongs thereto?
Thou shalt have Wych and Wellesley
Easton Town and Pinkeney.

The verse seems a little reminiscent of early mummers' plays and could well be a corrupted oral account of how the manor of Sherston was acquired by an early landowner.

There is some disagreement as to whether Rattlebone did die or, as one tradition holds, survive to claim his lands. The verse quoted evidently indicates the hard bargaining that took place before the battle and would indicate that Rattlebone had a sizeable following of men to command such a high price for his service. There is a later medieval timber chest in the church traditionally supposed to have held his armour; the initials 'R.B.' are upon it, while near the south door is a small figure which is reputed to be him but has been proved to be a monk holding a book and not a stone tile. A more substantial commemoration is The Rattlebone Inn which offers extensive accommodation for those who wish to eat or drink under a wide range of mugs, jugs and tankards hanging from beams above your head.

The fine church of the Holy Cross dates from c1170 and has had additions and alterations from many periods until the mid-18th century. The school, of 1845, is in the main street and on an autumn afternoon I stood and watched while a large group of mothers, and a few fathers, waited to collect their offspring. The doors opened and the children poured forth, but what impressed me was that most of the families walked home. Only those from outlying farms and houses used their cars and I found this a very pleasant surprise. Next door is a barn which was once used as a rifle range but which now houses the Community Centre.

Nearby is the result of a very good piece of community work. In 1935 the stone walls around the Fennymead, off Court Street, being in a state of disrepair, were voluntarily rebuilt by H. Sherwood, aged 76, assisted by P. Snell, aged 71, and H. Evans, a mere youngster of 60. The walls, surrounding what is now the village playing field, are substantial and this was obviously a considerable undertaking.

Sherston is thriving. There are several shops, including post office, stores, a butcher's where guinea fowl, wild boar, emu and quail may be purchased alongside more traditional meats, and four garages. Wiltshire Tracklements had their 'Mustard Manufactory' here where the renowned Urchfont Mustard was produced, among other varieties, but the company has moved into business units set up on a farm at Pinckney, still in the parish. It is surprising to find a business such as the Sherston Wine Company in this rural setting but they have been here for 18 years. Importing a wide range of wines, with an excellent selection of Spanish riojas, they ensure that Sherston can offer a better selection of wines than most towns. Even more exotic is a business which bottles quails' eggs, while on the modern front there is a computer company. This latter occupies the former Angel Inn and is well known as Sherston Software. Largely staffed by educationalists, they produce an impressive range of multimedia CD-ROMs in the fields of science, literacy and numeracy.

SHREWTON

Shrewton has a fascinating history, much of which is still waiting to be unravelled. The present parish is made up of seven early settlements: Maddington, Rollestone, Addestone, Homanton, Bourton and Netton, as well as Shrewton itself. Shrewton, however, was by no means the largest or most important settlement and even today the old area of Maddington is probably larger and still retains its church as does Rollestone. Addestone remains as a farm name but the others are only remembered by their area of downland still named after them.

The remaining village is set in the valley of the River Till, quite a deep stream considering that we are close to its source. Nowadays, rather than the river, it is the busy Devizes to Andover road that commands most attention, although fortunately many of the houses are sited on two minor roads leading north and south from the village centre. In the middle is the church of St Mary, Shrewton. Nearby is Shrewton House, built c1830; it has some fine ironwork in its balcony and terracing.

As with most of the Salisbury Plain villages, the early houses tend to be of flint and stone with brick taking over by the early 19th century. This is a large

Blind House
Shrewton

village with much modern development and the population is now approaching 2,000. It is the commercial centre for a large area and this is reflected by the garages, shops, post office and newsagent although the small outpost of Lloyd's Bank closed a few years ago and the small and unusual building it occupied is now an antiques and bric-a-brac shop. Three pubs, The Catherine Wheel, The Plume of Feathers and The George serve the village.

In the village centre, on the main road, is the mid-18th century domed blind house, or lock up. Besides being an immediate prison for village wrongdoers, it is believed to have offered secure accommodation for prisoners being escorted between Devizes and Salisbury. Unfortunately, in the 20th century its position on the edge of the road caused it to be the unwilling participant in various accidents involving lorries and tanks. A few years ago it was therefore moved back a few yards from the roadside.

At the northern end of the village is Elston and, if seven settlements in one village isn't confusing enough, Elston is in the parish of Orcheston. Building here tends to be of banded flint and stone while tucked unobtrusively away is the Shrewton Steam Laundries. Elston House is a very substantial and interesting complex with large ranges of stables and loose boxes. From here there is a road and a track leading through the wooded valley to Orcheston which passes Appleford School, founded by Gerald Trump, as a co-educational school for dyslexic children aged from seven to seventeen years.

Orcheston itself consists of two parishes: St George and St Mary. The Perpendicular Church of St George is disused and derelict, suffering from falling masonry. At the other end of the village is the church of St Mary, approached by a narrow path through trees and hedges. It is of flint and rubble and dates from the 13th century with later additions. The Crown is also built of flint with stone chequerwork and further caters for visitors with its separate restaurant. Proving that a hidden village can attract holidaymakers is the Stonehenge Caravan Park with its Village Shop while our feline friends can take their ease at the Stonehenge Cats' Hotel a little further down the road.

Opposite St Mary's is what must have been the old school, now a private residence which was called, with a nice touch of humour, 'Form III'. More prosaically it is now known as the Old School House The 'big house' of the village is most unusually of very pale colour brick but the pleasant Old Rectory is a more traditional mixture of stone, flint and brick in bands. In

1998 there was a scarecrow family of four in an attractive floral garden set above a bend in the road.

SLAUGHTERFORD

This peaceful little settlement has seen both the violence of battle and the growth of water-powered industry. In the year AD 879 King Alfred defeated the Danes here; legend has it that the river ran red with blood and so the village was named. Sadly though the facts are more prosaic. The name comes from Old English meaning the ford by the blackthorns. The industry was attracted by the clear powerful waters of the By Brook which also turned the wheels of mills at Castle Combe, Long Dean and Box. In the late 16th century there were three fulling mills and cloth was produced until 1827.

It is paper-making for which Slaughterford was best known. Rag Mill, now derelict, can be reached by walking upstream from the bridge. Here in a litter of industrial remains can be seen the nine foot iron wheel and its now empty mill leat. It was here that the 'stuff' was prepared; rags being cut, boiled and broken into individual fibres, then stored in the steep tanks. The stuff was transported in vats of elm mounted on bogies to Chaps Mill by the bridge. Paper was made here from 1790 to 1815 and again from 1827. Until recently the modern paper mill of W. J. Dowding and Sons worked on this site, sometimes using a water turbine powered by a massive waterwheel. The site is now the centre of controversy with a plan to build 14 dwellings and garages by the banks of the By Brook.

The village also possessed a brewery, that of Little and Sons, though by the 1950s this had been converted into a private house. The settlement can boast one of the few wall post boxes from the reign of Edward VII, while on the bridge there used to be an old cast iron highways sign that unfortunately disappeared a few years ago. Under the Highways and Locomotives Amendment Act of 1878, it stated: 'Notice is hereby given that LOCOMOTIVES are PROHIBITED from passing over this bridge as such would be attended with danger to the public'. Fortunately, however, the bridge took the weight of the paper mill lorries without harm.

At the time of the Commonwealth, Cromwell's soldiers passed through Slaughterford from Chippenham, on their way to Bristol for embarkation to fight in Ireland. In what was regrettably the practice of their Puritan kind, they despoiled the church. Instead of merely smashing statues and stained glass as was their normal action, they destroyed the whole church before they were satisfied. It was in ruins for 200 years before being rebuilt in 1823, and restored in 1883. During the churchless two centuries, worshippers had to walk or ride the two miles to Biddestone for church services.

SOPWORTH

Approached only by narrow roads that no longer seem to lead anywhere, the fortunate village of Sopworth slumbers through modern times. Here, I wrote eleven years ago, 'a dog may take his untroubled rest in the road for more than half an hour uninterrupted by the internal combustion engine. The only noticeable sounds are those of farm animals; a blissful oasis of peace in the modern world.' On a recent visit I did not see the dog but it was still a peaceful village with little traffic. Cattle, sheep, horses and hens are all around for the village has retained its farms and farmyards in the centre. Northend Farm has a fine range of stone barns and outbuildings, while elsewhere until recently there were two early farmyards looking much as they did 100 years ago. They are still there but now the old stone farm buildings have been converted into desirable residences.

Being in the Cotswolds and mostly surrounded by Gloucestershire, the buildings are in the famous warm mellow stone of the area, although a few have been rendered. Many have been well restored, particularly Tavern House, once the village pub and still with an open area before it where once sat the village elders with beer and clay pipes on fine summer nights. The village is now too small and too far away from any centre of population to support a pub. The school went the same way and now its building of 1880 makes a fine residence, The School House.

Away from the road and surrounded by farm and fields is the little church of St Mary. 'Drastically restored in 1871', to quote Pevsner, the only part of the exterior that still looks early is the Perpendicular tower. Nearby is the beautiful Manor House with its early 18th century frontage while across the road is a late 17th century rendered house with mullioned windows and stone quoins. In the south is the large pink-washed Manor Farmhouse with a further good range of outbuildings. In all, a lovely small village with a pattern of small fields enclosed by drystone walls to the north and slightly larger fields bounded by hedges to the south.

SOUTHWICK

Southwick is in the shape of the letter 'T', with the tail being the North Bradley road and the top the A361 from Trowbridge to Frome. Here there is much scattered development with isolated farms and small groups of dwellings all around a large common. The road which crossed the River Frome at Tellisford is said to be the packhorse route from Bristol through Wellow and Norton St Philip and then on to Salisbury through North Bradley and Edington. It was still used by drovers in the 1880s.

Until 1937 the southern part of Rode Hill, now in Somerset, was in the parish and in 1824 the vicar of North Bradley raised money to erect a new church there. This meant that the Road Hill House murder of 1860 took place in Wiltshire and explains why the accused half-sister, Constance Kent, was taken to Trowbridge Police Station, rather than to a Somerset town. The murder of the four year old Savill became the sensation of England and there were many suspects. Most people believe that, although Constance Kent confessed to the murder and served 21 years in prison, she did not commit the crime. This interesting story can be read in *Saint - with Red Hands?* by Yseult Bridges (1954) and *Cruelly Murdered* by Bernard Taylor (1979).

A Baptist church existed in Southwick as early as 1655 and as its members were numerous and influential it must be supposed that it was not a new foundation. The first Baptist church as such had been founded in London in 1633 and it is believed that the church at Southwick was only a few years more recent. Dissenters enjoyed much freedom at this time but, with the death of Cromwell in 1658, a period of great persecution followed, lasting until the Glorious Revolution of 1688. During this time many Baptists met in a natural dell in Witch Pit Wood on the Cutteridge Estate; William Trenchard, the owner, was the Member of Parliament for Westbury and a zealous Dissenter. In 1669 congregations of between 200 and 300 people were meeting there.

In October 1815 the old thatched chapel was taken down; on 15th May 1816 the foundation stone of the new one was laid. It was completed in a few months and dedicated on 31st October. Materials from the old chapel, which had stood for 106 years, were re-used in building a new vestry. There is still an open air baptistery which, until recent years, was used for adult baptism, by complete submersion. At the turn of the 20th century these were attended by up to a thousand people and I can well remember one in the 1950s when some hundreds were present. Quite a frightening sight this, for a small boy, with grown-ups, dressed all in white, being pushed below the water.

In 1861 the Providence chapel was built by a group who had split from the main Baptists; a common habit this, particularly in the 19th century. There was no other church in the village until the Rev. Were of North Bradley erected a small iron church near the crossroads in 1881. This was destroyed by fire in 1897 and in 1903 the 14th century style church of St Thomas was built. Despite it having a 14th century font from Chilton Foliat, a sunken tank for baptism was included at the western end as a concession to the strong Baptist principles of the village.

The village now contains extensive modern development and is mainly a dormitory for Trowbridge, from which it is separated by only a field or two. Southwick, however, has several shops, a well-used recreation ground, and a village hall. An independent pub, The Farmhouse, has been opened in recent years, a replacement for the old Fleur de Lys that once stood on the opposite side of the road and is now remembered by a road of that name. More recently a country park is being developed on open ground between Southwick and Trowbridge.

SOUTH WRAXALL

South Wraxall is a beautiful stone village with a glorious manor house in a most successful amalgam of styles; the 15th century combining with the Elizabethan and Jacobean periods. It was in the ownership of the Long family from the early 15th century until quite recently. In the late 16th century Sir Walter Long built the grander parts of the house, including the large drawing room. There is a story, although I am sure it is told of many country houses of the right period, that it was here Sir Walter Raleigh first smoked tobacco in this country. On a visit to Sir Walter Long he is believed to have persuaded that gentleman to join him in a pipeful of the leaf of the exotic weed. Whether he enjoyed it is unfortunately not known.

To the north of the Manor is Manor Farmhouse, much of which was a 14th century hospice, extended in the 17th century. The village to the south is clustered around the church of St James. A most unusual sight this church, with an enormous stair turret and a large saddleback roof. The tower of c1300 is not tall, only ten feet higher than the ridge of the nave roof, but the saddleback roof on top makes it most distinctive and eye-catching.

Next to the church is the old school of 1841, now converted into the village hall, while all around are houses of the 16th and 17th centuries. The pleasant Longs Arms has a double bay window of the 18th century and throughout the summer a charming array of flowers before its facade. In fact the floral display takes over the front of the pub and even extends along a high retaining wall which is topped by flower tubs. When eating or drinking one can view the church through a colourful Arcadia.

To the south lies Lower Wraxall, now the larger part of the settlement. The two are most directly connected by tarmac footpaths leading through fields where inquisitive heifers or bullocks may inquire your business, or a pony may eye you up as a possible provider of apples. These paths provide an opportunity to take in the delightful setting of small hedged fields of pastureland and admire the outbuildings of Mison Farmhouse. This is a splendid farmhouse dated 1576 over the doorway and inscribed with the words: 'God save our Queen Elizabeth'. In the orchard is a most unusual circular stone barn or granary. On the other side of the path is an excellent example of modern Cotswold building in a house, newly constructed in 1998, with fine attention to detailing.

A stream runs through Lower Wraxall and again there are many good houses of the 16th and 17th centuries. In a house as old as most in the village is the South Wraxall Working Men's Club, quite a surprise in this small village.

STANTON ST QUINTIN

Today Stanton St Quintin can be a fairly noisy place. To the south is the drone of the M4 providing constant noise throughout the day; doubtless if you live here you don't notice it, only feeling that something is wrong if the sound of the traffic suddenly ceases. In the north-east is Hullavington Airfield with its camouflaged turf-covered aircraft hangars and extensive housing; now closed but until recently providing both a busy hum and employment in the area.

It was very different in the latter half of the 19th century when James Hickerton, my great grandfather, lived here. Then it was a tiny peaceful place having so few people that my great grandfather had to go courting further afield. In the 1870s on his days off he would walk to Trowbridge to see a Crockerton girl who was in service there. His devotion, with the return journey totalling about 33 miles, was obviously effective for in September 1879 they were married!

Arch, St Giles
Stanton St. Quinton

More than a century earlier a murder was committed here which was still well remembered 200 years later. The full story is told in Countess Badeni's book *Wiltshire Forefathers*. William Jacques, supposed to be the rascally son of the vicar of Leigh Delamere, was a sailor who had been paid off from *HMS Stagg*. He met a former crew member, a black man by the name of George Hartford, in the Green Dragon Inn at Malmesbury. After drinking there and at Hullavington, George Hartford set out through Stanton Wood to walk to Chippenham. In the wood, by the side of a little pool called the Black Pond, he was murdered by Jacques for the remains of his £28 seaman's pay. The body was swiftly found, Jacques was arrested at Chippenham and tried at Salisbury where he confessed and was hanged on Stanton Common before a large gathering of people. A not uncommon story in the 18th century but well remembered, I suspect, because the village would hardly have seen a black man by 1764.

The old moated manor house to which Stanton Wood and Stanton Park belonged was demolished in 1856. Until this date the present Stanton Court was the rectory, originally built in 1780. Next door is the church of St Giles with its central Norman tower; high up on this is a sheela-na-gig.

In the main street are houses and cottages from the 17th, 18th and 19th centuries. To the east of the Chippenham to Malmesbury road and the far side of Stanton Common is Lower Stanton St Quintin with its houses and chapel. Just recently there has been substantial building work here with various barn conversions. Barns, where my ancestors worked in the winter threshing grain with a flail, are now luxury homes. Farther east off the road is a medieval, or possibly Norman, moated site. Built originally to defend a large farmstead or small manor house, it was later associated with a hermit, according to John Aubrey, in the 17th century.

STEEPLE ASHTON

Steeple Ashton has long been a favourite village of mine. It is the most obvious timber framed settlement in west Wiltshire, grouped around its triangular green, with many appealing houses. Its fortunes were built on ecclesiastical influence and wool, two economic factors of great importance in medieval times. A weekly market and fair were held from 1266, and the Middle Ages saw Steeple Ashton as the local centre of the large estates of Romsey Abbey. The former wealth of the clothiers can be estimated by their magnificent

Perpendicular church, but there was no water power in the village and, as the woollen industry became more dependent upon rivers, it quickly declined locally. By the end of the 16th century it had completely gone and was concentrated in the river valleys.

The church of St Mary is certainly the most impressive feature, impressive enough for its steeple to have apparently given the village its name when added to the original Ashton, or Ash Farm although this is not the case. Originally there was a spire on the top, giving a height of 186 feet but this came down during July of 1670. Built on the early 15th century tower between 1480 and 1500, it survived well until struck by lightning. Repairs were being completed in October 1670 when lightning struck again, killing two men and causing substantial damage to the roof and fabric of the church. This second occasion was obviously taken as a divine omen for there was no further attempt made to rebuild. Much of the 15th century building was paid for by two local clothiers: Robert Long and Walter Leucas. Inside there is a church library, not the modern type with a collection of recent religious works in the west end of an aisle, but an accumulation of early works and documents which have been preserved here.

In the centre of the village is a green complete with market cross and blind house. There has been much dispute over the age of the cross with one optimistic suggestion being 1071. As it stands it is late 17th century and the carving dates from 1679, although there have been many restorations. The octagonal blind house, or lock-up, is of 1773 and is another indication of the size and importance of the village. Around the green are many fine houses dating back over five centuries.

The settlements at Ashton Hill and Ashton Common came about from encroachments on the common land and were known to exist by 1773. There are still a few small brick houses, which could indicate original settlement, some farmhouses and a most interesting complex of buildings on Ashton Common, just off the road leading to Stoney Gutter crossroads.

From the 17th century comes a story of a well known sheep stealer, John Brewer. In 1661 John Haskins, a serjeant at law in London, wrote to John Aubrey as follows.

> Mr Aubrey, - I have bin told that in the time of Baron Tanfield, about 1620, there was indicted one John Brewer, of Stiple Ashton, for sheep stealing, who had a trick to keep the mutton sweet seven weeks without salt, but would not tell his way to the

> judge, no not at his trial. He was acquitted. Now will you oblige me and some other of your servants, if you can enquire how this was done. - Your servant, John Haskins'.

Aubrey did not know but being an intensely curious man, particularly when his native Wiltshire was involved, made enquiries of Robert Beach of Steeple Ashton. The answer provided an example of how the countryman, even when on trial, liked to have a laugh at the expense of learned men. The sheep, when first stolen, were taken to Claverton, near Bath (a distance of between eight and ten miles), and kept alive in caves near the stone quarries. Whether it was the possession of this supposed secret that intrigued the judge and saved Mr Brewer's skin, or whether it was that the sheep, being the evidence, were so well hidden that they were never found, we shall never know!

STERT

I shall always think of Stert as the hidden village. From the Devizes to Upavon road little of it can be seen and the road into the community very sensibly peters out into a bridleway so that no through traffic disturbs the peace. I first walked around Stert when I was trying to identify a picture from the 1930s showing a farm labourer being greeted by two small girls at the gate of a cottage. That was in 1982 and, until then, the village was as unknown to me as I am sure it is to most other Wiltshire folk.

Stert village tumbles down a steep hillside, each house having been built on a precarious platform with a garden following the steep contours of the hill. The name comes from the Anglo-Saxon, Steort, meaning a promontory point or tail of land and is an extremely good description of the village. Looking to the south and south-west, there are superb views, especially from the churchyard, which is at the highest point of the old village.

It was in the west, around the church, that the village grew. Here there are many timber-framed white cottages with thatched roofs, most dating back to the 17th century or earlier. Also, next to the church, and forming a very pleasant group with it, is the gabled Manor Farmhouse. The house also dates from the 17th century and with its farmyard, duck pond and tree-lined drive to the main road presents a very attractive picture. The church itself is recent having been rebuilt in 1845-46 by J.R. Hakewill, who kept the Perpendicular two-bay north arcade.

The way to see Stert is to walk and there are pleasant footpaths leading to the lower ground, which eventually find their way to Devizes and Potterne. Indeed, there is quite a network of footpaths between Stert and Potterne which provide a pleasant circular walk for anyone starting from either village. On the other side of the parish, on the Lydeway, stands the Clock Inn. Once the home of the Raymonds, a clockmaking family, it was originally a low thatched building. The clock, which had a diamond-shaped wooden dial, dated from 1773 but disappeared a few years ago.

STOCKTON

The pretty village of Stockton lies on the pleasant road of the Wylye valley; the other being the A36 trunk-road on the eastern side of the river. It is a square-shaped parish whose boundaries are apparently little changed from when a Saxon lord, Wulfhere, held the manor in AD 901. As with all river valley parishes, a large area of downland is included and this stretches south to Stockton Wood. Nearby are Stockton Earthworks, a very large settlement which was begun in the Iron Age. It was continuously occupied from then and throughout the Romano-British period. Just to the south is the old Roman road along which Mendip lead was carried to Old Sarum.

The present village was originally settled at the eastern end around the church where there is still a range of much altered 17th century thatched cottages. The western end was developed later as a street village and until the mid-20th century there was open land between the two. Most of the houses on the street are early 19th century and there has been little building since 1815, apart from a row of council houses and a very few others. Around 1604 the village cross was moved into the eastern area where its stump remains near the lane leading to the church. Also here is the old school and an 18th century house which, in its porch, has a late 15th century mantelpiece from a Codford house. To the south of the street are two 17th century farmhouses, one dated 1693 and the other restored in 1966.

The church of St John the Baptist dates from the 12th to 15th centuries and there has been much later rebuilding. Inside there are many ornate and interesting monuments. One is to John Topp (died 1640) who in 1630 gave the piece of Elizabethan panel velvet that is in the north aisle. He was a clothier who by a bequest founded the Topp Almshouses in 1641. Hidden from the road they are up a little lane to the south, small, of stone and around three sides of a forecourt.

It was John Topp who built the Elizabethan Stockton House in the 1590s. A fine square house faced in bands of flint and stone it has a most delightful setting in parkland near the river. A later addition, in the time of the Commonwealth, was a chapel, while throughout the house is particularly rich in its plasterwork and fireplaces.

Among many other attractive houses are Long Hall which has a good 18th century brick frontage on its timber framed range and Glebe Farmhouse which is dated 1740 but which looks a century earlier. There is still much thatch in the village and in 1984 a thatcher was working here on many houses, including one whose roof had caught fire. As a result there is now some very tidy thatch in Stockton. The parish is still almost entirely devoted to agriculture as are many of the residents and in The Carriers, formerly The New Inn of the early 19th century, men closely connected with the land still meet together.

STOURTON WITH GASPER

To my mind the phrase 'the parish of Stourton with Gasper' has a fine ring to it; though it can bring to mind the somewhat foolish picture of someone coughing over a cigarette! But Stourton is far nobler than that for it contains the fine gardens of Stourhead. The lakes here date from 1448 when Sir John Stourton was granted a licence to enclose 1,000 acres to create a park. Included was the valley containing the source of the River Stour and the stream was dammed to create a series of fish ponds. The Stourtons suffered during the Civil War for being both Royalist and Catholic and were forced to sell their estate in 1704 for £11,000. By 1717 it was resold to the banker, Henry Hoare for £14,000, in a possible example of early 18th century property speculation. In 1718 he demolished the old large house, of whose architecture John Aubrey did not think highly, and had built only the second Palladian style house to be erected in England.

For a detailed history and description of its famous gardens the book to read is *The Stourhead Landscape* by Kenneth Woodbridge (1982). Making the lake, planting, and commissioning buildings in the grounds was begun in 1744 by the second Henry Hoare. The gardens are very compact with picturesque individual features being so designed to be viewed in sequence around the lake, one vista leading on to another.

Within the grounds, near the cottages on the road, is the Bristol High Cross. Erected here in 1765, it was originally at the junction of Broad Street with the High Street in Bristol. Dismantled as an obstruction in 1733, it was rebuilt on College Green in 1736 and dismantled again in 1762 when it lay neglected in a corner of the Cathedral until rescued by Henry Hoare in 1764 and brought to Stourhead in six wagons.

In the 1780s Stourhead was left to Sir Richard Colt Hoare. He further improved the grounds and was a far greater horticulturist than his grandfather, Henry Hoare. He is, however, better remembered as an antiquary and archaeologist, although his habit of opening up barrows for any treasures within and leaving no adequate record is of course an anathema to modern archaeologists. Among his greatest contributions to Wiltshire were his *History of Ancient Wiltshire* and *History of Modern Wiltshire*. The latter is contained in six great volumes and would more correctly be called the history of southern Wiltshire as it covers only that half of the county. Colt Hoare also added parapets to the small Perpendicular church of St Peter thus making it more picturesque and in keeping with his landscape design.

Outside the gates of Stourhead is the pleasant little stone village of Stourton. To some extent the village now exists to cater for the visitor and there is a large inn and a good National Trust shop nearby. Not many visitors penetrate to the southern end of the lakes where a scatter of houses and cottages along a ridge comprise the hamlet of Gasper. There are good woodland views and walks along this part of the Wiltshire border.

One must cross this border to visit Alfred's Tower in Somerset. Designed as part of the Stourhead landscape, it is supposed to mark the spot where King Alfred rallied the Saxons before the battle of Edington in AD 878. There is a statue of Alfred on the front. The project was begun in 1762 and completed by 1772 and commemorates the peace with France and the succession of George III in 1760. It is 160 feet high and the small spire on the top has recently been restored after a wartime accident when it was struck by an aeroplane.

SUTTON VENY

For thousands of men Sutton Veny Camp provided a temporary home during the Great War. Today virtually no trace remains, apart from a few survivals such as the name of Camp Farm. In 1914 the Army had begun building the camp and hundreds of men, called navvies by the villagers, swept into the village, living and sleeping rough, to create a small town of huts, tents and a hospital. The first troops came to the village on 27th April 1915 and, when the camp was complete and fully occupied, it contained 30,000 men. It covered an enormous area and a railway line three and a half miles long was constructed from Heytesbury to help troop movements and bring in supplies.

Internees were held at the camp and later in the conflict prisoners of war were incarcerated. Both groups were used for work parties. Thirty nine German prisoners did not survive the war and were buried at the local church until in 1963 they were removed to the German POW cemetery in Staffordshire. It was a great time for spy rumours and one such local suspect was in fact arrested, and later shot in the Tower of London. He was the local schools' Attendance Officer. The Army built two cinemas for the entertainment of the troops but one did not last too long. One evening when the projector had broken down the manager was ordered by his wife to disappear with the night's takings. Her announcement that the money could not be returned but that free tickets would be issued was not well received as many of the men were embarking for France the next day. They took their revenge by setting fire to the picture house.

The military hospital was greatly extended during the war and many were the men recovering from their 'Blighty ticket' that convalesced in the village. Towards the end of the war in 1918 a tragedy struck. Influenza raged at the camp for six weeks and many servicemen, including over 100 Australian soldiers and five Australian nurses died.

Today nearly 600 people live in the village which, like the others of the Wylye valley, has undergone a considerable degree of gentrification in the last few decades. Reminders of ruder days were the brick gutters on either side of the road which had replaced open ditches in 1868 when the Parish Vestry was most concerned with the insanitary state of the village streets. However, the brick gutters were still used as open sewers into the 20th century.

Sutton Veny has two churches. That of St Leonard was allowed to become a picturesque ruin from 1868, when it was decided to abandon the unstable structure on its low damp site and build the church of St John the Evangelist on higher ground. Sutton Veny House, dating from the 17th century but refronted in Georgian times, is now a nursing home, while for a time Polebridge House was a boarding school.

SWALLOWCLIFFE

An attractive quiet village, lying to the north of the A30 Salisbury to Shaftesbury road, Swallowcliffe is in a small valley and is mostly sheltered by low hills. Like its neighbouring parishes of Sutton Mandeville, Fovant and Compton Chamberlayne, where an impressive small range of hills rise steeply to over 200 metres to the south, the downland pastures of the parish were on this high ground. It was here that men first settled and a substantial site was occupied in the Iron Age but later generations shunned the hills and settled in the river valleys.

It was by the little stream, that flows northwards into the River Sem, that the first church of St Peter was built. It was certainly in existence by 1150 and in the 19th century was known to have Norman work, including pillars and arches, while much of the church had been altered or built in the 14th and 15th centuries. In later centuries the church suffered from its position in one of the lowest parts of the village. Writing in 1829 Sir Richard Colt Hoare says, 'The pillars are so very short in their proportions that they are supposed to have sunk half their length or more into the ground: but this supposition will admit of a doubt. But others suppose that this church . . . has either sunk so much, or the ground around it has risen by accumulation of sediment from the waters, that the pavement has been raised above the water, which even now is sometimes two feet deep in the church . . .'

From Colt Hoare's words it would seem that the church had been periodically flooded for some years. It is now believed that the church had indeed sunk into the water-bearing soil of its site and that the blocking of a drainage ditch probably caused the floods. The operations of an adjacent tannery, the sluice gates of a fish pond upstream and the working of a watermill downstream may have provided some secondary causes. The floods deposited mud on both pews and floor and at times the church was unusable but the churchwardens had been advised not to make any substantial repairs in case the whole church fell down. A new site for a church was given by the Earl of Pembroke, the old church was declared unfit for divine worship, the vicar applied for grant aid and plans were drawn up for a new church costing £1,260.

This was built in 1842-43 and is one of Gilbert Scott's early works. He intended to use old piers and arches and to preserve as much as possible of the early form. It is believed that stone from the old church was re-used but as Scott made old stones look like new by re-tooling them it is difficult to know. The church is larger than its predecessor and stands proudly on higher ground presenting its tower and transept to the road. Entry to the church is through the tower and there is probably more of interest here than in the rest of the church. Brought from the old church is an effigy, thought to be that of Sir Thomas West who was born before 1290 and died overseas on 1st November 1343. Below him is a large stone, with an indentation for a brass, set into the floor. It is thought to be of an abbess and is one of only two such memorials in England. It is likely to have been removed, for safe keeping, from either Wilton or Shaftesbury Abbey at the time of the Dissolution. The incised and decorated stone below the three bellropes is probably a 13th century coffin lid.

Above the effigy is a large board with an interesting story. On the enclosure of the common waste in 1662 was 'set out 20 acres of said common grounds for the poor people of the said parish to be employed and remain the use and benefit of the poor of the said parish for ever'. By order of the High Court of Chancery on 4th November 1675 it was decreed that the overseers of the poor should hold the 20 acres for the benefit of the poor. In 1853, when the board was erected, the land was let for an annual rent of £20. Inside the church there are two fonts, both believed to have been in the old church, and, nearby, two framed rolls of honour. When looking at such rolls you normally find that more men in a parish have died in the First World War than in the Second, but not so in Swallowcliffe. In the First, although seven men were wounded and two gassed, only one man was killed whereas four lost their lives in the Second, when five women also served.

The secular buildings are of stone with thatched or slate roofs; good examples being Chaldon House and Alfords. The manor house, to the east, is of the 17th century and is probably the earliest structure. The Royal Oak in the centre of the village and adjacent to the site of the old church, is a good combination of materials. The walls are of painted stone while the taller part of the building is thatched and the lower is of slate. They run Sunday charity quizzes here and, when I visited in the autumn of 1998, had raised £485. A continuation of the spirit which set aside 20 acres of land for the poor.

The little stream which once caused so much trouble now flows peacefully and has been made a feature of some of the gardens through which it flows. Near the road is a convenient seat on which you can sit and contemplate the water and the pleasant family garden behind the pub and maybe speculate on the village name. I had always assumed that it referred to the summer-visiting swallows but it also seems as likely to have been an early name for the stream below the 'cliff' of hills to the south.

 THE TEFFONTS

The Teffonts are two of the prettiest small villages in Wiltshire. Set along a north to south road, they merge together and are further connected by the small River Teff flowing past the doors of many of the houses on its way to Teffont Park and its confluence with the River Nadder.

Teffont Evias is the southernmost and smaller of the two. The Manor House has a four-bay facade with battlements at the top. It is a very imposing structure and has now been converted into flats. On the lawns of the Manor House stands the church of St Michael and All Angels with its imposing 125 foot steeple. The upper part of the steeple was added a few years after the main rebuilding of 1826 and originally boasted a weather vane. This blew down in the 1920s, when it was found to have a bullet hole in it. The impact of the bullet had damaged the spindle, making rotation difficult and this eventually caused its fall. Perhaps an example of idle marksmanship from a soldier stationed nearby during the First World War.

John Aubrey wrote that there was a quarry of very good white freestone, not long since discovered at Evias. In this he was probably misinformed as, in the acres of underground workings, large numbers of Roman coins have been found. The quarry supplied stone for Salisbury Cathedral and for the rebuilding of the spire of Chichester Cathedral.

At the top of the village we meet the turnpike road, c1820, from Dinton which now brings most traffic through Teffont Magna instead of skirting the northern end, by the church, on its way to Hindon. At this road junction stands The Black Horse which became an inn when the turnpike road was built, having previously been a small farmhouse since its construction early in the 18th century. In 1939 it was owned by the People's Refreshment House Association Ltd but now it is closed and the barn, to the rear, houses the Francis Frith Collection which provides modern copies of Frith photographs of places throughout the United Kingdom. An inn of the same name had previously stood on the south side of the old Dinton road. This 17th century stone building is now a private house.

There are some attractive cottages of the 17th century in the main street but the most interesting building is Fitz House. The late 16th century house was used as a farmhouse until 1920. The attractive house, with its pollarded limes and stream in front and delightful extensive gardens to the side and rear, made a great impression on the author Edith Olivier. She was determined to live there and after 1920 an opportunity arose for her to lease it. A later literary occupant was Siegfried Sassoon. On quite a steep slope, the gardens are superb and require a great deal of time spent on their upkeep and maintenance. In the 1980s I greatly appreciated the cream teas sold at the entrance cottage; it was here I enjoyed the only cream tea I have ever had served on bone china.

At the top of the village we leave the present main road and go straight on past the old school (open from 1859 to 1936) which is now used as a village hall. This leads to a small green and a large yew, behind which is the simple structure of the church of St Edward. The present church was rebuilt in the late 13th century after an earlier one, c1200, had been destroyed or damaged.

There are other interesting points about this church. Up to 1922 the dead of Teffont Magna had to be carried along a path through the woods for burial at Dinton. The church contains a narrow-waisted 13th century bell, rare in England, and a pre-Reformation chancel screen, one of the few to have survived in this part of the world. On the door jambs of the 14th century south porch there are scratched representations of two medieval ships: a rarity for an inland church.

The Teffonts had to wait long for piped water to its houses – 1962, in fact. Prior to that, from c1896, water was piped from Springhead (to the north), where four or five springs rise, to standpipes in the villages.

Pleasing features in each village are the thatched wooden bus shelters while Magna still retains a long-handled thatch hook, a necessary piece of equipment when thatch was afire and threatening surrounding roofs.

On 16th April 1987 a new venture began in the village when the late animal writer and broadcaster Johnny Morris performed the opening ceremony for the Wessex Shire Park. The Park was the brainchild of John and Rosemary Webb who farmed 1,000 acres locally and owned the Wylye Shire Horse Stud. Unfortunately this splendid venture ran into difficulties and the Park, with its modern replica of a tithe barn is now closed and renamed the Long House.

Teffont, however, is determined to provide a farm park and now has the Farmer Giles Farmstead. This good conversion to a farm park in a working dairy farm is sited just off the A303 road.

TILSHEAD

Near to the village is the source of the River Till and it might be thought that so the village was named. Unfortunately, the derivation of English place-names is rarely as simple as this. 'Til' comes from the personal name Tidwulr and refers to his hide, a household or an area of land that could support one free family. It is one of the upland villages of Salisbury Plain set in a dry valley. Nowadays the busy Devizes to Salisbury road runs through the settlement and nearby is the army presence of camp and firing ranges encountered everywhere on the Plain.

Many buildings exhibit the traditional use of flint and stone, some using a chequer pattern and others alternating bands. The church of St Thomas of Canterbury is part chequerwork and its squat stumpy Early English central tower looks out from the middle of the village. On the south wall of the chancel is a small lancet window with no glass; the wooden shutter is original and gives a reminder of how churches looked when glass was too scarce and expensive to be used.

Of special interest are the Flood Cottages, built in 1842 from public funds to sustain losses by the poor in the Tilshead and Shrewton parishes in the Great Flood of 1841. Twelve trustees were appointed to spend the rents raised from these cottages on fuel and clothing, which was to be distributed among the poor of each parish on 16th January, that being the anniversary of the 'Aweful Visitation'.

On reading the inscription the visitor may pause in some bewilderment for there is no surface water to be seen anywhere in the vicinity. Special circumstances created this great flood. Two days after a heavy snowstorm there was a rapid thaw and at about five o'clock on 16th January a torrent of water several feet deep rushed down the valley over the still frozen ground that was unable to absorb it. It is said that the water was ten to fifteen feet deep as it poured through the village, sweeping some cottages clean away and only leaving a wall or chimney stack standing of others. The damage amounted to many thousands of pounds for besides houses, barns, walls, fences and animals were destroyed. Fortunately the people did have early warning of the disaster, and managed to escape the torrent.

Before leaving Tilshead it is worth reflecting that in 1086 the Domesday Book recorded the settlement as a prosperous town. With 66 burgesses, it was one of the largest boroughs in Wiltshire and doubtless owed its wealth and fortune to its position in the middle of the Plain with massive sheep farming operations all around it.

TISBURY

Many people think of Tisbury as a town but those who have always lived there regard it as a village and so shall I. When I first visited it in the mid-1960s I felt that here was a place some years behind the other parts of Wiltshire that I knew. Time and wider experience have not entirely altered that impression and today I have the agreeable feeling that the pace and quality of life is that of earlier, more halcyon times.

Don't let me mislead you into looking upon Tisbury as a quiet backwater. It is busy, commercially successful and cars line the streets. There are more than a score of shops, small supermarkets, garages and a laundry and dry cleaners. Agricultural machinery is also manufactured here and there has been much modern development too, mainly on the outskirts of the historic community. Just off The Square is the imposing brewery, rebuilt in 1885, where the independent Wiltshire Brewery Company operated until recently.

Leisure and social facilities are available; halls, a youth and community service, a sports centre and a library; finance is represented by banks and an accountant. If we take a closer look at the shops we find some to be more specialised than we might have thought in a rural area. There is a furniture showroom, a wet fish shop, a flower shop, two clothes shops, an electrical shop and a chemist. Tisbury is fortunate in that it has been able to keep such a wealth of business activity and not be drained of its community life blood by becoming a dormitory village for the largest nearby town.

To me, one of the glories of Tisbury is its attractive jumble of houses and shops that cascade down the line of its main street into The Square. Rather small by some standards, this square nevertheless still maintains a traditional role of being a place to stand and watch the world go by. To help the world on its way, there is an old iron lamp standard which still wears its collar of wooden fingerboards pointing in all directions. Off The Square there is a very nice range of buildings around the church. Probably dating from the late 17th century they include the most attractive Crown Inn with its offset coaching arch. At right-angles to The Crown are some very substantial stone and brick almshouses of 1887 bearing a stern message for the inmates from Joshua XXIV, 15; 'As for me and my house we will serve the Lord'.

The cruciform church of St John the Baptist, built of Portland stone, is much larger than the normal village church and is the largest in this part of Wiltshire. There is an excellent church history, by Ralph Harold Jackson, available in the church. In the western wall of the nave is a porch with stone seating where the poor are supposed to have sat whilst awaiting alms. This is still called 'The Beggars' Porch'.

The 1970s saw the production of some very fine green and red kneelers by a small group of lady embroiderers. The bright colours of these give a reminder of the colour that was ever-present in medieval churches, while the carved pew ends indicate that post-medieval man preferred not to stand throughout the whole of the service. Recently the church has forged a link with Holy Trinity church in Tottenham.

The most notable feature of the churchyard is a huge and ancient yew tree with its split trunk filled with concrete. It is reputed to be 1,000 years old and its circumference measures 31 feet.

On the eastern edge of the village, where the roads to Chilmark and Chicksgrove diverge, is the remarkable survival of a grange of the nunnery of Shaftesbury, with the farmhouse, barn, gatehouses and outbuildings, dating from the 14th and 15th centuries. It really is a most imposing group with an outer and inner gatehouse (just like a castle). In the farmyard is the largest barn in England, built of stone in the 15th century with 13 internal bays and large porch entrances in the middle of both long sides. Roofing material was originally stone tiles but it is now thatched – 1,450 square yards of thatching as calculated by Alec Clifton-Taylor. The barn was re-thatched in 1971 in a slightly more ornate style than before.

TOLLARD ROYAL

In the centre of beautiful Cranborne Chase lies Tollard Royal, a small village set around a bend in the road between Ringwood and Shaftesbury. Enclosed by high valley sides, it is peaceful here and there are good walks along quiet tracks and lanes, both on the high hills and along the valley bottoms. There is grand open country on the hills from where you look down into the wooded valley and catch a glint of sunlight on the pond set in the middle of the village. Some houses and cottages are thatched, there is a general store and post office and the inn (The King John) provides refreshment, although the village pond sometimes does not, for it is dried up for part of the year.

King John's House, Tollard Royal

The church of St Peter ad Vincula (in chains) is one of the very few with this dedication in England; another is most appropriately in the Tower of London. The church has had many alterations made over the centuries and its architectural history is much obscured.

Next to the church is the magnificent King John's House with its narrow vertical timbering and panels of apricot-coloured wash. The central part is c1240, while the medieval north-west wing was remodelled in the late 16th century. Traditionally this was a hunting lodge used by King John whilst hunting on the Chase and thus the village received the Royal addition to its name. In the 18th century the house passed to the Pitt-Rivers family and hence to General Pitt-Rivers who freely allowed the public to come and view its splendours.

General Pitt-Rivers is quite rightly known as the father of modern archaeology. Interested in anthropology, he used his well-trained military mind to bring precision and order to the technique of archaeological excavation. He well understood the need to record each item and its relationship to everything else, even though it might seem meaningless at the time. He conducted many excavations on the Chase; some of the material can be seen in the Pitt-Rivers Museum at Oxford, but the General's own collections of artefacts, drawings and model reconstructions are now housed in Salisbury Museum.

The General himself lived in the late Georgian or early Victorian 'Rushmore' and opened up the Larmer Tree Grounds 'for the recreation of the people in the neighbouring towns and villages'. He provided a temple in 1880, six houses for people to picnic in, a bandstand and, in 1895, a theatre. There was a paid caretaker and crockery and cutlery were loaned free of charge to picnic parties. On Sunday afternoons a band, composed of 16 workmen from the estate, played and the grounds were open to the public every day of the year without payment. The provision of these grounds for public use was a fine philanthropic gesture by a fine and distinguished man. Incidentally, the larmer tree was probably a wych elm and in Tollard Royal was believed to be the tree beneath which King John met his huntsmen. After the General's death the grounds decayed but at their peak, in 1893, there were over 24,000 visitors.

Sandroyd School is now here and, most recently, the Rushmore Park Golf Club has been created. Adjacent to the Larmer Tree Grounds is Tollard Park, now Tollard Park Arabian Stud and Tollard Equestrian Centre.

UPAVON

Upavon has grown up at the junction of the four roads from Salisbury, Devizes, Marlborough and Andover, being also the halfway point for traffic travelling from either Salisbury or Amesbury to Devizes or Marlborough. This traffic brought trade to the village and, combined with the important medieval market, created a prosperous community. Although the market ended early in the 19th century the old market square is still evident in the High Street while the surrounding buildings which date from the 17th century remind us of the commercial worth of this village that is eight miles from the nearest town. The Antelope, which was rebuilt in the early 18th century, was first mentioned in 1609 and clearly benefited from both the market and travellers. In 1648 the trade of The Antelope and the other two licensed victualling houses was threatened by the proliferation of between 20 and 30 unlicensed alehouses in the parish. John Newman, the minister of Upavon, petitioned the Quarter Sessions saying that, 'God Almighty is greatly dishonoured, his sabbaths profaned, good laws condemned and the infinite of youth extremely corrupted'. Furthermore, he said, 'there was a great complaint of bastardies, sheep-stealers, hedgebreakers, quarrells and the like'. Upavon must have been a lively place in the 17th century.

In the 20th century a different type of transport to the wagons and coaches appeared when 425 acres of Upavon Down, to the east of the village, was acquired for an airfield. In June 1912 the Central Flying School of the Royal Flying Corps was opened to provide military training for qualified pilots. After the First World War all RAF flying instructors were trained here while between 1924 and 1934 the station became a base for fighter squadrons, when night flying techniques were developed. The station was very active during the Second World War and in 1942 the Central Flying School was replaced by No 7 Flying Instructors' School and the same year saw the HQ of No 38 Group Transport Command based here.

After the Second World War transport and strike commands were still based here but by the 1970s the station had become mainly administrative. The impact of the RAF on this area has been considerable, not least as an employer of labour. To accommodate this civilian workforce council housing was built to the south of the village and the increase in population has certainly ensured that shops and services have been maintained. A combination of the RAF presence, the lack of a railway line and the four major roads has also meant that there is still a reasonably good bus service at Upavon.

In the centre of the village, by the bridge over the Salisbury Avon, is the church of St Mary. Typically built of alternating bands of flint and ashlar, in the 12th and 13th centuries, it had fallen into a ruined state by 1411, after which date it was restored. A Victorian restoration occurred in 1875-76. There is an octagonal Norman font richly carved and, most appropriately considering the dedication, featuring an Annunciation.

Within the parish, at Widdington Farm, was born Henry 'Orator' Hunt in 1773. After the death of his father he farmed here but it is as a Radical politician that he is known. He was a friend of Cobbett and, in 1819, he presided at the Manchester reform meeting that became known as the Peterloo Massacre after it was broken up by the Yeomanry. He entered Parliament in 1831 and presented the earliest petition in favour of 'women's rights'. He tended to alienate everyone, including Cobbett, however, and was hardly tolerated by his friends while his opponents' view of him was of 'a most unprincipled demagogue'. He died at Alresford, Hampshire, in 1835 and was buried in the family vault of his mistress, Mrs Gronow, at Parham. He had been married, at the age of 22, to a Miss Halcomb, daughter of the landlord of The Bear Inn at Devizes. After she had borne his three children he separated from her when he was 29 and eloped with a Mrs Vince, the wife of a friend. So although not a favourite with his colleagues, at least the ladies saw some hidden charms in him.

UPTON SCUDAMORE

The village has become much more obvious since the building of the Warminster bypass. It is not really a hilltop settlement but it is sited on a low mound rising out of the greensand ridge, commanding extensive views in all directions except the east. For to the east, and within the parish, the chalk scarp of Salisbury Plain rises some 650 feet, or 199 metres which sounds far less impressive, at Upton Cow Down. That the site has proved attractive to man in the past has been shown by early Iron Age finds to the south of the church which, itself, is near the site of a Roman building.

The church of St Mary the Virgin is on the south side of the village where the land falls away towards Warminster. Not a central position and not, apparently, a case where the village has moved away from its church as it is unlikely that there was early settlement on the lower ground. The earliest extant work in the church is Norman, being the surround of the north doorway and the decorated circular font which probably come from a time when there was only a small nave and chancel. Additions and rebuildings were carried out up to the 15th century and the tower was rebuilt in 1750. By the middle of the 19th century the church had become 'an offensive charnel house' with 'all sorts of deformities and material obstructions to worship'. In other words the old church which had evolved organically offended the Victorian sense of order and they removed many things we would find interesting and put in regimented rows of pews facing the altar and the pulpit.

The church was extensively altered and rebuilt in 13th century style under G.E. Street. In the north aisle remain two effigies of knights of the late 1200s and the late 1300s. These are probably members of the Scudamore family whose ownership of the manor added their name as a suffix to the simple Upton which means higher farm. The church and village have given their name to a type of small organ. After the 1855 to 1859 restoration the vicar, John Baron, did not have sufficient money for an organ and so designed one with only one manual and no pedals, which he based on medieval models. Nelson Hall, an organ builder living in the village made it and the architect, Street, designed the wooden case. The organ found favour with other churches as it was cheap and needed little space and Nelson Hall moved to Warminster and made several Scudamore organs. After his early death the well known London organ builder, Henry Willis, made them.

In medieval and early modern times the village was of a reasonable size while in the early part of the 19th century it varied between 300 and 400 in population. A decline began in the 1870s when farming was in a bad way and the village has remained small ever since. Today even the post office has closed and, apart from farming, the only apparent sign of commercial activity is The Angel, built in painted brick on the roadside with good iron bootscrapers at its doorways. This has always been an agricultural parish although doubtless there was some domestic spinning and weaving carried out until the early 19th century. Today one feels that most of the working population are employed in the nearby towns with only a handful working on the land.

The same John Baron who designed the organ is commemorated, with his wife, in a water tower erected as a memorial in 1906. There is good, if hard, water here and both Trowbridge and Melksham are supplied from boreholes in the splendidly named Biss Bottom. As the name suggests, it is here that the Biss Brook rises before becoming the River Biss flowing through Trowbridge and into the River Avon. Biss, or Bissie, means finger and this was an early surname in the area.

URCHFONT

A compact village lying on the B3098 to the west of the Devizes to Salisbury road. There are many attractive houses, the earliest dating from the 16th century with fine examples of the 18th and 19th centuries. These houses are worth more than a second glance and the best is Urchfont Manor, said by Sir Nikolaus Pevsner to be one of the best houses of its type in Wiltshire. It was built for Sir William Pynsent, c1680, and is of brick with stone dressings, with an impressive doorway.

Nowadays many people have the opportunity to stay at the Manor as it has been an adult residential centre of Wiltshire County Council since 1947. A variety of courses are held, on such subjects as natural history, art, geology, archaeology and cookery. It really is a splendid setting in which to imbibe knowledge.

The most attractive features of this village are its greens. By the church there is a substantial pond maintaining a flock of ducks. Urchfont thinks highly of its ducks and they are a great attraction for visitors and locals alike. Adjoining the pond are the farmyard gates of Manor Farm. The farmhouse itself is of the 19th century.

The church of St Michael and All Angels is approached by what at first sight appears to be a private drive. The. church is built of local sandstone with limestone dressings and, although the chancel arch is of c1200, the present church is largely the result of rebuilding and enlargements from 1300 to 1500. The church contains some good monuments. That to Sir Robert Tothill (1753) is a standing wall monument with a black sarcophagus and block obelisk and is by P. Sheemakers. That to James Long (1768) is of coloured marble with an obelisk reminding us of his monument on Etchilhampton Hill.

In 1523 an Urchfont tailor, John Bent, was unable to believe that the Eucharist bread and wine could be converted into the body and blood of Christ. In an age when men wore their religion more openly, he publicly proclaimed this. He suffered martyrdom at Devizes for his beliefs when he was accused of denying the doctrine of the transubstantiation.

The Lower Green, the larger of the two, is surrounded by houses, many of 17th century origin and is a most peaceful and attractive place to live. From here the road leads to Cuckoo's Corner, so named on the Tithe Award map of 1840, and a name redolent of the promise of spring and early summer. Take this road and you will travel through a landscape little altered through the last 150 years. With hedged broad verges the road leads through pastureland with hedgerow timber and curls around an old thatched brick farmstead before reluctantly delivering you into the present at Potterne Wick.

The name Urchfont has had several variations over the centuries, Ierchesfonte, Archesfunte, Erchfount, Ushant among them. It is believed to derive from the spring of Eorich and the village has possessed several springs including one that has never run dry. In 1930 the name was Erchfont when the local people built their village hall entirely by their own labour and recorded, on the facade, this fact for posterity. At that time the village was very much a self-contained community but since the end of the Second World War it has become a dormitory area for Devizes.

In the 18th and early 19th centuries a small inn called The Shepherd and Dog stood on the Lydeway. While Thomas Burry (died 1842) was landlord the inn had an evil reputation, for it was said that peddlers and other solitary visitors were often never seen again after entering its doors. There is a story that more than a dozen bodies were exhumed from shallow graves behind the inn, victims of the landlord's greed. Thomas Burry does not seem to have been brought to justice, however, but there is a tradition that the bells of old Stert church refused to ring at his funeral.

WANBOROUGH

The village name seems to come from the Old English indicating a hill or barrow, or in this case maybe a group of four barrows on Sugar Hill. Of later date is the Roman road, Ermine Street, which runs from Silchester to Cirencester and around which was the town of Durocornovium which was occupied for most of the Roman period.

The modern village lies slightly to the south of the Roman town with Lower Wanborough still on Ermine Street. This was a resting place for drovers taking their cattle to London, often 800 head passing through in a week, and there were many hostelries catering for them. Two of those remaining, The Harrow and The Plough are attractively thatched and very close to one another.

In *Villages of the White Horse* Alfred Williams mentions two great festivals connected with Wanborough in past times. Lot Mead took place at mowing time when there was much merriment and games and, after mowing, each of the mowers was provided with a pound of beef and a clove of garlic. The latter

item would seem to indicate that Englishmen were not as averse to garlic as has been supposed; unless, of course, they used it to wear as a protection against witches. The Cow Fair brought in cattle from the Welsh borders whilst at the Autumn Fair the booths for entertainments and sporting contests extended for a mile along both sides of the road. This was followed by a great feast at which the village band played after the local champions of wrestling and back-swording had been proclaimed.

Alfred Williams also talks of the cottage industries that were such a part of village life until the early 19th century. Spinning and weaving, straw plaiting, soap making and candle making, while locally grown flax was spun by the farmers' wives and woven by the villagers into sheets and dress material. Blankets and carpets were manufactured and the villagers 'finished' cloth that had been woven in Oxfordshire.

Upper Wanborough is the older part of the present village and is set well on its hillside looking over the broad clay vale to the north-west. The church of St Andrew has both a west tower and a spire over the east end of the nave; a popular legend explains these as having been built by a man whose wife was childless. If they were blessed with a boy he would provide money to build a tower, for a girl the spire. When his wife presented him with boy and girl twins he kept his vow and built both!

From an age which considered all millers dishonest, there is an unusual epitaph to one Thomas Robins who died in 1760:

'God works his wonders now and then
Here lies a miller, an honest man.
This world's glory he did not mind,
Nor was his Heart to Pride inclin'd.
Vile enemies him oft oppress'd.
God set him free, as he thought best.'

A mill had clacked at Wanborough since Saxon times and was still working into the 20th century. Its remains can still be seen on the River Lyd.

In the church porch an interesting sign is preserved. It says: 'All females are requested to take off their pattens on entering this door', and it conjures up a time of unpaved roads, deep ruts and much mud.

WARDOUR

The name Wardour is synonymous with the Arundell family and Roman Catholicism. From 1592 it has been in the family's possession, apart from a brief hiatus during the Civil War. Today the spectacular ruin of Old Wardour Castle is a direct result of that war. The licence to crenellate (fortify a house, turning it into a castle) had been granted to Lord Lovel in 1393 but the present castle is from the reconstruction of Sir Matthew Arundell in 1578.

By the time of the Civil War the estate was in the hands of Thomas, 2nd Lord Wardour, a Royalist, naturally. While he was at Oxford with the King in 1643 his castle was besieged by Sir Edward Hungerford of Bromham. It was defended by Lady Blanche Arundell with 25 men and some women and children against a force of 1,300 men. The castle held out for six days before surrendering, whereupon much wanton destruction was carried out by the Parliamentarians. The castle was then garrisoned for Parliament by Edmund Ludlow of Maiden Bradley, and was besieged in 1644 by Henry, 3rd Lord Arundell, who had succeeded to the title on his father's death in 1643. Mining and counter-mining had caused great damage to the castle by the time it was surrendered on 18th March.

The hexagonal castle is in a superb setting, overlooking its large fishpond and surrounded by wooded hillsides. It is now in the care of the Department of the Environment. When the Arundells returned at the Restoration, there was no attempt made to restore the castle. Instead, they built a small undistinguished house on the south side of the bailey wall. Typical 18th century landscaping has enhanced the effect of a picturesque ruin and in 1792 a grotto was constructed of stone, brick and plaster by Josiah Lane of Tisbury, a famous Wiltshire grotto builder.

New Wardour Castle, by James Paine, was completed in 1776 for the 8th Lord Arundell. It is the largest Georgian house in Wiltshire and is built of stone. Naturally a private Catholic chapel was included as the family and their people always remained true to the old faith. The village school is still a Catholic one. On the death of John, Lord Arundell, in 1944, after being wounded and suffering imprisonment in Colditz, the house was sold and in 1960 taken over by Cranborne Chase School. The school is now closed and extremely fine and costly renovations and conversions have taken place to provide luxurious flats and apartments.

WEST ASHTON

The village of West Ashton, situated on a hill to the south-east of Trowbridge, is built along the roads to the south-west and south-east of its crossroads.

Uphill from West Ashton crossroads are five pairs of houses, c1850, called Doreen Cottages, that were built for estate workers; other pairs and groups are scattered through the village. The design is fairly typical of those found in Victorian books of house plans for the landed gentry who wished to re-house their workers in something better than the damp leaking cottages that were all too common. At the crossroads itself there was a garden with a few fruit trees which only recently disappeared when the crossroads, an accident blackspot, were improved and traffic lights installed. This was the site of an alehouse where, in the 19th century, residents of Trowbridge were wont to walk and take refreshment. Looking back along the road, while they drank their pints of beer, they could contemplate the dominating woollen mills where they earned their money.

Refreshment of a different sort was marketed in the 18th century when a mineral well was discovered in 1731. In 1733 the *London Evening Post* carried advertisements for the water, making claims that more than 100 people had been cured of such diseases as leprosy, sore eyes and the King's evil. There was a tenuous link with another beverage, coffee, in 1694 when Thomas King was born in the parish. He gave his name to King's Coffee House in Covent Garden, which became a fashionable meeting place of the 18th century.

Today the chief concern of the village is the traffic that thunders along the A350, especially at holiday times. The Trowbridge to Frome bypass would alleviate the problem. It was first suggested in the 1920s. Seventy years later the Frome section has been built but the Trowbridge part is still being discussed. The only tangible evidence of interest is in Yarnbrook and is over 60 years old. It is the former police house which has its back to the existing road, for it was built to front a road which never came.

Above the village is the little that remains of Rood Ashton Hall. Designed in 1808 by Jeffery Wyatt, it was altered and extended in 1836 by Thomas Hopper. The estate had been in the Long family since 1597. In 1923 Walter Long, Viscount Long of Wraxall, recorded that it had always been the rule on the estate, concerning the farms, that a son succeeded a father, and failing a son the tenant had the right to nominate a successor. In the 19th century the Longs spent much money on improving agriculture on their estates but were not always fortunate in their schemes and saw little return on their expenditure. On the death of his grandfather in 1867, Walter Long's father inherited the Wiltshire estates and the family moved to Rood Ashton.

Walter Long, who had a distinguished parliamentary career both in Ireland and as First Lord of the Admiralty, died in 1924 and the estate was broken up, the mansion being sold in 1930. It was used during the Second World War by the Services and was again sold in 1950 when it was stripped of most of its fittings, including the roof.

In the late 1970s most of the Hall was demolished. One part remains and has been converted into a private house while the crenellated stable lodge to the east still looks much as it did when the Long's carriages rolled under the arch into the cobbled courtyard.

In the first half of the 20th century Rood Ashton Park was open at weekends for the recreation of the people of Trowbridge. Families would walk through the ancient Biss Wood and enter the Park at Castle Lodge. Here they had acres of wooded parkland in which to walk or sit, plus the attraction of a lake with two small islets. The only danger was the roofless remains of an old deep icehouse but this was well hidden in the middle of a copse.

WEST DEAN

The best way to approach West Dean is along the minor road from Whiteparish in the south. Then one can stop at the top of the scarp slope of Dean Hill and enjoy extensive views of woodland with small patches of fields and very, very few buildings. Leaving the hill we note that much of it is an armament depot and there are large black iron fences with notices warning the walker of guard dogs.

In the village there is evidence of this being border country; the western half of The Red Lion is in Wiltshire and the eastern part in Hampshire as indicated on the front of the building; an interesting problem for council tax collectors! There are some pleasant houses here but the best thatched cottages are in Hampshire, leaving Wiltshire with the railway level crossing. In front of The Red Lion is a shallow stream, with ducks a-dabbling, and a well kept village green: an ideal place for refreshment and meditation on a summer's evening, surrounded by pink flowering chestnut trees.

The village has two churches, both dedicated to St Mary, although only parts of the first remain, having been restored as a mortuary chapel. The new church of 1866 is of red brick and flint with clay tiles and a wooden belfry.

The seat of the Evelyns was West Dean House (now demolished) which later became the home of the Duke of Kingston. His daughter, Lady Mary Wortley Montague (1690-1762), wrote concerning the local squires and gentlemen thus:

> '... insensible of other pleasures than hunting and drinking. The consequence of which is, the poor female part of their family being seldom permitted a coach, or at best but a couple of starved jades to drag a dirty chariot, their lords and masters having no occasion for such a machine, as their mornings are spent among hounds, and the nights with as beastley companions, with what liquor they can get in this country, which is not very famous for good drink.'

In this letter, written before her marriage in 1712, Lady Mary, already well known as both a beauty and a wit, compared the area and its men most unfavourably with Nottinghamshire.

In the village centre, there is the canal wharf of the Southampton and Salisbury Canal Navigation. Begun in 1795, this suffered from flooding, poor workmanship, bad management and lack of money. Given all this, it is not surprising that the canal never reached Salisbury! It only got as far as Alderbury, although it carried some traffic from the River Test to West Grimstead until 1808.

West Lavington

West Lavington is now a very long street village which has joined up with that of Littleton Pannell along the Devizes to Salisbury road. However, the most interesting parts of the village are not easily seen from the main road and you must walk around Stibb Hill, Rutts Lane and the network of little roads around the church to appreciate its charms.

Where Rutts Lane joins the main road is Dial House, a very good brick building of 1691 with the sundial which named it over the doorway. At the bottom of Stibb Hill is a long timber-framed house set on a stone plinth and with stone gable ends. Nearby is Pyt House which is late Georgian in style while to the south of the church is the early Georgian Old Vicarage and the late 17th century brick Parsonage.

Alderman William Dauntsey endowed almshouses and a school opposite the church of All Saints. Dauntsey House is nicely built of stone with the family coat of arms on the gable while the present brick almshouses in the west wing were erected in 1831. They became derelict in the 1970s but have recently been renovated and now have bathrooms.

The present Dauntsey's School is further north and is contained in buildings dating from 1895 with many newer blocks including the Memorial Hall, chapel and library. It is a mixed public school which attracts many local children who are collected daily by coach from a wide area.

Back in the older part of the village a stream runs alongside the road and the nearby pub is called The Bridge, but the singular lack of pavements here makes walking an exciting if not dangerous pastime. Scattered around are many houses from the 18th and 19th centuries while some of the outlying thatched buildings, such as Cliffe Farm Cottage on Stibb Hill, are much earlier.

There are two ghost stories connected with the Salisbury road out of West Lavington. The Easterton ghost was a headless woman who was accustomed to vanish into the graveyard. In the late 19th century the wall of this graveyard was demolished and the headless skeletons of a woman and young child were discovered. Whether this was the cause of the ghost or of the ghost story who can say? After this find local people may have been minded of the time when perhaps great uncle George encountered a headless woman dressed in white on his way home from Salisbury market. On the other hand, folk memory could have retained the knowledge of a suicide buried just outside consecrated ground. Perhaps an unmarried mother and the child she took with her rather than leave to the scorn of the Parish.

The other story concerns a drummer boy who was murdered in the 1770s. Some years later a colour sergeant was walking past the scene of the murder when he believed that he saw and heard the drummer boy. It is said that he was so frightened that he broke down and confessed that it was he who had murdered the boy for his pay. I do feel that an 18th century sergeant would have been a rather hard-bitten character unlikely to worry overmuch about a murder he had committed some years before, even if his victim's ghost did appear at the scene of the crime. However, it could indicate the grip of superstition on the peasant mind of a comparatively well travelled man.

WESTWOOD

The old stone village of Westwood lies to the south-west of Bradford on Avon. The beautiful unspoilt Westwood Manor contains architecture from four periods; c1400, c1480, early 16th century and early 17th century. For a proper appreciation of the building, the intending visitor should read Denys Sutton's *Westwood Manor*, published by the National Trust. For the Trust now maintains the Manor, having been left it by Edgar Graham Lister in 1956. Today the house remains much as it was in the 1650s with 16th century ceilings of oak beams in grid pattern, moulded plasterwork of the 17th century and the extremely ornate King's Room. In the decorative plasterwork of the latter is what appears to be a Red Indian on a totem pole.

The church of St Mary dates from the 13th century but was enlarged in the 15th century when the superb Perpendicular tower was built. An early 16th century feature is the 'old lad of Westwood', otherwise known as the 'Westwood imp'. This is a stone representation of the devil under which are carved the words, 'Resist me and I will flee'.

If, however, you do wish to yield to the temptation to have a drink you will find The New Inn very conveniently situated. There is even the good excuse that you can examine copies of old village photographs and some local documents which adorn the walls. Pause before entering though and note the most unusual sign for the 'Ladies'. The letters are beer bottle tops set in cement on the wall. Inside the pub there is a real international flavour as you can try kangaroo, ostrich, emu, crocodile and wild boar imported from Australia, Africa and France.

In the early days of the Second World War the War Department built 94 bungalows for people employed by the Enfield Motor Cycle Company at Upper Westwood. These were acquired by the Council in 1960 and since then there has been much housing development in the parish. During the war use was made of the underground stone quarries when the company turned to war work and at many times of the year workers needed sun lamp treatment as they never saw daylight.

As its name suggests, Avoncliff is set on a hillside overlooking the River Avon. From the mid-18th century to the late 1930s there were mills connected with the textile industry and there is a fine ancient weir. One remaining mill is now a house while the other has only two floors left of its original four. It is a most attractive area and one much frequented by visitors. The best way to get here is to walk or cycle along the tow path, or canoe along the canal from Bradford on Avon, and you can then feel you really deserve your refreshment in the pub or nearby tea rooms.

The valley is spanned by the John Rennie aqueduct of c1804 which takes the Kennet and Avon Canal across the river. Naturally it is of Bath stone and is in the Georgian style but for many years there were problems with the water running out of it. This has now been conquered and boats can once more cross the valley between Bradford on Avon and Bath. Climbing around this hillside is thirsty work so it is fortunate that The Cross Guns is perched on the hillside. It is a picturesque 17th century building providing a wide range of beers which can be enjoyed while appreciating the fine views in the valley.

To the west of Westwood, and partly in Somerset, is the tiny community of Iford. Three roads lead to it and they are all narrow and mostly single track. In a tranquil setting by the River Frome stands Iford House. The fine classical front was added c1730 by William Chanler, a salter and mill-owner from Bradford on Avon, but earlier parts could date from c1500 with extensions during the reign of Elizabeth I. The house was in a dilapidated state when, in 1899, it was bought by Harold Peto, an architectural partner of Sir Ernest George and Sir Edwin Lutyens, who became more and more interested in garden design and was responsible for many in this country and abroad. He believed that for the highest development of beauty a garden must be a combination of architecture and plants. At Iford he put this into effect making most attractive use of his collections of antique fragments. The results can be seen on Wednesdays and Sunday afternoons during May, June and July, when the gardens are opened by Mr and Mrs J.J. W. Hignett.

Much of Iford is in Somerset and the county boundary actually runs through the house, parallel with the classical front, and outside bisects a fish pond. The gardens are now the venue for popular concerts during the spring and summer when a wide range of musical tastes is catered for. Take a hamper and you can picnic in beautiful surroundings whilst listening to music in the open air.

WHITEPARISH

The village of Whiteparish has a long and interesting evolution as a settlement on the edge of the forest. This is explained in masterly fashion by Christopher Taylor in an article in the *Wiltshire Archaeological & Natural History Magazine, Vol. 62*, 1962. It is a story of the slow clearing of the forest which enabled the two Saxon communities of Frustfield and Cowesfield, with their open fields, to grow into six hamlets plus farmsteads with 2,800 acres of land under cultivation by 1350. In the 18th century the village and its farms were almost completely rebuilt in brick, thus destroying the variety of styles that is a pleasing feature of many villages.

The present church of All Saints is of flint and stone and has a wooden belfry which is clad with wooden hanging tiles. The exterior is Victorian but inside there is a Norman priest's doorway in the chancel with a mixture of Early English and Perpendicular work elsewhere.

The community is well provided for, having four pubs; two of them, The Fountain and The King's Head are next door to one another. For more athletic pursuits there is a playing field and sports ground on the green.

The parish is still substantially wooded, especially to the south and east where the open field system never gained a foothold. The north-west is more open but to compensate it has the folly known as The Pepperbox on the top of Brickworth Down, also known as Pepperbox Hill. Built in 1606, probably by Sir Giles Eyre, it stands on land now owned by the National Trust and is an excellent picnic site with extensive views to both west and east.

WINGFIELD

The village of Wingfield is hardly visible from the main roads, the A366 from Trowbridge to Farleigh Hungerford and the B3109 from Bradford on Avon to Rode. A few hints of a thriving community - the war memorial, a pub and a few houses - are the only advertisement to the hurrying traffic. For Wingfield is sensible and stands back from the modern world, hiding itself down small lanes and in green fields. At first these lanes seem most prosaic, Church Lane, Chapel Lane and Shop Lane; surely named long ago by men whose long agricultural labours left little time for flights of imagination. But look a little further and the poet takes over from the ploughman with Pomeroy Lane, Magdalen Lane and, finally, Love's Lane. What matter that the latter was probably named after a Mr Love who farmed at the end of the lane, today we can believe that it was down this lane that young couples dallied as night closed around them.

In this fair-sized parish, 120 homes lie scattered, from cottages and modern bungalows to farmhouses and manors. One of these may be known by people in every country which has an English-speaking community; it is The Poplars, a hostelry which managed to retain everything that made the village pub such an important institution. It is a whitewashed stone building, parts of which were a farmhouse in the early 18th century; a barn still stands in the car park. Inside there is an open fire and a dartboard but no piped music, no fruit machines and no computer or video games. Instead beer, served from hand pumps, which has been allowed to stand for 24 hours after being tapped, and the art of good conversation and community spirit are much in evidence.

The landlord, until April 1986, who must have stood in direct line of descent from Chaucer's Harry Bailly, host at The Tabard Inn, was Fred Haywood who, with his wife Marge, ran The Poplars from 1961. One of Fred's early deeds was to make a cricket ground, attached to the pub, where one of the best village teams in south-west England play their home matches.

Because of the nearness of the main road there is one interesting variation of the MCC code. Anyone who hits a six is credited with the score but is then out; a rule that brings a swift end to an innings. Apart from its cricket, such is the reputation of The Poplars that people from all the local towns drink there and visitors from throughout the country and from abroad find their way to its hospitable doors, now opened by Mike and Sue Marshall.

There is another residence in this village which is internationally known: Midway Manor, on the Bradford Road, was the home of the late Chairman of the World Wildlife Fund. The Manor was also once the home of General Shrapnel, the inventor in 1785 of the bomb which bears his name. He is commemorated by stone replicas of the bombs on the gateposts at the entrance to the drive.

Within the parish, on the Farleigh Hungerford road, lies Stowford. This small settlement has buildings which date from the early 16th century, one a clothier's house and now a farmhouse and another that was a mill. A late 18th century fulling mill on the site was in use until the 1840s. Nowadays the farm is host to the Annual Village Pump Trowbridge Folk Festival; an event each July that attracts an international cast of singers, dancers and entertainers who provide something suitable for every member of the family. At other times of the year excellent cream teas are provided and craftsmen have workshops on the site.

WINSLEY

The stone village of Winsley is huddled around its twisting tortuous main street through which traffic passes only with difficulty. The history of the recently built bypass is long and filled with acrimony and recriminations from both highway planners and villagers but, after many years of delay, the through traffic is now taken away from the pleasing historic centre.

The general impression of that centre is of stone cottages of the 17th and 18th centuries with more substantial residences of the 19th century. The best feature of the church of St Nicholas is its detached Perpendicular tower with a saddleback roof reminiscent of that at South Wraxall. The rest of the church was built in 1841 and is pleasant enough from the outside but within appears more like a church hall than a church.

The substantial Winsley Manor House has 16th century mullioned windows but much of the present building probably dates to 1612. It formerly housed the Sutcliffe School, a special school for boys from Wiltshire and neighbouring counties. It is now Dorothy House, a hospice for cancer sufferers in the Bath and west Wiltshire area, and a subject for much local fund raising. The other large house is to the north of the village. Conkwell Grange built in 1907 is in the William and Mary style and has a substantial model farm complex. Among the delights of this area are the small wandering roads that pass between dry stone walls on their way from Winsley to Conkwell to Hartley to the Ashleys and so to Bradford on Avon.

The road north from Conkwell enters the slopes of Warleigh Wood through which are also good tracks and footpaths.

Back in the village the narrow footways are mostly of hard-wearing pitched paving; it is pleasant to see these not yet covered by tarmacadam. Near to the war memorial, which is in the style of an old village cross, is the substantial Manor Farm. One of the more ornate buildings is the Methodist church of 1902 which has a most interesting doorway and arch on the south-west corner of the building.

In the 1960s much modern development took place, mainly to the west of the village centre and not detracting from it. This did raise the population by about 1,000 (it is now nearly 2,000) and provided homes for people working in Bath and the towns of West Wiltshire. Two features for which Winsley has always been noted are bowls and cricket and there is still a good bowling green and clubhouse in the village while the cricket club has one of the better local teams.

Down a minor road, by the old Winsley Vicarage, lies the delightful small village of Turleigh. Set on the slopes of a hillside that falls away into the valley of the Avon it is a place of warm mellow stone and beautiful gardens on terraces cut into the hillside. Once again there are narrow roads and pitched paving and all the houses have been well renovated.

The house names in Turleigh are often indicative of earlier occupations and some are unduly modest. The trades that the village has lost can be seen from the Old Post Office, the Old Bakery (both with bow windows) and the Old Tannery.

THE WINTERBOURNES

The three Winterbournes: Gunner, Dauntsey and Earls, are often regarded as one village and apart from the markers in the pavement by the church wall, it is impossible to see where Dauntsey ends and Earls begins. The two have shared the church of St Michael from 1868 when the early churches of both villages were demolished and a new one built astride the parish boundary. The greater part, however, is in Winterbourne Earls and so they can claim the parish church.

In Dauntsey is a very imposing 18th century Manor House in red brick of three storeys. In the garden is a weatherboard barn set on staddle stones. Between the Manor House and the church is a very nice early 18th century red brick house, The Elms. Elsewhere there is a mixture of thatched cottages and modern housing.

The name of the pub here is The Tything Man. A tithing was a group of householders, often ten, who were bound to act as law keepers for one another and the pub name is of some antiquity. The Methodist chapel here is thatched while the attached house is appropriately called 'Canaan'.

Winterbourne Gunner in the north, unlike the others, lies mainly away from the busy Marlborough to Salisbury road. The church of St Mary remained blessedly free from the influence of the Victorians and is mostly Early English with a stumpy unbuttressed tower which is most likely Norman. This is appropriate as the village name comes from a mid-13th century manor holder called Gunnora de la Mare and Gunnor is a Norman woman's name. The others acquired their names from the 13th century Roger Daunteseye and the Earls of Salisbury.

Also in the 13th century a certain Thomas Becket was a young parish priest here and used to walk over to Clarendon Palace to take services in the chapel. To the south the road bridge over the River Bourne is still called St Thomas's Bridge. The path which St Thomas used to take remains mysteriously green throughout the year thus being distinguished from the surrounding countryside. Still called St Thomas's Path it is an unusual memorial to the man who was murdered in Canterbury Cathedral.

THE WINTERSLOWS

Winterslow is a rarity among Wiltshire villages for it is built on a hill top. Or rather, I should say, they are built on a hill top as there is East Winterslow, which has slipped slightly downhill onto The Common, Middle Winterslow and West Winterslow. The latter has the only Anglican church, that of All Saints, whose exterior is the 1866 restoration but whose interior contains work from the 13th century and also some Early Norman architecture.

There are many early remains here. To the north-east, on Easton Down, are Neolithic flint mines, while on the surrounding downs are many barrows and field systems. The Roman road from Old Sarum to Winchester passes through the parish. Near the church, the site of a Roman villa has been found. In the north of the parish, on Roche Court Down, are two Saxon cemeteries. So we are in an ancient landscape and it is likely that there has been continuous occupation here since the Iron Age, and possibly from much earlier.

Today the Winterslows present a pattern of houses set amid fields and woods, farms and plantations. There is much recent housing, particularly on The Common which presents a most unexpected sea of brick and tile, rather than the waving corn one is expecting whilst travelling from West Winterslow. On The Common are many older small houses and cottages, some dating from the first settlements in the late 18th century. These were built by independent smallholders who, like most common dwellers, became enthusiastic nonconformists - two chapels bear witness to this. At the end of the 19th century the Poore family of Old Lodge set up a Land Court which was able to reclaim common land and let it to the smallholders on 999 year leases.

The Earls of Holland, descended from Sir Stephen Fox of Farley, held lands here until 1912. In the 18th century they had tried to create a country mansion in a great park but after two houses had been destroyed by fire on separate occasions they gave up in 1744 and built on an estate near London. That was Holland House and the estate contained what became Mayfair and a great deal of the West End.

On the main Salisbury to Andover road stands The Pheasant Inn, better known to many Wiltshire folk and students of English literature as the Winterslow Hut. A famous coaching inn where William Hazlitt once resided and wrote his *Winterslow Essays* and which, at different times, was visited by Charles and Mary Lamb and Rudyard Kipling. It was here that the Exeter mail coach was attacked by a lioness in 1816. The lioness was part of a menagerie on its way to Salisbury Fair and severely mauled one of the horses plus a large Newfoundland dog before being recaptured. The coach passengers with great presence of mind locked themselves inside the inn while the keepers recaptured the lioness from under a granary.

WISHFORD

'Grovely, Grovely, Grovely, and all Grovely', is the cry to be heard on the morning of 29th May, Oak Apple Day. On this day few villagers are still abed after sunrise (before 5 am) and those that are will be brought unwillingly to wakefulness by a local 'band', using drums, dust-bin lids and pots and pans to ensure that everyone is ready for the village's greatest festivity of the year. At first light people climb to Grovely Wood and bring back green oak boughs to decorate their houses. An especially large bough is hoisted to the top of the slim church tower to bring good fortune to future weddings, solemnised there during the coming year.

Later in the morning representatives go to Salisbury Cathedral and lay an offering of green branches before the altar and perform a traditional dance on the lawn afterwards. This part, however, is the sedate modern outcome of a much livelier festival for, until the 19th century, most of the villagers would dance their way the eight miles to Salisbury and then perform their dance in front of the altar. Booths and side-shows would be erected in The Close and it was a riotous and joyous occasion.

The great feature about the Oak Apple Day celebrations in Wishford is that it is not a modern revival but is the product of a tradition that could stretch back into the remote past. The festivities are to commemorate the victory over the local landowner, an Earl of Pembroke, who tried to interfere with the village's long held right to gather green branches in Grovely Forest. However, documentary evidence in the *Sum of the Ancient Customs belonging to Wishford and Barford out of the Forest of Grovely* (1603) suggests otherwise. In it the freeholders and tenants are said to 'fetch and bring away Boughs at their pleasure from the woods of Grovely, from May-day in the morning until Whitmonday at night . . .' It was stated that this practice, and several others, had happened from time out of mind.

Several historians have shown that the customs date to a pagan period and were connected with May Day celebrations, the worship of tree spirits and a recognition of the life force whose sap is rising strongly at this time of year. So don't lie slug-abed but go to Wishford on Oak Apple Day. There you will see a living link with prehistoric times. But don't make yourself obtrusive for this is taking place for the village and not for the benefit of tourists, although all visitors are welcome. The proceedings are now organised by the Oak Apple Club (formed 1892) whose motto is 'Unity is Strength' and whose members have to live in the parish.

That has dealt with one day in the village year but there is much to see at other times. The community is set on a charming stretch of the River Wylye and has three pleasant streets of houses around which you can wander without being too disturbed by motorised traffic.

The most interesting concentration is around the church of St Giles. Rebuilt in 1863-64, except for the chancel and lower part of the tower, it has many early objects of interest inside. Two effigies represent Nicholas de Bonham (died 1386) and his wife. In front of this there were brass plates let into the floor, now mostly represented by indentations only, representing Thomas de Bonham (died 1473), his wife Edith and their nine children. Local tradition had it that on his wife presenting him with twins, Thomas absented himself from her for seven years but after his return she presented him with septuplets. They were all brought to the church for baptism on a charger (dish) and John Aubrey, writing in the 17th century, said that men could still remember the dish hanging in the church. A monument in the chancel is to Sir Richard Grobham (died 1629) and his wife. In 1623 he had provided land to build almshouses for four poor people and one housekeeper. The almshouses are still there, to the side of the church, although they have been made into two dwellings.

Next door is the school of 1722, built from bequests made by Sir Richard Howe and, like that of Sir Richard Grobham, recorded on a brass plate in the church porch. It states that he provided for a master to teach 20 poor boys to 'write, read, cost accounts and to learn to say the church catechism', and for a mistress to teach 20 poor girls to 'read, work, learn and say the church catechism'. In the 18th century girls were not expected to need the art of writing which was regarded solely as a male occupation or profession. There were many well born young ladies who could read a book without difficulty but would struggle to write little more than their name; the X as a woman's signature in the parish register did not necessarily mean that she was illiterate but merely that she could not write.

In the church wall are set the bread stones. These record the price of bread from 1800 in gallons. The gallon measurement was used in a local bakery until its closure in 1982; it represented four standard two pound loaves. The earlier stones represent the Napoleonic Wars, 3s 10d a gallon in 1801, 2s 8d in 1920 after the Great War; in 1971 the first price in decimal currency was noted. Within the church stands a rather splendid early fire engine, made entirely in wood by Richard Newsham in 1728. With twelve men pumping, it could provide 65 gallons a minute and it cost the Churchwardens £33 3s 0d. Remarkably, the engine was used as recently as 1970 to fight a fire!

THE WOODFORDS

A more delightful setting than that of the three communities that make up Woodford is most difficult to imagine. They seem to have everything. A broad meandering clear river, lush pastures, valley slopes, a prevalence of mature trees and a valley scattered with attractive houses. They have been fortunate in that the two major roads to Salisbury in this area follow the ridges on either side of the Avon Valley, leaving this small section between West Amesbury and Old Sarum well off the beaten track.

The only way to really see the Woodfords is to walk. There are minor roads on both sides of the river and, using bridges at Upper Woodford in the north and Lower Woodford, Little Durnford or the Avon Bridge in the south, pleasant walks of between five and ten miles are available. Upper Woodford makes an excellent starting point for here is The Bridge Inn and, hopefully, on your return it will be opening time. The Inn looks across the placid flowing river, ringed by rising trout and rippled by swans and cygnets, to the meadows beyond.

One of the architectural treasures of Middle Woodford is hidden by trees from many viewpoints. This is the 17th century Heale House, a beautiful brick house greatly enlarged in 1894 by Detmar Blow who made such a superb job that the recent additions are indistinguishable from the original. Here are eight acres of gardens, open weekdays from Easter to the autumn, including a Japanese park with the Nikka bridge that was made in Japan. There are many unusual trees, shrubs and plants, including a collection of musk roses.

Heale House is best known for sheltering King Charles II after the Battle of Worcester in 1651. It would seem that he was safe here in the Avon Valley for he was apparently able to visit Stonehenge on one of the few days he spent here. In Lower Woodford there is again much use of flint and brick in the cottages but here one of the more striking features is the number of chalk cob walls. Many of these surround the numerous farmyards and these indicate that a number of lives here are still connected with farming. On the other side of the river are Netton and Salterton; Netton was once much larger than it is today and employed a considerable number of people in the wool trade.

There are some lovely tiny villages nearby. Little Durnford with its 18th century stone and flint chequer frontage and Great Durnford with its large rich Norman Church of St Andrew. Wilsford, whose Norman church tower displays herringbone patterned flintwork and where Detmar Blow built Wilsford House in 1906 in the style of the 17th century and using local labour. West Amesbury with a beautiful range of stone and flint houses fronting the road and where West Amesbury House hides a medieval house behind its later facade. And lastly, and perhaps the most beautiful, Lake with the most imposing Lake House originally dating from the latter part of the 16th century.

WOOTTON RIVERS

Wootton Rivers sounds as though it should be a one horse town in an American western and not a beautiful English village in a peaceful countryside. And it was a pioneer village in Saxon times. The name Wootton indicates it was the farmstead by the wood; Rivers comes from the family who were 13th century lords of the manor. The wood is Savernake Forest to the north where wolf and wild boar would have been a danger to early settlers while later, in Norman times, this corner of the Vale of Pewsey was under the harsh forest laws.

Basically this is a one street village with many thatched houses and cottages from the canal bridge in the south to the northerly parts of Forest Road. It is difficult to find unpleasing houses here and it would be invidious to mention a few when so many are worthy. Space must be made for the attractive and greatly expanded Royal Oak with its wide ranging menu and its family of ducks waddling along the ridge of its deep thatched roof. Full of thatch and with little through traffic this remains a quiet unspoiled Wiltshire village. There are farms in the street, one with the only local example of hanging tiles, which give the appearance of a working village while other evidence, such as the frequently used village hall indicates a good spirit of local participation.

The village is at least one mile distant from any major road but at one time commerce passed through the southern end of the village on the Kennet and Avon Canal. Near the bridge is the beautifully restored Wootton Rivers lock and Lock House, the old brick and slate lock keeper's cottage. From here one can walk the towpath to the little village of New Mill, one mile away, or to Burbage Wharf, one and three-quarter miles distant. A little further to the south is the railway that was the commercial death of the waterway.

The church of St Andrew is well hidden. Surrounded by trees, it is barely visible from the road and can only be clearly sighted from the railway bridge. It is approached by a footpath to the side of the entrance to Manor Farm. A narrow path leads through a pair of gate piers, with gate and wall long gone, into a most pleasant old-fashioned country churchyard surrounded by farm, fields and trees. It is shut away from the internal combustion engine and really does give that sense of tranquillity that all such churches once possessed.

The most interesting feature of the church is its clock in the wooden belfry. It has three faces. Two are conventional but the third has the words: 'Glory be to God' around the edge of the dial in place of numerals. It was made by Jack

Spratt, a countryman with a most inventive turn of mind who became famous locally as an amateur clockmaker. He lived, until his death in 1935, in a thatched house with dormer windows standing back from the road. He made and placed a clock on the front of his house - only the '3' and '9' were on the dial; above these was the word 'Clock' and below 'House'. He filled his house with clocks, one of which was a grandfather clock that could play over 100 tunes and possessed twelve sets of chimes; the beautiful case had been carved with a table knife.

The story of the church clock is fascinating. In 1911 the village wished to commemorate the coronation of George V by providing the church with a clock but were unable to do so because of the expense and local apathy. At this point Jack Spratt offered to make the clock for nothing if the villagers would provide him with several hundredweight of scrap iron, steel, brass and lead. Apparently the offer was received with some hilarity but nevertheless he received quantities of fire irons, brass weights, gunmetal and lead pipes. A London firm was approached about making wheels and pinions, but on being sent a description of the clock and its escapement understandably never replied!

So, with the help of the local blacksmith, and with castings made by a Pewsey firm using wooden patterns, Jack Spratt constructed his clock. He used a broomstick for the pendulum and gave the clock a unique set of chimes. All the hours between twelve and six have different sets of quarter chimes which are then repeated between six and twelve. After 80-odd years Jack's clock is still keeping good time and is an amazing memorial to a truly amazing man. There is another of Jack's clocks with the words 'TOGODBEGLORY' on the dial in place of numerals. This is on the Methodist chapel of 1881 but, alas, this clock has stopped.

Above the village looms Martinsell Hill and, until around 1860, a fair was held here on Palm Sunday. Two sports are recorded from this fair. 'Bandy', a form of hockey, was played on the north slope of the hill with the ball being hit up the hill from one player to another. In the other, boys used to slide down the hillside sitting astride horses' jawbones, steering with their feet. The latter practice is reminiscent of the Scottish game of hurley-hackit, riding a cow's skull down a slope, dating back at least to the 15th century. Though what their mothers thought of the state of their footwear after this sport is open to question.

WORTON

Approaching Worton from Seend you might miss a most unusual thatched farm as you sweep around one of the bends which guard this approach to the village. If you do miss the farm it is a shame and a return journey on the same road would be advisable. For this is Marsh Farm, displaying a rare example of early 19th century picturesque taste. A 17th century timber-framed farmhouse was altered and the thatch swept down low over a deep veranda and held up by five rustic supports. A little further along the road a turning to the right leads down Mill Road, past The Old Mill of c1850 now converted into flats, to the attractive village of Marston which is linked to Worton in many ways.

As you enter Worton you are conscious of modern housing and indeed this is true at both the eastern and western approaches. For it is basically a street village, and one which suffers in the early morning for being used as a 'rat run' to avoid considerable traffic delays in Devizes and, at other times of the day, from heavy vehicles travelling from the Salisbury area into western Wiltshire. To drive through Worton is to miss many architectural delights and pleasant footpaths and it is well worth parking, thus slowing down that through traffic, and spending an hour walking in the parish.

At the western end are what can be thought of as the public buildings - Worton and Marston Village Hall, black and white, with a war memorial to the three local men who died in the Second World War; and Worton and Marston County Primary School in an attractive rural setting for learning and with good playing fields. Opposite is the former Wesleyan Methodist chapel of 1848, which replaced the original one of 1829, which is now the Anglican Catholic church of St Brihtwold. The large modern house next door nicely retains the original link by its name, Wesley House.

Church Lane leads off from the village hall and at the end is the lovely little hidden Christ Church. For many years I had not realised that there was a church in the village; indeed there was not until 1843 when Christ Church was built as a chapel of easement. The path is lined by 14 lime trees and from its platform graveyard the church looks out across fields and a small lake. I have never rated the diocesan architect T. H. Wyatt highly but here, with the help of David Brandon, he has designed a most fitting simple church in a Gothic style. A simple cruciform plan, plain stone ashlar, wide nave, no stained glass so plenty of natural light, box pews and a small west gallery are a far cry from some of the excesses of the 19th century. The total cost was

£1,100 and the builder was Mr Jones of Bradford on Avon.

Both Worton and Marston were formerly tithings of the parish of Potterne and it was not until an Order of Council in 1852 created the district chapelry of Worton, from the tithings of Worton and Marston, that they became an ecclesiastical parish in their own right. It was in this year that Christ Church became an official parish church and in 1894 Worton civil parish was placed under the aegis of a parish council. Although local administration is new the landscape is old. The land is generally flat, about 200 feet above sea level, and both watercourses and village development are roughly on an east-west axis. The village extends from Mill Road in the west to Cuckold's Green in the east. The latter was so named by 1773 and one feels sorry for the man who lived there and has had his misfortune remembered for more than 200 years. The name for the village itself comes from the Old English for herb enclosure or kitchen garden which conjures up a far pleasanter domestic scene.

The area is well blessed with footpaths. From the church, Church Lane becomes a footpath, crosses the substantial waters of the Lavington Brook and continues to Marston. From the High Street many paths begin, some cross Worton Common while others head towards Potterne and Poulshot.

In the High Street are many fine houses and cottages and there is much use of Bridgwater tiles. From the 16th century is the timber-framed Manor Farmhouse, encased in the 18th century and now rendered. More remain from the 17th century. The timber-framed Rose and Crown, refronted with red brick a century later, still with a cobbled area in front and providing both a skittle alley and a function room; The Old Forge; The Grange; Park Farmhouse; and Ashton House, all timber-framed and the latter two with hipped thatched roofs. The 18th century saw many alterations to existing houses and also the building of The Little House, Worton House and The Old Coach House. Both 17th and 18th centuries must have been prosperous times here but the real surprise comes from 1912.

A century later than the alterations to Marsh Farm is Prince Hill House. It is an unusually elaborate neo-Georgian house with elaborate detailing outside and fine fittings of early 18th century style inside. It has been very nicely renovated recently and the roughcast painted timber facings are in very apt and subtle shades of blue and grey.

Two others deserve mention. The Old School House is of brick and vaguely ecclesiastical looking with its pointed windows. Not surprising as it began life as the Sunday school room of 1844 and became the village school by 1859 when 50 children were attending class. It was not until 1931 that responsibility was transferred from the church and parish to the county council. Next door is the attractive Fowler's Cottage of brick with stone decoration.

WROUGHTON

In the year AD 823 the Battle of Ellandune was fought between Egbert of Wessex and Beornwulf of Mercia in the fields now covered by Wroughton's modern housing estates. The King of Mercia brought thousands of men against the hundreds of Wessex but as the *Anglo-Saxon Chronicle* says: 'Egbert's men were pale and lean, Beornwulf's well fed and ruddy, but inexperienced and rash.' Mercia was overwhelmed by the well-trained men of Wessex and, in the words of a West Saxon poet; 'The Brook of Ellandune ran red with gore, it was choked with slain, and became foul with the carnage.' The brook, now known as the River Ray, winds through West Swindon on its way to its assignation with the Thames.

The older part of the village lies around the A361 road from Avebury to Swindon which flows down Wroughton Hill until checked by a left-hand bend and its junction with the Chisledon road. At the top of the hill stands the church of St John the Baptist and St Helen.

Horses were a great interest in Wroughton and there are still racing stables to the south and west of the village. One of the most famous of locally trained horses is commemorated in the name of the 20th century Brown Jack public house, which is built of brick as is its contemporary The Ely Inn. It is now most unfortunately renamed The Wroughton, a meaningless name compared with that of the horse formerly commemorated. Slightly earlier is The Three Tuns, whose appearance I find to have been spoilt in recent years yet it still retains three tablets let into the wall proclaiming 'Kingsdown Ales and Porter'. The earliest pub appears to be The White Hart, a Wadworth's house which is of stone and thatch and is most attractive.

There are several shops in the old part of the village and of course a shopping centre in the new development. An imaginative conversion of an old property is Fairwater House which, with its stables and outbuildings, has been well altered to provide office and other accommodation. The stream, which powered five mills at the time of the Domesday survey, still flows openly through the lower part of the village. Nearby is a scheduled ancient monument, the moat, of which little now remains save a hummock, a pond and the modern Moat Walk.

To the north lies the M4 and it is this which will save Wroughton from being absorbed into Swindon and losing its own identity, even though it is now part of the new Swindon Borough Council. To the south is a substantial RAF presence, the major part of which is now the RAF hospital. On the airfield site is a store of the Science Museum which can be visited on an open day each September.

WYLYE

The parish of Wylye spans the river valley of the same name and extends onto Salisbury Plain in the north and Wylye Down in the south. This is unusual in this valley for each parish normally keeps to its own side of the river but the reason is easily found. To the north was originally the manor of Deptford and its land on the Plain is still called Deptford Down. The remains of the hamlet are scattered around the A36 and the A303 and its chapel of ease is now used as a barn.

Wylye itself is on the minor road to the south of the river and contains many attractive houses of stone and flint. In Teapot Street (it would be nice to know the origin of this name) stands an old chapel in flint and stone while most of the houses of similar construction are thatched. At the end of Teapot Street is the junction with the Dinton road which crosses the railway line and rises over the downs providing fine views, especially to the west. To the east is Bilbury Farm, set in the earthworks of the Iron Age hill fort of Bilbury Rings and sheltered by a circular belt of trees.

The church of St Mary the Virgin was rebuilt in 1844-46, except for the 15th century west tower whose rainwater spouts are carved as gargoyles. Inside there is a splendid pulpit, dated 1628, with carved trees and which came from the church at Wilton.

In the churchyard is a large tomb, by the south gate, with iron railings but no inscription. A story concerning this is told by Sir Richard Colt Hoare thus: 'a person by the name of Popjay, of mean extraction went abroad in his early youth, and after some years returned to Wily in his carriage, and with a show of having acquired considerable wealth; he caused this expensive tomb to be built, and the bodies of his mother and sister, who had been dead for some time, to be disinterred and placed within it, but shortly after he left the country, and the tomb remains still unpaid for.' The tomb is of the late 17th

Flint & stone Cottage, Wylye

or early 18th century and there is a local tradition that the vicar of the time paid for it and was buried there himself.

Nearby is The Bell, an inn whose foundations date from the 14th century, while at the eastern end of the village was The Lamb which was thatched but was burned and had to be rebuilt. It is now a private house.

On the river the mill still stands with its mill race while in the river is the statue of a naked man blowing a horn. Believed to be 18th century, it represents a postboy who had fallen from the mail coach into the river and drowned. The village is now separated from the A303 which once passed through it and the streets carry only local traffic. Until recently, though, there was an event which saw a great influx of people for one weekend every year, the Wylye Horse Trials. That September weekend always seemed to be cold yet it didn't matter as the cross-country course for the three-day event, and in later years the carriage driving, was set on a hillside and superb views of most of it could be obtained from many vantage points. Organised by Sir Hugh and Lady Russell of Bathampton House, it only ceased through their ill health. Many of Britain's equestrian teams have come here when training for Olympic Games and World Championships and the Bathampton Equestrian Centre still provides excellent facilities.

YATESBURY

In the 19th century Yatesbury was described as 'one of the smallest, humblest and most retired parishes on the Wiltshire Downs' (Rev A.C. Smith). Cottages fell derelict in the early years of the 20th century and the village became even smaller. Today it is still tiny. In the past, severe snow storms cut off the village for many weeks, notably in 1859 and 1881 and even in the 20th century it was isolated for several days at a time. This isolation was to change during the Second World War when the RAF camp saw many thousands of men pass through the area. Today it is hard to imagine the teeming activity that was here only 50-odd years ago although some of the buildings are being converted into an aircraft museum.

Another source of great activity in those days were the rabbits which thickly populated the downs. My father, who was stationed here during the war, related that one member of the RAF Regiment owned a whippet which, on being introduced to this abundance, chased around in all directions for a few moments and then sat down as though he knew when the odds were too great for him! On the downs there are many footpaths and trackways and in earlier centuries there were even more. They were greatly favoured by the smugglers when transporting their contraband across Wiltshire from the south coast to the Midlands.

Around Yatesbury they were also the favourite places of highwaymen who used them as approaches to a place of attack on the main road or as a convenient means of escape. Until the early years of the 19th century the Cherhill gang operated here and as a warning to them a gibbet stood nearby with the iron-bound skeleton of a highwayman creaking and clanging in the wind. One member of this gang used to make his attacks completely naked, saying that the effect of him springing naked into the moonlight had a most terrifying effect upon his victim. He also reckoned that a naked man was less easy to identify afterwards than one fully clothed; presumably his victims would not be looking at his face.

YATTON KEYNELL

'97 miles to Hyde Park Corner. To Sodbury 11', was how the passengers in a coach and four may have regarded Yatton Keynell. Just one more village in an uncomfortable journey with maybe a quick stop for refreshment. The traffic still rushes past the old cast iron mile marker on its way to the village or motor racing circuit of Castle Combe. Most houses are on this road and that to Grittleton, although two others, from West Yatton and Biddestone, come into the centre of the village.

Like all Wiltshire villages on the edge of the Cotswolds, the earlier buildings are of stone and there is little that is under 200 years old. On the road to West Yatton is the most beautiful, the Manor House, dated 1659, with three gables. It sits facing a very attractive stone barn and other outbuildings, reminders of its deep involvement in local farming. To the south-east, on the Chippenham road, The Old Dairy proclaims its former use with two milk churns placed on top of a stone loading platform. There are several former farmhouses in the village.

The Bell appears to be an old farmhouse while The Book House has old stone cattle stalls on the roadside; the stalls are now filled with colourful hanging baskets, rather than lowing cows. Opposite is The Old Farmhouse, a pleasant 18th century building with a Tuscan porch.

In the centre of the village, with cottages tucked around its churchyard, stands the church of St Margaret. Of the 13th and 15th centuries, it was drastically restored in 1868 which has led to much of the interior appearing very plain. It is the only local church I know that has iron gates outside its wooden doors.

It was in this village that John Aubrey went to school. He recorded that 'he entered into his grammar at the Latin School at Yatton Keynell in the church where the curate Mr Hart taught the oldest boys Virgil, Ovid, Cicero etc.' Although due reverence was paid to the classics it did not extend to medieval illuminated manuscripts. Aubrey says that old missals from Malmesbury Abbey were destroyed by being used for book covers! These missals were books containing the whole order of Catholic services for the year and would doubtless have been considered worthless, if not dangerous, by the Reformed Church. In 1998 the present school was replaced by the newly built By Brook Valley CE School which will serve several villages. It was on a visit to the old school in October 1998, when it was housing children from four village schools, that I discovered the whereabouts of the intriguingly named 'Tiddley Wink'. I was leading some classes of children through the intricacies of Victorian life in the village, making use of the 1891 census, and remarked that there were seven houses at this place but I had no idea where it was. Immediately I was informed that it was a row of cottages near the new Golf Academy, but neither the children nor I could guess why it was so named.

It is well worth taking the narrow road alongside the church to visit West Yatton and Long Dean. West Yatton is set at the head of a wooded coombe and contains many good houses, barns and outbuildings. Most noteworthy is Ivy Farmhouse, dated 1706, while to the south-west of the road one cottage contains a 13th century one-light window. Beautifully situated at the lower end of the coombe is West Dean with some very pretty cottages.

ZEALS

There are very few place-names in England beginning with 'Z' and they are all in the West Country. An indication of our habit of pronouncing 'S' as a 'Z', for they all originate from early words beginning with 'S'. Zeals first makes its appearance in its present form in the mid-17th century and comes from the Old English word 'sealh' meaning a willow, sallow or sally. There are few willows left in the parish now but some may be noticed in the lower part of the village. What will most definitely be noticed is the constant traffic on the

A303 which bisects the village. Many of us in Wiltshire have regarded this road as a means of getting traffic from the south-east through Wiltshire as quickly as possible without it encroaching on to our other roads. Zeals and a few other villages, which do not have a bypass, unfortunately have to bear the brunt of it.

Three counties meet at Zeals and in fact the southern part of the village is in Dorset, as is the next-door settlement of Bourton, while neighbouring Penselwood is in Somerset.

For some centuries Zeals appears to have been the village without a church. It was mentioned in 1220 as being dedicated to St Martin and the last reference to it was in 1558. There are no known remains of this edifice and for some time the faithful were shepherded from Mere, although doubtless many walked across the county border to a nearer church. The foundation stone of the present church of St Martin was laid on 11th September 1845, on land which had been given by the Duke of Somerset. It was consecrated in 1846 and its building cost £2,000. The design was by a young Gilbert Scott, before he received his knighthood. A notice in the porch points out that seating for 296 persons had been provided in the chapel and that this should be free and unappropriated for evermore.

In the churchyard is a Glastonbury Thorn, grafted from the original. You'll find it in the south-west angle of the porch and the nave. Since 1962 it has been considered unsafe to ring the bells and since 1977 the summons to prayer has been effected by the sound of bells being broadcast electronically.

The older houses of the village are a mixture of stone and brick with a little thatch amid the more modern roofing materials. On the main road, and successfully attracting the passing trade, stands The Bell and Crown. Opposite are the brick almshouses of 1865 built in Tudor style with gables and superb chimney stacks which were in a precarious state in the 1980s but are now nicely repaired. The large Zeals House was substantially added to in Victorian times but contains features from earlier centuries.

Index